3000 800030 6
St. Louis Community College
D0075029

Why Did the Soviet Union Collapse?

Why Did the Soviet Union Collapse?

Understanding Historical Change

Robert Strayer

M.E. Sharpe
Armonk, New York
London, England

Library of Congress Cataloging-in-Publication Data

Strayer, Robert W.
Why did the Soviet Union collapse? : understanding historical change / by Robert Strayer.
p. cm.
Includes bibliographical references and index.
ISBN 0–7656–0003–X (cloth : alk. paper). —
ISBN 0–7656–0004–8 (pbk.: alk. paper)
1. Soviet Union—History—1985–1991.
2. Soviet Union—History—Philosophy. I. Title.
DK286.S77 1998
947.085′4—dc21
97-46087
CIP

Printed in the United States of America

The paper used in this publication meets the minimum requirements of American National Standard for Information Sciences—Permanence of Paper for Printed Library Materials, ANSI Z 39.48-1984.

MV (c) 10 9 8 7 6 5 4 3 2 1
MV (p) 10 9 8 7 6 5 4 3 2 1

Contents

Preface

Endings are endlessly fascinating, perhaps because they call to mind the fragility and passing quality of so much that we encounter in our brief journeys, including of course our own lives. So it is no surprise that metaphors of ending—death, fall, collapse—frequently punctuate historical analysis. This book explores one of the most significant of twentieth-century endings—the demise of the Soviet Union—placing this enormous event in the perspective of Russian, Soviet, and occasionally world history. And it uses the collapse of the Soviet Union to illustrate how historians seek to understand and explain that largest and most general question of their profession: How does change occur in human societies?

Accordingly, the Introduction sketches a set of historical and comparative contexts for thinking about the terminal phase of the Soviet experience and examines why it has occasioned so much controversy and debate. Then Chapter 1 highlights the major legacies of the more distant Russian and Soviet past that continued to echo in the late Soviet period, and Chapter 2 outlines the social processes and historical conditions of the post-Stalin era that provide the immediate background to the Gorbachev experiment. Those three decades now assume great importance, for they disclose, at least retrospectively, those cracks in the Soviet foundation that later widened and deepened to bring down the entire communist edifice.

Chapters 3, 4, and 5 chronicle the Soviet Union's final six years—

the Gorbachev era—in a thematic rather than a strictly chronological fashion. Chapter 3 presents the evolving Gorbachev reform program, a sometimes cautious and sometimes bold attempt to rescue Soviet socialism from its assorted ailments. That program, however, did not produce what its designer intended. And so Chapter 4 turns the historical spotlight away from Gorbachev's plans and visions to the disastrous economic outcomes of that program and to a variety of social responses to it. Chapter 5 returns the focus to Gorbachev and the leadership of the USSR during the country's final two years, but now in their role of responding or reacting to conflicting pressures from society rather than initiating change in that society.

The Soviet collapse has triggered a great and continuing debate, both political and intellectual. How far back should we begin in our search for its causes? Was the Soviet experiment so seriously flawed from its inception that its demise was inevitable? In what ways did Gorbachev's reforms contribute to the country's death? Why did the Soviet collapse occur with such a surprising absence of bloodshed? Did pressure from the West, and particularly from the United States, push the Soviet Union to its grave? We seek to highlight these and other contested issues in this book, both in the narrative itself and in separate sections labeled "Questions and Controversies." A further feature of the book—boxed inserts marked "Voices"—provides commentary on many aspects of the late Soviet experience from jokes, songs, recollections, letters to the editor, political manifestos, and other sources.

That in short is what this book is about. And here is what it is not about. This book is not a textbook survey of all of Soviet history, but rather a more focused analysis of the Soviet collapse in the context of Soviet history. Furthermore, it is not an effort to present a single, unified explanation of that collapse, but rather to provide readers with enough information and ideas to weigh alternative explanations with some confidence.

Over the past decade I have had the rare opportunity of witnessing the amazing transformation of the Soviet Union and Russia to some extent "from the inside," and in the process I have developed a number of fine friends. In the course of numerous visits to the country, I have been warmly welcomed, intellectually enlightened, and personally enriched by these friendships. It is in part through the eyes of these people that I have seen the demise of the Soviet Union and the slow and painful emergence of a new Russia: Elena Brouk; Brunya and Anya Poleshchuk; the Sudakov family; Tanya and Natasha Kharkova; Lena Svinina; Yaroslav Kuzmin; Marina Yermilova; Liza Tsvetkova; Andrei and Lena Likhtarinkov; Yuri Goncharov; Alexei Getman; Alexander Savin; Yevgeni Ivanov; Ilya and Lena Popeko; Alexander Poleshchuk and Olya Andreyenko; Sophia Petrovna Poleshchuk; and Lena Lyunyova.

I should also like to recognize the encouragement of that extraordinary community of scholars and teachers in the History Department of SUNY, College at Brockport, among whom I have worked now for more than a quarter century. They have supported me in times of personal tragedy; they have provided a stimulating intellectual environment in which to teach and write; and they have enabled me to enter the field of Soviet history in the middle of my career and have facilitated the retraining which that change made necessary. Many thanks also to the College at Brockport for funding several of my trips to Russia and to the SUNY/UUP Professional Development Program, which assisted in my retraining.

Finally, I want to acknowledge my wife, Suzanne Sturn—a marvelous actress, a fine teacher, a woman of spirit, and a wonderful companion for the journey. Her work in calling characters and situations to life on stage parallels my work in recalling events and people to life on paper. The intersection of our lives and our work has vastly enriched the process of writing this book. I am grateful beyond measure.

Robert Strayer
Rochester, New York

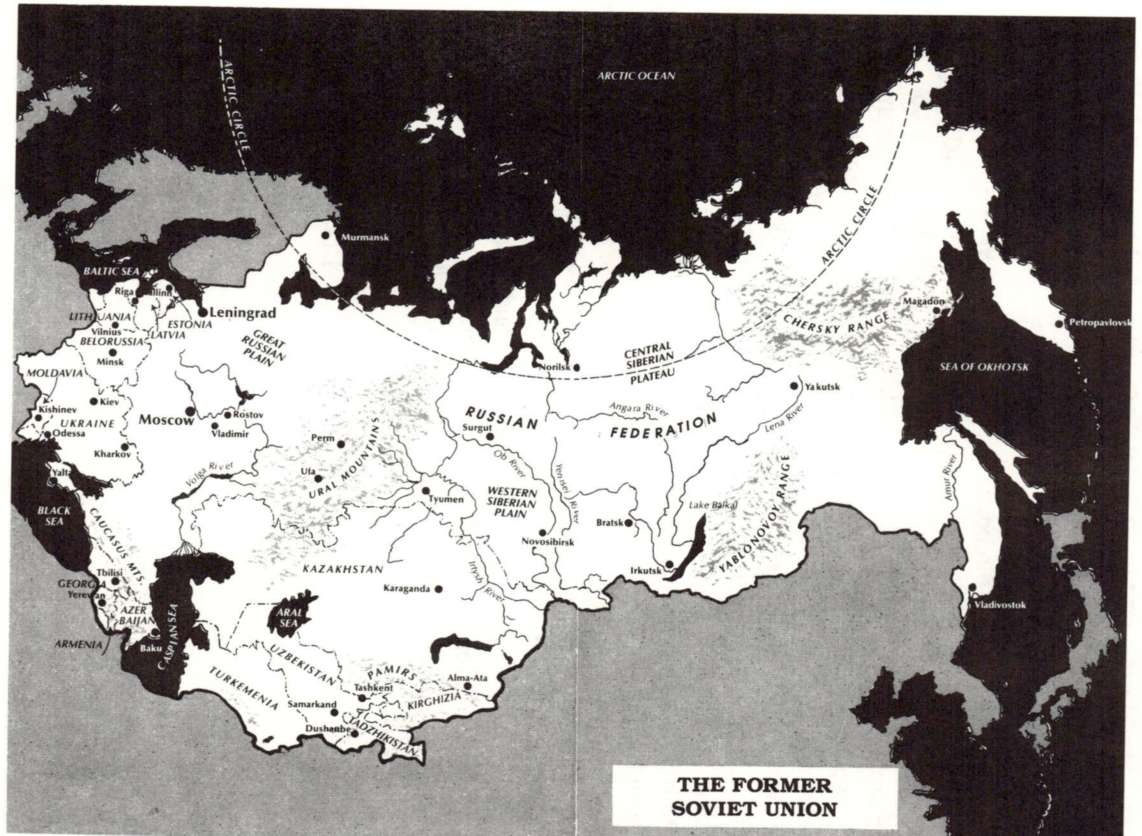

From Michael Kort, *The Soviet Colossus: History and Aftermath*, 4th edition (Armonk: M.E. Sharpe, 1996).

Why Did the Soviet Union Collapse?

Introduction: Contexts and Comparisons

A little after 7:30 on the evening of December 25, 1991, the red banner of the Soviet Union was lowered for the last time from its flagpole high above Moscow's Kremlin, while the white, red, and blue tricolor, now the emblem of the new Russian state, was raised in its place. President Mikhail Gorbachev had just delivered a televised farewell address to the citizens of a now vanishing country. And outside the Kremlin, on that spacious stone plaza known as Red Square, a small group of communist demonstrators protested the demise of their country before the tomb of the man who had founded it. Otherwise, only a few passing citizens actually witnessed the moment. If we need to fix the precise time when the Soviet Union, and the vast social experiment it represented, ceased to exist, the lowering of that flag will serve as well as any.

The demise of the Soviet Union, an event of profound consequence in its own right, illustrates an even larger historical pattern—the process by which all human societies constantly change, sometimes slowly and unobtrusively and at other times with revolutionary speed and dramatic impact. Understanding that process in all its infinite complexity is the central task of historians, political scientists, sociologists, anthropologists, economists, and others. While this book focuses primarily on those historical changes that led to the demise of the Soviet system, it also illustrates how historians and social scientists seek to describe and explain the processes of social change more generally.

Defining the Soviet Collapse

In embarking on an exploration of why the Soviet Union collapsed, we might well ask at the outset what, precisely, it was that collapsed. What, in short, are we seeking to explain? Most obviously, of course, it was a political entity—the world's largest country, encompassing fully one-sixth of the world's land area and officially entitled the Union of Soviet Socialist Republics—that passed away on that cold December evening. As its title implied, that country was a "union" of fifteen constituent republics, each of which now assumed an independent existence, claiming full sovereignty within the larger international community. The Union that disappeared on that day had grown out the Russian Revolution of 1917 and had been a central fixture of international political life for more than seven decades. It had exited the First World War to preserve the revolution, had struggled to a painful and costly victory in the Second World War, and had vigorously contested the Cold War that followed. It had at various times and for various people inspired hope for a more just world and provoked fear of a Dark Age to come. It was a state of enormous consequence for the world of the twentieth century. And now it was gone.

Behind the Soviet Union, however, lay the Russian Empire, with far deeper historical roots, and it too had now collapsed. Centuries in the making, that empire had grown from a small Russian principality in the vicinity of Moscow to become an enormous imperial domain—ruled by a Russian tsar, spanning both Europe and Asia, and embracing ancient, highly developed peoples in Eastern Europe, the Caucasus, and Central Asia as well as the less technologically sophisticated cultures of Siberia and the Far East. Lenin's Soviet Union had inherited that empire and preserved it largely intact. Now, from a Russian viewpoint, as 1991 drew to a close, the territorial gains of the preceding 250 years had been stripped unceremoniously away. So too had the so-called satellite states of Eastern Europe, officially independent but under clear Soviet control since the end of World War II. From the viewpoint of those "subject peoples," however, whether within the USSR or adjacent to it—Latvians, Ukrainians, Georgians, Kazaks, Poles, Hungarians, and many others—the collapse of the Soviet Union represented an exhilarating liberation from "the prison of nations," the denouement of long and ardent desires for a more independent political existence.

The Soviet Union, however, was no ordinary country, nor even an ordinary empire, for it was a state devoted to an idea. That idea was socialism, and it too had largely collapsed or lost its appeal by 1991. The socialist dream of equality, justice, and community has an ancient pedigree, but its modern expression took shape in the fertile mind of Karl Marx. His life (1818–1883) coincided with perhaps the harshest phase of capitalist industrialization in Europe, a time when an encompassing market economy was rudely shattering older institutions and traditions and before the benefits of this new and highly productive system were widely shared. It was a savage process, described by Marx as "naked, shameless, direct, brutal exploitation," but in it, he discerned the coming of a new world.[1] He celebrated in almost lyrical terms the productive virtues of capitalism, creating for the first time the real possibility of an abundant and humane life for all. But the fatal flaws of capitalism—private property, growing inequalities, bitter and worsening class conflict, competitive and individualistic values—prevented the realization of those possibilities. Capitalism would therefore be swept away in revolutionary upheaval, while its vast productive potential would be placed in service to the whole of society in a rationally planned and egalitarian community. In such a socialist commonwealth, degrading poverty, conflicting classes, contending nations, and human alienation generally would be but fading memories. From the ashes of capitalism, Marx wrote, there will emerge a socialist society in which "the free development of each [person] is the condition for the free development of all."[2]

It was a grand, prophetic, utopian vision of human freedom and the end of history, and it inspired socialist movements of workers and intellectuals amid the grim harshness of Europe's industrialization in the nineteenth century. Nowhere, however, did these movements come to power, save in that most unlikely of countries, tsarist Russia, where autocracy still reigned, where most people still lived in rural poverty, and where industrialization had only recently begun. It was an inhospitable environment for building the first socialist society. But the Bolshevik revolutionaries of 1917 possessed a rock-solid conviction that they, and they alone, could undertake that monumental task. In the process they would trigger socialist upheaval in the rest of Europe and ultimately the world. Such a powerful vision of Russia's world historical role seemed to justify, in their own minds, whatever was necessary to promote and then to preserve the revolution.

This socialist ideal remained at the core of Soviet ideology from Lenin to Gorbachev. And in the twentieth century that ideal in varying forms spread widely, most notably to China but also Southeast Asia, parts of Africa and the Middle East, Cuba, and elsewhere. But the realities of Soviet life over the course of seven decades—Stalinist brutalities, a new elite of party functionaries, the almost total absence of personal freedoms, and later, economic stagnation—badly tarnished the socialist idea. By the 1980s few people in the Soviet Union, and rapidly decreasing numbers outside of it, retained their belief in the world-changing character of socialism, despite its continued propagation through official channels. The power of socialism to inspire the making of a just, or even a tolerable, society seemed to perish together with the first country officially to embrace those ideals.

As the ideology of socialism lost its appeal, so too did the Communist Party that carried that ideology and had provided for more than seventy years the organizational glue for the country. It had begun as a splinter group of radical Marxist revolutionaries in the early twentieth century; it came to power, quite unexpectedly, in the upheavals of 1917; it became the central political structure of the Soviet regime, far more important than the official government apparatus; it penetrated every nook and cranny of the country. Yet by 1990 millions were resigning their membership in that party. And in the aftermath of the failed coup of August 1991, in which elements of the party leadership were clearly implicated, the Communist Party was officially banned in the country it had long governed. It was a stunning political reversal.

If the party collapsed as an organization, so too, though less completely, did the centrally planned economy that was the party's proudest achievement and the heart of Soviet socialism. It had been designed to avoid the wasteful and chaotic competition of capitalism and to move the country quickly toward industrial development. At least in this last respect, it succeeded after a fashion. The Soviet economy had provided the material foundation for victory in World War II and served as a model of rapid industrial growth for many countries in the Third World. But by the 1970s, its performance was clearly slipping and its momentum seemed exhausted. Gorbachev's entire reform program was designed to remedy its deficiencies but wound up exacerbating them as the country slipped ever deeper into economic crisis. As the Soviet experiment expired, its vaunted planned economy lay in ruins. The market, not the Five-Year Plan, was now celebrated around the world as the best agency for promoting economic growth and creating an abundant society. Economic failure thus contributed much to the erosion of the party and to the declining legitimacy of socialism itself.

December 1991 marked as well a sharp diminution in the country's international stature. It had been Leonid Brezhnev's proudest boast that the Soviet Union had caught up militarily with the United States during the 1970s and achieved the status of an equal global superpower. But a faltering economy soon exposed the hollowness of such pretensions. By the mid-1990s, the Russian state that had emerged from the ashes of the Soviet Union could make no such claim at all. The country's population and territory had shrunk dramatically; its armed forces were but a quarter of the size of the Soviet military only a few years before; and these forces were unable to contain even the uprising in tiny Chechnya. Only its nuclear capacity, enormously powerful but of little diplomatic utility, gave post-Soviet Russia a claim to great-power status.

All of these changes, of course, coincided with and helped to promote the end of the Cold War. Rooted in the ideological challenge of the Russian Revolution and in the political-military challenge of postwar Soviet foreign policy, that East-West conflict represented one of the world's deepest and most enduring divides in the second half of the twentieth century. By 1991, however, the major expressions of that conflict—sharp ideological antagonism, a divided Europe, an escalating arms race, and rivalries in the Third World—had been substantially tempered. To the immense surprise and relief of an astonished world, the Cold War was over.

Here then, concretely, is what expired as the Soviet Union passed into history: a state and an empire; a socialist ideology and a utopian dream; a dominant party and a centrally planned economy; a global superpower and a pattern of international conflict that had shaped a half century of world history. Each of these elements and the relationships among them require explanation.

Questions and Controversies: *The Roots of Argument*

The task of historical analysis involves describing what happened, explaining why things turned out as they did, and assessing the signifi-

Voices

The Soviet Collapse and Children's Play

The enormous changes that overtook the Soviet Union in the 1980s and 1990s have been difficult for scholars to define with precision. Here is one description from a Soviet journalist and former political prisoner, based on the games his daughter played.

The children have come home from school. From the hallway I can hear our younger daughter, Katya, and our favorite little neighbor boy, Lyovochka, telling each other some pleasant nonsense and laughing quietly. Several years ago, when I was arrested and the children were younger, they used to play "prison" day after day. They put together some building blocks, boards, and construction sets and called the whole thing "a prison for Katya's papa," that is, for me. . . . Now our children play "manager." They buy factories and railroads, offer goods on the exchange, count and change money. . . . It is strange for us adults, who have counted crumpled rubles our whole lives and stood for days in lines for basic necessities, to see children with 100,000–ruble bank notes in their hands.

Could we be expected to have any interest in commercial profit, if for three consecutive generations the chief dream and hope of millions of people was to survive to the end of their labor camp term, to be released from prison, to return home from exile, and to hide somewhere far away in some burrow, barricade oneself in, roll up into a ball, so that the ever-present KGB would stop noticing them and forget about them? Will our children really be free of this feeling? We, at least, will certainly never be free of it.

From Lev Timofeyev, *Russia's Secret Rulers* (New York: Alfred A. Knopf, 1992), pp. 3–4.

cance of historical events and processes. All of this is forever laced with controversy and dispute. The earlier notion of scientific objectivity in historical analysis—the idea that detached and trained observers might reconstruct the past "as it really happened" and come to final consensus about it—has largely vanished. Most scholars now recognize controversy as an inescapable and enduring part of the historian's craft, even while they struggle to sift the evidence with care and put aside obvious bias. But the various perspectives associated with differences in class, gender, nation, ethnic group, and generation provide no common vantage point for understanding the past and ensure that lively debate continues on virtually every historical question imaginable. History is society's memory, but it is at virtually every point contested memory.

Nothing more clearly illustrates this observation than the effort to explain the demise of the Soviet Union. Why exactly has this question provoked such heated controversy and debate? What passions has it raised and what vested interests has it engaged?

On one level, the death of empires and great powers has always captured our imagination, perhaps because of the sharp contrast between the size, splendor, long duration, and apparent invincibility of these creations during their heyday and the decay and ruin to which they succumb at their demise. We are all intrigued by the fall of the mighty. The collapse of the Roman Empire, for example, continues to provide occasion for endless commentary on politics and morality some fifteen hundred years after the event. The dissolution of the Soviet Union will likely exercise a similar power over human imagination for a very long time.

But in the Soviet Union itself, and in its successor states, the collapse of country—either potential or actual—has been for a decade a political issue of consuming interest and for many a deeply personal matter as well. No wonder it has animated intense public debate and endless private conversation. Non-Russian nationalists, of course, rejoiced as the Soviet "prison" disintegrated and long-captive nations emerged into the bright light of freedom. Even some Russians welcomed the end of the Soviet Union that Russia had long dominated. Aleksandr Solzhenitsyn, the great exiled dissident writer who revealed the horrors of Stalinism, argued passionately that Russia could never recover from the multiple wounds of communism unless it could rid itself of empire. "We don't have the strength for sustaining an empire," he wrote. "Let this burden fall from our shoulders: it is crushing us, sapping our energy, and hastening our demise."[3] In the early 1990s, many Russians agreed.

Bitterly rejecting such thinking, "Soviet patriots" despaired as they watched their great country—a global superpower, heir to centuries of a proud Russian tradition, and avatar of revolutionary socialism—disintegrate before their eyes. They sought political revenge on Gorbachev, Boris Yeltsin, and others they held responsible for the disaster. In the tumultuous years since 1991, nostalgia for the Soviet Union has become widespread in Russia as the stability, security, and global prestige of the Soviet era vanished in favor of impoverishment, criminality, prostitution, growing social inequalities, and the loss of superpower status. In 1996, a reviving Communist Party, which won 40 percent of the vote in the presidential election of that year, adopted a platform calling for the voluntary restoration of the Soviet Union. And the Russian parliament voted overwhelmingly to condemn the agreement that had dissolved the Union less than five years earlier.

Still another voice within the former Soviet Union proclaims the collapse of the communist system largely an illusion. It simply did not happen. Even during the communist era, writes journalist, human rights activist, and former political prisoner Lev Timofeyev, a "web of secret connections" involving the party leadership, the KGB, the military-industrial complex, and the criminal underworld, really ran the country with the Communist Party operating only as an "outer screen." That hidden elite pushed Gorbachev forward to shore up a weakening system. And despite the collapse of the Union, those "secret structures," in this view, have continued to dominate Russia and many other newly independent states after 1991. Rooted in a widespread belief in vast conspiracies and a shadow government, such ideas have had a considerable appeal in contemporary Russia, where many of the old elite have obviously done quite well for themselves while millions of ordinary citizens became even more impoverished and insecure. According to Timofeyev, "few Russians doubt that besides the visible political machinations obvious to everyone, there is another hidden level of intrigue" wholly outside of public control.[4]

In the West, controversy about the demise of the Soviet Union has drawn energy from long and bitter academic debates about the nature of the Soviet experience. To simplify a complex set of arguments, on the one side stood the "conservative" scholars who viewed the Soviet Union as an illegitimate experiment in totalitarianism, originating in a conspiratorial Bolshevik coup, sustained largely by violent repression, and issuing in an unspeakable tragedy. They wrote from a position of moral outrage and political anticommunism, finding few if any redeeming features in Soviet history and little basis for believing in the

Armenian artist Levon Abrahamian depicts the USSR's collapse in terms of the many Soviet values being violated in front of Lenin's tomb. The signs in Russian from left to right read as follows: "Down with the Communist Party," "Miss USSR," "Lenin." Reprinted with permission of the artist, Levon Abrahamian.

possibility of real change or reform in that system. They were academic cold warriors, supporting a "tough" Western posture, and proud of it.

On the other side were the "revisionists." While not denying the horrific elements of the Soviet experience, they saw themselves as rescuing Soviet studies from the stranglehold of such Cold War thinking. Revisionists understood the Bolshevik revolution in large part as a popular upheaval, criticized "totalitarianism" as an inadequate concept for describing Soviet society, and understood the Cold War as the joint responsibility of the United States and the USSR. Furthermore, they saw the Soviet Union after Stalin as a maturing industrial society in which the pressures of modernization were creating a professional middle class and a more pluralistic political life, similar to that of other modern societies.

Here was the crux of the argument. Conservative scholars, focusing largely on politics, viewed the Soviet Union as an ideologically driven totalitarian system, wholly different from that of other western industrial nations. Revisionists, focusing on social and economic processes, understood the Soviet Union as one variation on the modernizing theme and increasingly converging with the West. The Gorbachev reforms and the subsequent collapse of the country imparted a new focus and intensity to these controversies. Revisionists applauded the Gorbachev reforms as a vindication of their views that the Soviet Union was in fact changing rapidly, and they accused conservatives of failing to foresee and being unable to explain how a genuine reformer such as Gorbachev might arise from within the Soviet system. But conservatives saw the Soviet collapse as proof positive that a rigid totalitarian system could not be reformed, but only replaced. They charged that revisionists, grossly overestimating the stability of Soviet society, had failed to predict the Soviet collapse and were subsequently unable to explain it adequately.

In both the former Soviet Union and the West, those debates continue with no real consensus in sight. Throughout this book we will repeatedly highlight specific controversies and interpretative questions, often in separate sections called "Questions and Controversies." They serve to illustrate the major disputes surrounding the demise of the Soviet Union as well as the various approaches scholars have taken toward the even larger problem of explaining how human societies change.

Questions and Controversies: *Was the Soviet Collapse Historically Unique?*

Since the Soviet Union was so large and so globally significant, its collapse, and the events leading toward it, have had a singular and distinctive quality, placing recent Soviet history in a category of its own. But should we view its passing from the historical stage as a wholly unique phenomenon? Or can its demise be usefully compared with the experience of other peoples and countries? Do the final years of the Soviet Union find a place in any larger patterns of historical change?

For those who have seen the Soviet Union as the world's last empire, its collapse marked the final chapter in a global process of imperial disintegration or decolonization that has reshaped the world of the twentieth century. Of the three great land-based, contiguous empires of the nineteenth century—the Austro-Hungarian, Ottoman, and Russian—only the last survived the devastating impact of World War I, albeit in a new Soviet guise. The others fell apart under the twin blows of military defeat and the assertive nationalism of subject peoples. Following World War II, similar forces destroyed the overseas empires of Britain, France, Belgium, Italy, and Portugal, leading to the creation of dozens of "new nations" in Asia, Africa, and the Middle East.

But if the Soviet collapse represents a continuation of that process, it differed from the earlier cases in several important ways. Why, for example, was the Russian/Soviet empire able to persist into the final decade of a highly nationalistic twentieth century, when other empires had long ago succumbed to the forces of particularistic nationalism? The speed and suddenness of the Soviet collapse also contrasts with the much more extended disintegration of other empires. The Roman, Byzantine, Austro-Hungarian, and Ottoman Empires, for example, endured in decline for centuries, while the Soviet collapse took place within a few years and with little overt warning. That it occurred without military defeat and with relatively little violence also distinguishes it from many other cases.

But was the Soviet Union really an empire? The country's leadership strongly denied the imperial label, which they associated with capitalism. To them the Soviet Union was a multinational or multiethnic state, like many countries containing a culturally diverse population. In fact, countries such as Japan, France, or Germany with a largely homogeneous population are the exception. Far more common are those like India, Indonesia, Nigeria (and most other African states), the United States, and many others in which conflict among politicized ethnic or cultural groups, sometimes leading to civil war, represents a major element of domestic politics. If the Soviet Union is viewed in these terms, it joins only a handful of such countries that have actually broken up in the postwar world—India, Pakistan, Ethiopia, Yugoslavia, and Czechoslovakia. The demise of communist regimes, which had previously proven effective in holding multiethnic states together, now led three of these six to dissolution. In terms of how that process unfolded, the Soviet Union occupied a middle space, somewhere between the "civilized divorce" that split the Czechoslovakian union and the horrendous civil wars and ethnic cleansing that wracked Yugoslavia.

Yet another recent global pattern into which late Soviet history may fit involves the worldwide democracy movement. In the 1970s and 1980s, dozens of noncommunist countries have made a transition from highly authoritarian single-party government or military rule to multiparty democracy with contested elections. Spain, Portugal, and Greece in Europe, most of Latin America, the Philippines, and a number of African countries testify to the extent of this trend. Under Gorbachev in the late 1980s, the Soviet Union too moved toward contested elections and competing parties and thus joined these other countries in broadening effective political participation. And like many other transitions to democracy, the Soviet process began from within the repressive regime itself but subsequently gained momentum and moved well beyond the original goals of the leadership.

But the Soviet transition was different, because reformers confronted an unparalleled degree of state control and the almost total absence of a civil society. Elsewhere, even in highly authoritarian states, a variety of civic organizations had maintained at least a semi-autonomous existence: chambers of commerce, labor groups, peasant associations, churches, newspapers, universities, and sometimes political parties. And in most of these authoritarian states, private property was an established institution. In the Soviet Union, however, the party-state owned or controlled virtually all productive property, officially prohibited all independent organizations, and attempted to monopolize and dominate society in ways that even the most highly authoritarian noncommunist states did not. All this highlights the immense difficulties attending the Soviet transition to a more democratic political life. Far more than elsewhere, it was a matter of building "democracy from scratch."[5]

A further unique feature of the Soviet transition lay in the multiple tasks that confronted a reformist leadership. Not only was the Soviet Union attempting political democratization, but also *and at the same time* it was partially dismantling an elaborate centrally planned economy, while introducing against substantial resistance elements of a market economy; it was dealing with assertive nationalist demands for greater autonomy or even independence; and it was making radical adjustments in its foreign and military policy while managing its decline from global superpower status.[6] The simultaneous timing of these various transformations distinguished the Soviet transition from virtually all others and almost guaranteed some "overload" in its political system.

If the Soviet Union participated in a global revival of democratic practice, it also joined a number of other communist states in efforts to reform, and thus preserve, those regimes. In China, Vietnam, Eastern Europe, and even Cuba, as well as in the Soviet Union, party leaders initiated various economic and political changes intended to address long-standing problems and in some cases to respond to growing popular pressures. The Soviet Union, of course, had been under communist rule at least thirty years longer than any of the others. Unlike its Eastern European satellites, where Soviet military forces ultimately guaranteed party control, the communist system in the USSR had been imposed from within and thus had far deeper domestic roots. And unlike China, where the Cultural Revolution of the 1960s had badly disrupted and weakened the regional Communist Party structure, local functionaries in the Soviet Union had grown entrenched in office and even developed a measure of independence from central party and state organs by the 1970s. All of this meant that the potential for resistance to serious reform from above was greater in the Soviet Union than elsewhere.

The nature and sequencing of the reform process in the Soviet Union likewise differed from many of the others, particularly China. While both initiated reform from the top, the Chinese, following Mao Zedong's death in 1976, focused almost wholly on economic reform and forcefully silenced popular demands for serious political change in the Tiananmen Square massacre of 1989. By contrast, the Gorbachev program in the Soviet Union explicitly coupled economic reform with democratization and greater cultural and intellectual freedoms. In the aftermath of the Soviet collapse, many of Gorbachev's critics ardently wished that he had followed the Chinese model more closely.

Even within the economic domain, Soviet reform strategy differed sharply from that of China. While China in the early 1980s moved quickly and with relative ease away from collective agriculture to family farms, Soviet agricultural reform took a distinct back seat to urban and industrial change, while resistance to private farming from officials and farmers alike has been intense. As a consequence, the Soviet Union came to an end with little change in its agricultural sector and nothing at all like the impressive economic growth and booming rural incomes that have propelled Chinese development in the 1980s and 1990s.

The outcomes of the Soviet reform process have distinguished it most sharply from China. In the USSR, the party lost its dominant position as a tenuous and fragile democracy took hold; the country's socialist commitment lay in tatters; and the state itself disintegrated. In China, on the other hand, the party has maintained its political control; socialism, though largely devoid of serious content, remains the official ideology; and the country has retained its unity. A more dramatic contrast between the two communist giants of the twentieth century would be hard to imagine.

Two obvious factors offer a beginning point for an explanation. The Soviet Union contained an enormously diverse population within which lay many "nations in the making." China, with its relatively homogeneous population, simply did not have to deal with the ethnic or national problem in any comparable way, though regional differences based on variations in economic performance have occasioned growing political conflict. Secondly, China's astonishing economic growth has greased the skids of reform and provided at least some solvent for the tensions of that process. By contrast, the deepening crisis of the Soviet economy from 1988 on, and declining standards of living for most people, exacerbated all of its other problems and contributed much to the country's collapse in 1991.

The reform process in Eastern Europe provides yet another contrast to the Soviet experience. Some of the early reform efforts in the several decades after World War II were initiated from above, but always with an eye on the Soviet reaction. Thus, Hungary experimented with elements of a market economy; Poland permitted private agriculture and a role for the Catholic Church; Romania practiced a relatively independent foreign policy; and Czechoslovakia inaugurated a broad reform package in 1968, quite similar to Gorbachev's *glasnost* and *perestroika* some twenty years later, that ultimately provoked Soviet intervention. By the 1980s, however, the initiative for change was coming almost wholly from below, most notably in Poland's Solidarity movement. And in the miracle year of 1989 popular upheavals swept communist regimes from power almost overnight all across Eastern Europe. It was quite a different sequence from that of the Soviet Union, where Gorbachev's reforms from above initiated the social awakenings that ultimately brought down the communist regime but rather more slowly than in Eastern Europe.

Yet another large-scale process of historical change that provides a context for understanding the Soviet Union's final years is "the rise and fall of the great powers" within the system of European states.[7]

Emerging after the Renaissance, the great-power system featured endemic rivalry, ceaseless competition, and frequent wars as the political-military position of its various members rose and fell relative to one another. The Hapsburg dynasty, which linked Spanish and Austrian realms, first threatened to dominate the continent (1519–1659), until checked by a coalition of opposing powers. The Dutch Netherlands in the early seventeenth century, France under Louis XIV and again under Napoleon, Britain in the nineteenth century, and Germany in the first half of the twentieth—each in varying ways had a period of efflorescence, only to lose that position to a new rising power, often amid harsh military conflict.

In trying to explain this kaleidoscopic pattern, historian Paul Kennedy has emphasized the relationship of economic and political power. "There is a very clear connection *in the long run,*" he wrote, "between an individual Great Power's economic rise and fall and its growth and decline as an important military power (or world empire)."[8] He coined the term "imperial overstretch" to describe the situation in which a state's international obligations—military expenditure, colonies, and foreign bases, for example—undermine its domestic economy and thus contribute to its political-military decline.

Such an analysis helps to explain the changing Russian and Soviet role in the international arena. Russia joined the European great powers in the eighteenth century on the basis of Peter the Great's modernizing reforms and the country's large population. Its relative power declined during the nineteenth century as the Industrial Revolution, and Russia's slowness in reproducing it, pushed Britain, France, Germany, and Japan to the fore. Military defeats in the Crimean War (1854–56), the Russo-Japanese War of 1905, and World War I painfully disclosed its comparative backwardness. By the mid-twentieth century, however, the Soviet Union had been bolstered by Stalin's ferocious drive to industrialize, had struggled to a bloody victory in World War II—which decisively weakened Europe's other great powers—and had acquired both nuclear weapons and a buffer zone of satellite states in Eastern Europe. On these foundations, it emerged as one of the two superpowers in what had become a "bipolar" world. It seemed that the early-nineteenth-century prediction of Alexis de Tocqueville had come to pass—that Russia and the United States were "marked out by the will of Heaven to sway the destinies of half the globe."[9]

Despite its immense and growing military prowess during the Cold War, Soviet claims to superpower status rested on fragile and weakening economic foundations, as the 1970s and 1980s demonstrated. While the causes of this marked economic decline will be explored more thoroughly in Chapter 2, a form of "imperial overstretch" was clearly among them. An escalating arms race in both nuclear and conventional weapons together with expensive commitments in Eastern Europe and the Third World sent Soviet defense spending skyrocketing, undermining its domestic consumer economy in the process. Furthermore, the postwar recovery of Europe and Japan and the explosive economic growth of China made the Soviet position even worse by comparison. Particularly in the Gorbachev era, the Soviet leadership was quite aware of the relationship between its declining economic base and its international standing; and that perception substantially fueled the Soviet reform effort of the late 1980s.

Unchecked economic weakness would no doubt have assured a relative Soviet decline in the now global system of competing nation-states. But the sudden and quite unexpected disappearance of the Soviet Union marks its experience as sharply different from those of earlier declining states, where the process of decline worked itself out over many decades, leaving the core state intact. So, too, does the absence of clear military defeat, which had frequently accompanied and hastened the political decline of other great powers. Nonetheless, the Soviet Union joins Spain, France, Britain and other formerly great powers in the painful experience of international decline. None of its successor states, including the still huge and nuclear-equipped Russian Federation, occupies the powerful international position the Soviet Union had, for a brief time, enjoyed.

The terminal experience of the Soviet Union thus bears comparison with other disintegrating empires, other multiethnic states in crisis, other transitions to democracy, other reforming communist regimes, and other great powers in decline. But the country's sheer size and complexity and its historical centrality mark its passing as an event of unique significance in the world of the twentieth century.

The Uses of History

Historians believe, often with some passion, that the long view backward or "historical context" is essential for understanding contemporary events. But how exactly can historical inquiry assist us in grasping the complex events and processes that accompanied the final years of the Soviet Union?

In the first place, historical reflection reminds us of the many ways in which the past shapes and restricts the actions of people in the present, even if they are wholly unaware of it. The agenda of the Gorbachev reform program was largely a response to the legacy of Stalinism and invoked an even earlier Leninist version of the Soviet experience. The Stalin era in turn perpetuated in many ways the heritage of the tsarist political system that preceded it. And Russian autocracy of the late nineteenth century can hardly be understood without reference to the cultural heritage of Byzantium, the Mongol invasions of early Russia, or the reforms of Peter the Great. Thus, the past poses the problems those living in the present must confront, and it limits the alternatives available to them. Such a view of historical legacies highlights the constraints under which all of us operate and emphasizes the limits of human freedom.

But just how far should we take this understanding of historical legacies? Since the events we recount have already occurred, it is tempting, when looking back, to think that they were somehow inevitable, that things had to occur as they did. Some scholars, for example, imply that the growth of a more urbanized and well-educated society in the post-Stalin decades made political liberalization in the Soviet Union necessary and inescapable. In this view, Gorbachev's reform program was an inevitable consequence of earlier social changes. Others have argued that the "totalitarian" nature of the Soviet Union rendered reform impossible; thus Gorbachev's failure to revive the Soviet Union is more easily understood and the country's collapse may be thought inevitable.

This kind of thinking, however, leaves out the unexpectedness of historical change, minimizes the impact of individuals and particular decisions or policies, and ignores the vast uncertainty about the outcome of their actions that most people feel most of the time. Few people, if any, in the early 1980s expected that dramatic reforms were in the offing, and as late as 1989 or 1990 not many foresaw the imminent collapse of the Soviet Union. Historical reflection, then, is useful in reminding us that other alternatives seemed possible "back then," and that people living in the thick of things did not know what would happen. The hindsight of the historian, in short, can be misleading as well as revealing.

Echoes from the past can assist our understanding of more recent events in yet another way, for much of human culture is a dialogue or conversation with history, often contested with others who see the past very differently. In the endless creation of our constantly changing cultures, we continually make use of bits and pieces from the past—events, symbols, recollections—to construct a meaningful and livable world for ourselves and to serve our own interests in the here and now. Thus, Gorbachev invoked the memory of Lenin and the New Economic Policy of the 1920s to root his reforms in the soil of a respected past. Some of his radical critics, impatient with his desire to preserve a form of socialism, rejected the entire Soviet experience, including Lenin, and celebrated instead the last decades of tsarist rule when capitalist modernization and cultural westernization seemed to be taking root. That era, rather than the Soviet experience, offered to them a more solid historical foundation for building a new society. And millions of ordinary people, reeling from inflation, crime, empty shops, and enormous uncertainty, frequently described their situation in contrast to what they remembered as the stability and security of the Brezhnev era. Thus, historical knowledge is useful as we "listen in" on conversations from the past and about the past.

Notes

1. Karl Marx and Friedrich Engels, *The Communist Manifesto* (New York: Appleton-Century-Crofts, 1955), p. 12. (Originally published in 1848.)
2. Ibid., p. 32.
3. Aleksandr Solzhenitsyn, *Rebuilding Russia* (New York: Farrar, Straus and Giroux, 1991), p. 10.
4. Lev Timofeyev, *Russia's Secret Rulers* (New York: Knopf, 1992), p. 16.
5. For this argument, see M. Steven Fish, *Democracy from Scratch: Opposition and Regime in the New Russian Revolution* (Princeton: Princeton University Press, 1995).
6. Archie Brown, *The Gorbachev Factor* (New York: Oxford University Press, 1996), pp. 157–60; Sarah M. Terry, "Thinking about Post Communist Transitions: How Different Are They?" *Slavic Review* 52:2 (summer 1993), pp. 333–37.
7. This section draws on Paul Kennedy, *The Rise and Fall of the Great Powers* (New York: Random House, 1987).
8. Ibid., p. xxii.
9. Alexis de Tocqueville, *Democracy in America,* vol. 1 (New York: Vintage Books, 1945), p. 452. (Originally published in 1835.)

Chapter 1

Legacies: The Burdens of Russian and Soviet History

One way to think about why the Soviet Union collapsed is to ask the opposite question: How can we explain the persistence of the Soviet regime for more than seven decades despite what we now see as its all too apparent weaknesses? What held this sprawling, multinational country together for seventy-four years, while other empires disintegrated and other authoritarian or totalitarian regimes expired? A brief review of Russian and Soviet history can perhaps point to the changing sources of Soviet cohesion. With these in mind, we can then examine the processes that undermined and eroded the foundations of the Soviet experiment. This chapter then highlights major aspects of Russian and Soviet history that resonated still in the final years of the Soviet Union.

Legacies of Old Russia

Evolving for perhaps one thousand years before the revolution of 1917, the Russian state and the society it encompassed cast a long shadow on the twentieth-century Soviet Union and arguably continue to do so. Among the features of old Russia that shaped Soviet and post-Soviet society, none was more significant than its autocracy. The term refers to the enormous power that the old Russian state, embodied in the person of the tsar, came to assume over individuals, groups, and institutions in Russian society. In the centuries following the expulsion of the Mongols (1480–1750), the Russian state subordinated the Orthodox Church, subjected a previously free peasantry to a serfdom not far removed from slavery, and brutally stripped the nobility of its independence, requiring its members to render service to the tsar in return for their estates and the right to exploit their peasants. The victory of the tsar over all other sources of power likewise persuaded merchants, few in number and far removed from main routes of international commerce, that "the path to wealth lay not in fighting the authorities but in collaborating with them."[1] All this contrasted sharply with Western Europe, where the greater independence of the nobility, church, peasantry, and merchant class served to constrain royal power and to create more pluralistic societies.

Thus, private enterprise and civil society in Russia were weak as means of generating national wealth and power and as sources of social change. When Russia found itself confronted with the superior military power of a more dynamic and innovative Western Europe, it was the state that undertook the task of reform and "catching up" with its more powerful rivals. Peter the Great (1689–1725) initiated the tradition of "reform from above" and in the process enlarged, centralized, and strengthened the state even further. Later tsars in the nineteenth century followed suit, finally freeing the serfs in 1861 and initiating a state-led industrialization in the 1880s and 1890s.

How has this autocratic tradition of old Russia continued to echo in the Soviet era, after the revolution of 1917 had supposedly swept it decisively away? One answer, of course, is that Stalinism, with its assault on the peasantry, its brutal industrialization, and its effort to regiment and control an entire society, bore marked similarities to autocratic Russia. Many historians have argued that the revolution of 1917, committed to breaking with an autocratic past, actually replicated and magnified its absolutism, its paternalistic demand for obedience from subjects, its obsession with control, and its refusal to accommodate civil society independent of the state. Stalin, in this view, appropriated the political culture of old Russia. Thus, when Gorbachev took on the Stalinist legacy in the 1980s, he was simultaneously confronting a deeply established feature of Russia's political tradition.

But that tradition has been a source of pride for many, even during the Soviet era. Early on, various noncommunist groups such as former imperial army officers and educated specialists sympathized with the Bolsheviks as the only Russian force sufficiently strong and well organized to hold the empire together. Stalin himself, it seems, identified with Ivan the Terrible and Peter the Great in their efforts to build a strong state and to overcome Russia's backwardness. In the 1940s these early tsars were rehabilitated in Soviet textbooks and were presented as historically progressive figures. Popular attitudes toward Stalin as a strong leader, checking the petty bosses who tyrannized ordinary people, drew upon images of the "good tsar" who sought to protect his humble subjects.[2] Russia's autocratic tradition, in short, may have helped to sustain the Soviet experiment.

Russian autocracy lingers too in the 1990s as an explanation for the continuing difficulties of creating democracy in post-Soviet Russia. Russian political culture, with its fear of anarchy and disorder, its dogmatic, uncompromising style, and its deference to strong central authority, represents in this view a deeply rooted obstacle to the establishment of an effective democratic regime. The title of a recent book, *Eternal Russia: Yeltsin, Gorbachev, and the Mirage of Democracy,* conveys this outlook.

There is, of course, more to the legacy of old Russia than autocracy. Those who in recent years have believed in democratic possibilities for Russia pointed to examples from the past on which to build. The peasant commune, the workers' cooperative, organs of local self-government called *zemstvos,* the soviets of 1905 and 1917—all of these illustrated the capacity for practical social initiative at a local level.[3] And in the realm of political theory one scholar has defined an "alternative political tradition," with deep roots in Russian history, that sought to constrain tsarist authority through the countervailing power of the church and the aristocracy.[4] Furthermore, many observers have celebrated the ingenious capacity of Russians to circumvent authority, to create warm and embracing social life in the private sphere, and to survive enormous difficulties.

Others claimed to see actual movement toward western constitutional government, as Tsar Nicholas II, acting under great pressure following the upheaval of 1905, reluctantly established an elected parliament, the Duma, and permitted political parties and trade unions to operate legally for the first time. Had World War I not intervened to put enormous pressure on these fragile sprouts of democracy, perhaps Russia could have avoided the revolution and all that followed from it and evolved slowly toward western-style politics and society. It is one of the great "what if" questions of Russian history, and contemplating it has provided a source of hope for those who view the entire Soviet experience as a tragic and wasted epoch. For them, the late tsarist era with its vibrant aristocratic culture and its democratizing and modernizing tendencies represents a more solid historical foundation for building a new Russia than the crumbling remains of the Soviet age.

A further element of the tsarist legacy that echoed loudly in the final years of the Soviet Union was the question of empire. During the three centuries following 1555, Russia became the world's largest contiguous land-based empire, stretching eastward across Siberia to the Pacific, penetrating southward to incorporate ancient kingdoms and peoples in Central Asia and the Caucasus, and moving westward to seize the Baltic states, Belarus, Ukraine, part of Poland, and more. The result was an enormous multiethnic state, an empire comprising one-sixth of the world's land surface, and populated by people speaking well over a hundred different languages or dialects, among whom Russians numbered a little more than half at the beginning of the twentieth century. But Russians had created that empire, a historical task that occupied them for centuries. As a consequence, Russian national identity has been heavily imperial. A flourishing Russia meant an expanding empire.[5]

The vast cultural diversity among non-Russians had only begun to congeal into political consciousness or nationalism when the revolution broke out in 1917. This relative weakness of national feeling helped the victorious Bolsheviks to reconquer breakaway regions and to reconstitute the empire under Soviet auspices by the early 1920s. Thereafter, while the national question engaged Soviet policymakers repeatedly, it was never a major threat to the Soviet state until it erupted, with volcanic force and little warning, in the late 1980s to bring this last of the world's great empires to ruin.

All this poses fundamental questions that bear on the final years of the USSR. How did the Soviet empire escape until so recently a confrontation with non-Russian nationalism when so many other empires in the twentieth century had been shattered by that powerful force? Did the Gorbachev reforms actually stimulate nationalism or simply allow the expression of sentiments that had been brewing under the surface for decades? And how did Russians respond to the threat of losing their empire?

Weaving its way through all of these old Russian traditions has been a final legacy from the pre-Soviet era that continues to resonate in the

1990s. It is the question of Russia's identity, an issue posed by both its geography and its history. Spanning both Europe and Asia, Russia was by the eighteenth century one of the great powers of Europe, ethnically and religiously part of a larger European civilization. Its reforming tsars introduced elements of Western European technology, administrative machinery, and culture, all of which had a serious impact on the state bureaucracy, the nobility, and a small professional middle class. Yet Russia's history set it apart. Its Byzantine cultural heritage, the Mongol invasions, the pervasiveness of its autocracy, the absence of a Renaissance or Reformation, the weakness of its mercantile middle class, the lateness of its industrialization—all of this and more distinguished Russia from the other great powers farther west.

Here was grist for the mill of Russia's emerging intelligentsia—its educated and politically engaged elite—in the nineteenth century. They argued passionately about Russia's identity and its historical destiny. Was the country in fact part of Europe, destined to shake off its cultural backwardness and join the mainstream of the liberal, democratic, capitalist West? Or was it in some way essentially different from the competitive, driven, and materialistic West—uniquely Slavic, Orthodox, and Russian, with more harmonious communities, committed to social equality, and attuned to things of the spirit? This debate between so-called Westernizers and Slavophiles has engaged educated Russians ever since. And that distinction has been used as well to define political and ideological conflicts in recent Soviet and Russian life. Gorbachev, Yeltsin, and other advocates of democracy and capitalism represent, of course, the contemporary Westernizers, intent on living at last in a "normal" European fashion after wandering in the wasteland of Soviet communism for decades. Their conservative opponents, appalled by western cultural decadence, crime, and impoverishment, are the Slavophiles, seeking to find a moral compass and political and economic stability somewhere in the Russian past. Clearly the situation is far more complicated than this simple dichotomy will allow, but it illustrates again how elements of Russia's earlier history reverberate still in the vastly altered circumstances of the late twentieth century.

Legacies of Revolution

In the midst of World War I, which was going very badly for the Russians, the revolutionary year of 1917 unfolded dramatically. It began in February with the overthrow of the tsarist regime and ended in October with the seizure of state power by the Bolsheviks. There followed three years of brutal civil war, in which the Bolsheviks staggered to victory over their many enemies. The 1920s moved to a different tempo as the battered Bolsheviks, now calling themselves communists, moderated their policies and sought to consolidate their regime through the vehicle of the New Economic Policy.

The Revolution was an epic upheaval, comparable only to the French and Chinese revolutions in scope, depth, and consequence. It ended the monarchy, eliminated the old ruling group, engaged the energies of a still-small factory working class, projected a wholly new socialist order, created novel institutions of government, and threw down a challenge to the entire capitalist world. In short, it laid the foundations of the Soviet system. What were the legacies of revolution that persisted over the following seven decades, and in what ways did they continue to inform the final years of the Soviet Union?

One of them, initially, was enthusiasm. It is difficult, from the vantage point of the 1990s, to imagine a time when some people genuinely believed in communism. But despite the narrow base of active social support that the Soviet state enjoyed, especially after the Civil War, the regime was in fact sustained in part by energetic commitment, particularly among the young. Drawing on a belief in progress, inspired by the idea of socialism, and emboldened by an emerging mythology of the revolution as an opening to whole new worlds, enthusiastic Soviet activists imagined unrestrained vistas of freedom, justice, and human happiness and were willing to act on those beliefs. The flourishing of utopian science fiction, the establishment of alternative rituals such as "red" weddings and "revolutionary" funerals, the spontaneous creation of communes by veterans, students, and poor peasants—all these and more testify to the enthusiasm the revolution unleashed.[6] So too does the willingness of thousands of activists to immerse themselves in the difficult work of construction and propaganda on the new collective farms and industrial sites of the 1930s.[7] But as a source of support for the Soviet regime, revolutionary enthusiasm among Soviet citizens and even party members was a rapidly diminishing asset, not much in evidence after the mid-1930s and only a faded memory by the 1980s.

In the rhetoric of the Soviet regime, however, the utopian impulse, born of revolution, lasted far longer. Grand ideas—about the making of a "new Soviet man," about "proletarian internationalism," about the "building of socialism"—echoed constantly in parades and pageants, in the press and in school textbooks. And elements of the Soviet leadership no doubt believed in the ideals and felt that the Soviet system approximated them or that it certainly should. In 1961 Nikita Khrushchev's new party program confidently predicted that full communism would be achieved by 1980. The great contrast between this utopian rhetoric and the drab realities of Soviet life surely contributed to the erosion of belief in the system.

The revolutionary spirit also lived on in the political style of Soviet leadership. It was one of renewing society, of mobilizing the masses for grand projects, of summoning the energies and enthusiasm of the country for some wholesale transformation. Socialism, after all, did not build itself. It had to be constructed by the deliberate and energetic action of the party and the state. Stalin's industrialization, Khrushchev's de-Stalinization, and Gorbachev's perestroika all shared this common style, which also drew upon the statist tradition of old Russia. In these ways the legacy of revolutionary enthusiasm and utopianism played a role long after they had faded among ordinary people.[8]

A more enduring revolutionary legacy was Lenin himself. The undisputed leader of the revolution and of the Bolshevik or Communist Party during his life, he became, following his death in 1924, the focus of a massive cult intended to legitimate the Soviet regime. Many have commented on the quasi-religious character of the Lenin cult: ubiquitous portraits, busts, and posters were its icons; an idealized biography, its gospel; his writings, the sacred scriptures; and his mausoleum in Red Square, a shrine. There were Lenin corners in schools and public buildings; St. Petersburg became Leningrad; numerous other towns, streets, factories, and farms adopted his name; historical markers identified his every move; heroic statues were everywhere.

But Lenin's legacy was a sharply contested inheritance. Stalin presented himself as Lenin's successor and humble disciple. If Lenin's grand achievement had been the revolution itself and its defense during the Civil War, Stalin's would be the building of socialism, the industrialization of the Soviet Union by whatever means were necessary. Thus, Stalin invoked the ruthless and decisive Lenin of 1917 and the Civil War to legitimate his assault on the peasantry, his breakneck industrialization, and his ferocity in rooting out "enemies of the revolution" during the 1930s.

But throughout Soviet history, Stalin's opponents or his critics sum-

A woodcut of Lenin and a religious icon, displayed side by side in a small town Russian home in the early 1990s, illustrates the ability of some people to integrate these very different elements of Russia's historical experience. The books to the right of the woodcut are Russian translations of works by John Steinbeck. Photograph from the author's collection.

moned other Lenins. The contestation of Lenin's legacy took shape initially in the 1920s, as a struggle for leadership after Lenin's death coincided with a major debate within the party about the most appropriate strategy for building socialism. By the end of the decade that debate pitted Stalin against Nikolai Bukharin, who had emerged as the major spokesman for the gradualist, persuasive, and nonconfrontational strategy associated with the New Economic Policy (NEP). The NEP had established a conciliatory approach to the country's peasant majority, seeking to enlisting them gradually and voluntarily into more socialist forms of agriculture. This meant a slower pace of industrial development, a mixed economy of state and private ownership, and a considerable role for the market, though it allowed no place for rival political parties. The NEP was also associated with a more relaxed and experimental climate in cultural and intellectual affairs and a general atmosphere of gradualism and social harmony, rather than radical upheaval and class conflict. Lenin himself had initiated the NEP as a "retreat" following the agonies of the Civil War and the Bolsheviks' near defeat in it, but before his death he had come to believe that it would be needed "seriously and for a long time." Thus, it was this later Lenin that Bukharin invoked in his unsuccessful effort to protect the NEP against Stalin's more forceful and dictatorial policies, which were themselves justified by reference to an earlier Lenin.

The de-Stalinization process, begun in a limited way in the Khrushchev years (1953–64), occasioned the revival of the Lenin cult. Now Stalin was presented as a deviation from, rather than a perpetuation of, the path Lenin had established. Lenin's relative openness to conflicting opinion within the party and his refusal to use force against party members contrasted sharply with Stalin's pervasive terror.

Even more pointedly, Gorbachev presented his initial reforms in a Leninist package, suggesting that Lenin's bold, creative, and active style were also his own. Furthermore, major elements of the NEP experience were held up as precedents for Gorbachev's policies.[9] This fostered a major reexamination of the NEP era among Soviet writers and historians, and it generally came to be seen as a positive alternative to Stalinism. In this telling of Soviet history, Stalinism was not the necessary or only possible outcome of Lenin's revolutionary legacy. NEP, the argument went, could have provided a far more humane and no less effective framework for Soviet development than Stalin's brutal and wasteful policies. Here was a Leninist, and therefore socialist, foundation on which Gorbachev's efforts to revive the Soviet system could be predicated.

While Gorbachev's glasnost actively encouraged attacks on Stalin, it opened the door for some to go even further. By 1988 and 1989, there were growing criticisms of Lenin himself in the Soviet press. The horrors of Stalinism, they argued, had their roots in Lenin's ideas and practices. The single-party state, an "ends justifies the means" morality, the use of terror against enemies, the building of concentration camps, reliance on the secret police—all began with Lenin, and Stalin was the logical outcome. This had long been a popular view in the West; now it was embraced passionately by those Soviet writers who sought to discredit not simply the Stalin era but the entire Soviet experience. This public "desacralizing" of the mythical Lenin certainly played some role in eroding further the legitimacy of the Soviet regime.

Yet another revolutionary legacy serving to underpin the Soviet system was the development of an official ideology. While all societies generate legitimating ideas and values, the Soviet experience was remarkable for the extent to which such an ideology was elaborated, made explicit, and propagated through the educational system and state-controlled media. It was rooted, of course, in the voluminous writings of Karl Marx but supplemented and modified by Lenin's writings and later by those of other theorists and political leaders. What were the major elements and characteristics of this ideology, known officially as Marxism-Leninism?

It was, in the first place, an all-inclusive, comprehensive system of thought that claimed to explain virtually everything. Politics, social class, culture, religion, artistic expression—all were shaped by economic foundations of society, or the "mode of production." Marx had focused attention on class and class conflict as the driving force in all of history and, more particularly, on the factory working class as the revolutionary agent for the overthrow of a fatally flawed capitalist system. Lenin expanded this to include the peasantry in Russia and exploited colonial subjects in Europe's overseas empires as additional revolutionary forces.

This ideology presented the revolutionary transition leading from capitalism to socialism as an inevitable process, an immutable law of historical development. This "scientific" character of Marxism-Leninism reflected a progressive, optimistic, and modernist view of history, rooted in the Enlightenment, and gave it a certainty and a dogmatism that were, at least for a time, attractive to many. Lenin contributed to this body of ideas the notion of a "vanguard party," endowed with a uniquely authoritative Marxist understanding of history and prepared to make and guard the revolution. Drilled into Soviet young people in required school classes, in Komsomol (the official communist youth organization), and in an endless stream of publications, Marxism-Leninism explained the origins of the Soviet Union in an inevitable and heroic revolution led by the Bolsheviks, described the present as a period of hard work needed to build a socialist society, and projected a utopian future of communist prosperity and equality. In the global struggle against capitalism and imperialism, the Soviet Union had a mission of world historical significance.

Much of this blended easily with older notions of Russia's uniqueness as a distinctly Slavic, harmonious, and unified society. Soviet socialism also was building a "higher" form of human community, and it too was governed by a uniquely just ruler. The USSR's destiny, like that of old Russia, differed sharply from that of the West. This set of ideas, elaborated and modified slightly over the years and blended with the cults of Lenin and Stalin, was an attempt to create a new mythology, worldview, or even a substitute religion to explain, justify, and legitimate the Soviet experiment. It was an enormous cultural undertaking. Ultimately, of course, that effort failed, and its failure played a major role in the collapse of the Soviet regime. To what extent did Soviet citizens ever believe that ideology? What conditions undermined that belief? These are vital questions to which we will return more than once.

A final legacy of revolution lay in the political system the victorious Bolsheviks erected. It was an unprecedented arrangement, particularly in the depth to which it penetrated society and the extent to which it sought to transform and control every area of life. It claimed to be democratic in that it acted in the interests of the vast majority, especially workers and peasants, but it created a centralized autocracy far surpassing that of the tsars. The dual instruments of that system—the state and the party—both derived from the revolution. It was their unique relationship that marked the Soviet regime as a new type of political system.

The new state derived its very name from organs of revolutionary upheaval, the soviets. Spontaneously formed grassroots councils, soviets had sprung up first in 1905 and then again in 1917 all across the country. Bolsheviks came to control the major urban soviets and carried out the October Revolution under the slogan, "All power to the soviets." Within a few years, however, these lively, popular, and revolutionary bodies had lost their insurgent spirit and their independence to become the largely powerless legislative branch of the new Union of Soviet Socialist Republics, and they remained so until the late 1980s.

Soviets were organized on every administrative level—villages, towns and cities, regions, provinces, republics, and the union, some fifty thousand in all. The hierarchy of soviets culminated in the Supreme Soviet of the USSR, the country's national parliament. Elected periodically from a single list of unopposed, party-prescribed candidates, their members' formal function was legislative; in fact, they generally passed in rubber-stamp unanimity the laws and the Five-Year Plans developed by the party leadership.

The executive or administrative branch of the Soviet state was embodied in a huge and hugely complex bureaucracy. This is perhaps not surprising, since the Soviet state, from the late 1920s on, abolished private property in favor of state ownership, undertook the enormous task of industrializing the country, and was the effective employer of virtually everyone. Thus, ministries and "state committees" proliferated. Some were responsible for ordinary functions of government (health, education, defense, justice), but the majority served to manage the economy. At the level of central planning were agencies responsible for some general economic function at the national level: overall planning; prices; labor and wages; wholesale, retail, and foreign trade; finance and banking; quality control. Then there were ministries, dozens of them, in charge of some branch of the economy: electronics, oil, automobiles, light industry, construction, chemicals. By the 1980s some twenty separate ministries were involved with machine building of some kind. Each of these ministries supervised numerous state-owned firms (known as "enterprises" in Soviet terminology), where production actually occurred. A number of these ministries had branches in each of the republics as well as their central headquarters in Moscow. The ministers in charge of these agencies—about one hundred of them by the 1980s—constituted the Council of Ministers, whose chairman, the prime minister, was the formal head of the government. Collectively these ministries, with their advisory councils, their professional staffs, and their affiliated research institutes, comprised an immense bureaucratic machine with hundreds of thousands of employees and great technical expertise. Its task was nothing less than running the entire country.

The quasi-federal character of the Soviet state likewise derived from the revolutionary era. In response to a series of nationalist movements that broke out during 1917 and 1918, the Bolshevik leadership adopted the principle of federalism. In theory, the USSR was a "voluntary union" of its component "union republics"—ultimately fifteen of them—each having the right to secede. This was, of course, wholly fictitious, for the Soviet Union consistently operated as a highly centralized, unitary state. Still, the principle had been established. Even more important, each of the union republics—Georgia, Ukraine, Latvia, Uzbekistan, and so on—was defined in ethnic or national terms. Furthermore, smaller ethnic groups living in one or another union republic received recognition in distinct territories known as autonomous republics, regions, or areas, depending on their size. This was in sharp contrast to the administrative units of the old Russian Empire, which paid no attention to local historical or cultural realities. Thus, the principle of nationality was embedded in the territorial administrative units of the new Soviet state. To its leaders, this was a temporary expedient, for their ideology proclaimed loudly that ethnic or national loyalties would dissolve into an all-Soviet identity as socialism took hold in the country. Nothing of the kind, of course, occurred, and it is arguable that the decision to organize the Soviet state in this fashion contributed to the triumph of national over Soviet identity.

Perhaps the chief characteristic of the Soviet state was its subordination to the Communist Party. In theory, the party was the vanguard, quite separate from the state, with responsibility for establishing policy, appointing people to important state positions, checking up on the implementation of policy, and generally leading the march to socialism. It was, as its own rules proclaimed, "the leading and guiding force in Soviet society." The state apparatus, on the other hand, implemented policy and carried out the day-to-day administration of the country under party supervision. It was a relationship akin to that between the owners of a private firm (the party) and their hired managers (the state bureaucracy). But over the course of several decades, the party itself became a huge bureaucratic machine, paralleling and penetrating state institutions.

In numbers, it grew rapidly, despite great losses during the purges of the 1930s and during World War II. In early 1917 it had about twenty-four thousand members, and it peaked in the late 1980s with some 20 million, almost 10 percent of the adult population. Recruited with considerable care and subject to a rigorous screening process, party members were to be the country's "best and brightest." Personally upright, well schooled in Marxist-Leninist ideology, model workers, and active in public life, party members were to be the disciplined exemplars of socialist society in the making. In return they acquired, in varying degrees, elite status in that society. Membership generally meant public respect, a measure of visibility, and important contacts. At its higher levels it provided preferential access to housing, scarce goods, better schools, travel opportunities, and certain jobs.

Clearly, not all party members were equal. The vast majority were quite ordinary people who lived and worked much like their nonparty neighbors. But they paid party dues, attended and organized endless meetings, discussion groups, and lectures, got out the vote at election time, and otherwise took part in the routines of party life. The real party elite, known as the *apparat* and numbering several hundred thousand people in the 1980s, were those actually employed by the party itself in its top positions. And a much broader elite, encompassing the apparat, included those who held *nomenklatura* positions somewhere in the far-flung state bureaucracy. These were high-level political and administrative posts for which explicit party approval was required. Many, though not all, nomenklatura positions were filled by party members. Here, in the apparat and the broader nomenklatura, was the ruling class of the late Soviet Union.

The party penetrated Soviet society through an elaborate hierarchical organization. At its base were Primary Party Organizations (PPOs), party cells organized at virtually every workplace in the country—factories, collective farms, shops, restaurants, schools, and offices—and numbering more than 425,000 in the early 1980s. Through the party's "right of control," these PPOs monitored the operation of their respective enterprises, alert for problems, inefficiencies, and violations of party policy. They represented the local eyes and ears of the ever present party.

Above the PPOs rose a series of party committees at each level of administrative organization—district, region, republic, and all-Union. Since these committees met infrequently, day-to-day business fell to their political bureaus (politburo), headed by the first secretary, who was normally a very powerful figure. Attached to each of these committees was a secretariat whose various departments assumed responsibility for particular functions, such as agriculture, administration, propaganda, culture, or light industry. Finally, periodic party conferences or congresses at each level elected their respective party committees, chose delegates to the party conference or congress of the next highest level, and approved policies that came down from the top. The whole system culminated at the all-Union, or national, level in Moscow, where the Central Committee, Politburo, and Secretariat were the major institutions and the general secretary of the party was the most prominent person. There the leading figures hammered out the main lines of policy, while the apparat supervised and coordinated state agencies and managed the party's internal affairs.

The basic principle of party operation was known as "democratic centralism." But the democratic elements (lower-level bodies genuinely electing higher-level organs, and free and open discussion before decisions were taken) largely disappeared by the late 1920s. In practice, "centralism" prevailed in an almost military style of discipline, with lower organs absolutely subordinate to higher ones, electing prescribed delegates and endorsing prearranged policies.

Beyond its local party cells and bureaucratic hierarchy, the Communist Party of the Soviet Union (CPSU) was active in research and publishing, writing and rewriting the party's history to fit the current party line and issuing thousands of books, articles, and newspapers to correctly interpret current affairs. Furthermore, affiliated youth organizations (Pioneers, Octobrists, Komsomol) brought the party's message to millions of young people and recruited many of them into the party itself. The CPSU, in short, touched virtually every Soviet citizen in every republic and region of the country. Its significance as an integrative institution for the Soviet regime can hardly be overestimated. It was in many ways what held the Soviet Union together, and the erosion of its authority in the late 1980s contributed much to the country's collapse.

Questions and Controversies:
Was the Soviet Union Doomed from the Start?

Among the enduring problems of historical explanation is how far back to begin. Since historians generally view the past as a seamless web of events and processes, starting points for analysis are a matter of judgment. And since historians pride themselves on uncovering the deeper and less obvious roots of contemporary events, many are prone to push the search for origins and causes into the distant past.

At what point, then, should we start in our attempt to explain the Soviet collapse? Because the Soviet system ended so quickly, certain historians, particularly those with a strong anticommunist bent, have argued that some fundamental fragility or contradiction lay at the heart of the Soviet system, which rendered it unviable virtually from the start and made its collapse only a matter of time.

Historian Martin Malia has articulated one such "fatal flaw" approach, rooted in the core ideology of the entire Soviet enterprise. The origins of the Soviet regime, Malia argues, lay in a utopian commitment to "building socialism," to realizing fully the ancient dream of abundance and human equality. Unlike the modest welfare-state socialism of Western Europe, this full or "maximalist" socialism necessarily meant the complete transformation of human consciousness and the abolition of private property, profit, and the market, for these were the chief sources of social inequality. But this was an impossible dream of utopian social engineering that flew in the face of both history and human nature. No such socialism had existed or could exist. Thus, the Communist Party, in which that dream was embodied, had to rely on "a mixture of ideological illusion and raw coercion." The inevitable outcome was the "dictatorship of the Party" or, in short, totalitarianism—an effort to subordinate all of human life to an ideologically driven party-state. Nor could such a system be reformed into "socialism with a human face" without abandoning its ideological commitment to equality and to the party's monopoly on truth and power. It was all or nothing. The gap between the high moral pretensions of the system and the criminal means used to achieve them, together with accumulating practical failures in the 1970s and 1980s, created "an inherently fragile affair, a permanent house of cards awaiting its natural fate." The Gorbachev reforms merely exposed that fragility for all to see, destroying what remained of the ideology. Thus, the system collapsed with a startling absence of resistance.[10]

If Malia finds the fatal flaw of the Soviet system in the idea of full socialism, others have located it in the impulse toward nationalism.[11] The Soviet Union, in this view, had preserved and extended Russia's multinational empire far into the twentieth century, even while claiming that socialism would dissolve national loyalties into an all-Soviet identity. But *Homo sovieticus* was largely a myth, undermined by Soviet policies that recognized national cultures but refused them any real political expression. Furthermore, in the larger world of the twentieth century, nationalism was the primary language of political discourse, and national groups in the Soviet Union could hardly remain immune. Thus, it was "the rebellion of the nations," long ignored by the Soviet regime and even by Gorbachev, that finally destroyed the communist state.

Both versions of the "fatal flaw" approaches seek some "unique and enduring structural fragility" to account for the Soviet collapse and push the search for explanation to the very beginning of the Soviet experiment.[12] But while such views offer historical depth, they have also provoked considerable criticism. In the first place, they offer no particular explanation for the timing of the country's disintegration. If the Soviet Union possessed some fatal flaw, why did it collapse in 1991 rather than 1961 or 2021?

Furthermore, "doomed from the start" approaches risk turning historical hindsight into assertions of inevitability. Certainly, the further back we go in seeking historical explanation for any event, the more determined the outcome appears. And yet that awareness was far from the minds of most people who actually lived the Soviet experience. Even when Gorbachev assumed power in 1985, virtually no one, within or outside the Soviet Union, anticipated either the rapid disintegration of the state or the quick end of Communist Party dominance. Stability and slow decline seemed more likely than dramatic change and disintegration. Many people—scholars, policymakers, and ordinary Soviet citizens—pointed to the country's long-term weaknesses and its growing problems. But that was a far cry from predicting the system's inevitable and imminent demise. Many imperial states—the Roman, Ottoman, and Austro-Hungarian empires, for example—endured long periods of political or economic decline without a sudden collapse. Why did the Soviet Union not follow that pattern?

Thus, critics of the fatal-flaw approach argue that attributing inevitability to events, based on hindsight, robs historical actors of their "agency," their ability to act and make decisions freely. It is therefore unfaithful to the actual experience of those who lived through Soviet history. But whose consciousness should the writing of history reflect—that of the actual participants in the historical process or that of scholars whose retrospective judgments may both illuminate and obscure the events they describe? The debate continues.

Legacies of Stalinism

The creation of an enormous party-state machine was in large measure achieved while Joseph Stalin ruled the Soviet Union (1929–53). It occurred as Stalin's regime launched the country on a gigantic effort at economic modernization and at "catching up" with those western capitalist nations by which it felt encircled and threatened. That effort, referred to in the Soviet Union as the "building of socialism," set in motion an epic social transformation that in a generation propelled the country toward a unique form of modern industrial society. Accompanying these processes was an escalating search for internal enemies that shaped and misshaped the entire system in many ways. This was all a part of that singular phenomenon known as Stalinism, though it encompassed far more than the initiatives and personality of the ruler. It was the pivot of Soviet history; it fashioned Soviet society even more decisively than the revolution itself; and its multiple legacies were the primary object of the Gorbachev reforms.

Among the first areas to feel the force of Stalin's "revolution from above" was the countryside. The Soviet regime was in search of grain both to feed the cities and to export in exchange for industrial machinery. Stalin's answer to the problem was the rapid and coercive consolidation of privately held and widely scattered strips of land into large collective farms, often coinciding with old villages, furnished slowly, with tractors and combines, and required to deliver fixed amounts of grain to the state at a set price. The state ultimately got its grain, but at a price far higher than it ever imagined.

The initial cost was massive peasant resistance, which the regime overcame only with the widespread use of force and violence. Accompanied by the closure of many churches, the slaughter of much of their livestock, a bitter famine that cost millions of lives, and the deportation to remote areas of perhaps a million *kulak* (relatively rich peasant) families, collectivization seemed to many peasants nothing less than a "second serfdom." Active resistance soon gave way to lingering resentment at the second-class status that *kolkhozniks* (collectivized farmers) experienced. Through very low prices paid for their compulsory deliveries of food products, they were exploited for decades on behalf of the country's industrialization effort. They were denied until the 1970s the internal passports that permitted legal movement within the country. And they were refused the right to individual ownership of horses right up to the country's collapse in 1991. The results of kolkhoznik resentment were described by an outside observer in 1971:

> The collective farm "serf" discharges his labor obligation to the "master" carelessly, grudgingly. He refuses to concern himself with the fertility of the "collective" land. It is not his. He does not see the public weeds, nor the rust on the collective machinery, nor the private cow that grazes just inside the collective cornfield. He steals from the collective or habitually turns a blind eye when his fellows do so.[13]

Such attitudes contributed much to the consistently low productivity of Soviet agriculture and the overall weakness of the Soviet economy. It was a further cost of collectivization.

A final price was that of principle. While the Stalinist regime understood socialism as requiring full public ownership of the means of production and the elimination of market exchange based on supply and demand, it felt required by the mid-1930s to grant the peasants small "household plots" and permission to sell the produce grown there in open markets. Throughout the entire Soviet era, these household plots and farmers' markets remained important to peasant livelihoods and to providing produce to the towns. But they represented an embarrassing admission that a fully collectivized agriculture was impossible to achieve.

Collectivization in Stalin's USSR was part of a larger strategy—creating modern industry. This had always been a Bolshevik priority, both to strengthen the country militarily against its capitalist neighbors and to establish the economic foundations for socialism. But during the NEP years, a moderate pace of industrial growth prevailed, and production focused largely on consumer goods. By the late 1920s, Stalin had determined to break out of this gradualist approach and launched a massive drive to "put an end to [Russian] backwardness." "We are fifty or one hundred years behind the advanced countries," he declared in 1931. "We must make good this distance in ten years. Either we do it or we shall perish."

The means to this great leap was state ownership and central planning, and in this respect, Soviet economic development differed sharply from that of the rest of Europe, which had relied largely on the market and private enterprise. Thus, the Soviets created the first modern industrial command economy. Treating the country's economy as a whole, a series of Five-Year Plans established overall goals and determined what items should be produced, in what quantities, and at what price. Based on estimates of requirements from local factories and ministries, the central planning agencies tried to make available the right amount of raw materials, manpower, and equipment and to coordinate the activities of many ministries and their related enterprises. It was an enormous undertaking, made even more so as Stalin forced the pace of industrial growth by increasing the production targets and then urging factory managers to exceed even these high goals. The first Five-Year Plan, he demanded, must be completed in four.

By any economic measure, it worked, at least for a time. Soviet industrial growth rates in the 1930s were high, while the West was mired in the Great Depression. Between 1928 and 1938, iron, steel, and coal production almost quadrupled. New cities and whole industries were created, and the urban workforce grew rapidly. Much of this growth took place in the previously backward areas of Siberia and east of the Urals. By the end of the 1930s, the Soviet Union was clearly one of the world's chief industrial states. And victory in World War II lent credibility to Soviet industrial strategy.

Thus, the Plan became central to Soviet political culture. In late 1929 a senior party official spelled out what this should mean: "We need to organize a social and political mechanism with which 150 million people will act, guided by a single plan, a single concept, a single will, a single effort to accomplish what is laid down by the plan."[14] To implement the Plan, a vast expansion of the state apparatus followed, and to supervise that implementation the party bureaucracy grew to match it.

The great advantage of planning was the ability to concentrate resources and labor for specific purposes. Thus, the Soviet command economy in the 1930s focused attention on heavy industry while sacrificing housing and consumer production. But the central dilemma of a command economy has been how to combine control from the center, which the plan requires, with the flexibility, creativity, and incentives for hard work that modern and technologically sophisticated economies demand. It was a dilemma the Soviet regime never solved and the Stalinist style of industrial planning exacerbated. That style favored gigantic enterprises over smaller ones, ignored local realities in favor of dictates from Moscow, pushed the tempo of industrial development at the expense of careful cost-benefit analysis, and sacrificed safety and workers' living conditions to maximize output.[15] This kind of planning persisted long after Stalin's death and contributed increasingly to both economic stagnation and environmental disaster. Periodic efforts at reform in the Stalin era and later did little to substantially modify this Stalinist planning system and the culture it had created.

Accompanying this revolutionary effort at "building socialism" was a growing search for "enemies" who would obstruct or subvert that process. Between 1928 and 1931 the regime tried a number of "bourgeois specialists" for "wrecking" and sabotage. There followed in the early 1930s a series of party purges, designed to weed out undesirable members. The climax of the search for enemies occurred in 1937–38 as hundreds of thousands, perhaps millions, of top party, state, and military officials were arrested on charges of disloyalty and then tried, convicted, and either executed or sent to labor camps. A series of fantastic show trials featured prominent party officials confessing to a variety of horrendous and altogether unlikely crimes. While high-ranking communist officials were most vulnerable, many others were like-

Voices

Remembering Stalin . . . Favorably

For many citizens of the former Soviet Union, the memory of Stalin has no doubt been one of anger, bitterness, and shame. But clearly not for everyone. Here are two excerpts that show the continuing uses of Stalin's image in the uncertain and insecure 1990s. The first is from a Colonel Volkov, sixty-two years old, speaking to an American reporter in 1991; the second conveys the views of Yuri Belov, a leading ideologist of a reviving Communist Party in 1996.

In those days only one word of Stalin's was needed, and everyone understood, from kids to the oldest people. Since we in uniform are used to discipline, it seems strange to us now when orders and laws are not obeyed. . . . What have we come to that we have nothing in the stores? Farms and factories don't fulfill their plans. Some even say that we should bring Stalin back to life for a couple of months.

From Adam Hochschild, *The Unquiet Ghost: Russians Remember Stalin* (New York: Penguin Books, 1994), pp. 65–66.

We are told that Stalinism means mass-scale repression. . . . The fact is that in 30 years under Stalin's guidance, just a moment in history, we covered the road from the wooden plow to the atomic reactor. The fact is that we overcame all industrial backwardness, and if that had not been done, the last war would not have been won.

From the *New York Times*, May 3, 1996, p. 10.

---

wise swept up in the carnage—members of the intelligentsia, people with foreign connections or relatives living abroad, "former kulaks and criminals," and not a few ordinary people who had uttered unguarded remarks or made the wrong enemies.

Historians continue to debate the sources of the terror and the precise number of persons involved,[16] but the legacy of those terrible events has shaped, and haunted, Soviet society ever since. One outcome, of course, was simple fear, most prominent among high-level officials and party members. That fear became a major prop of the Soviet regime and lasted long after the overt terror had diminished. It contributed to the passivity and the reluctance to take initiative that so many observers have noticed in Soviet life from the Politburo to the factory floor. Institutionally, Stalin's terror enhanced the role of the secret police and diminished that of the party. It also greatly increased the population of the Gulag, the countrywide network of forced-labor camps, which held some 5 million prisoners by the early 1950s. This slave labor force provided the manpower for any number of Soviet economic development projects in the most remote and inhospitable regions where free laborers were difficult to attract.

Famine, deportations, purges, arrests, executions, slave labor camps, victims numbering in the many millions—suffering on such an epic scale, and created by the regime itself, was extraordinarily difficult to square with any conception of socialism, and much of it was therefore repressed and not officially acknowledged. It produced, in the judgment of one scholar, "a nation traumatized by its own past."[17] The need to reckon with that past, to come to terms with the crimes of the Stalin era, echoed repeatedly in the decades that followed. It was among the major legacies which that era bore to the final years of the Soviet Union.

The upheavals of the Stalin era led to a massive movement of people and the emergence of a new social structure. An enormous exodus from the villages to the new industrial centers and urban areas—some 12 million people during the First Five-Year Plan alone—drained the collective farms of their most energetic, ambitious, and "modern" elements. Many of those who remained were clearly demoralized, recognizing that the "good life" lay elsewhere. One rural official in 1937 put into words what many believed: "The clever ones left the collective farms long ago; all that remain are the fools."[18]

The urban working class grew correspondingly, but its mostly young, unskilled recruits, fresh from rural villages, gave it a far different character than the radical proletarians who had made the revolution in 1917. Stalin's desire to create a technically competent and thoroughly communist elite, drawn from the working class, provided great opportunity for hundreds of thousands of these young people—manual laborers and low-level white-collar workers—who streamed into the new technical schools that opened after 1928. These institutes, operating outside the older university system, were affiliated with particular industrial ministries and offered a narrow technical education, coupled with ideological instruction. Those who graduated (mostly in engineering of some kind) in the early 1930s experienced rapid promotion in the party, state, or industrial bureaucracies and considerable upward social mobility. The great majority of them survived the purges and terror of the 1930s and even benefited as their elders were removed. With Khrushchev, Brezhnev, and Alexei Kosygin among them, this generation of the administrative and specialist elite dominated Soviet society into the 1980s and provided the top post-Stalin leadership for the country. Social mobility thus provided, for a time, a measure of support and legitimation for the Soviet regime.[19]

This "new class" was privileged in many ways—access to special stores, hospitals, schools, and apartments; luxurious vacations and country homes; higher salaries; servants and chauffeurs; high social status. But these privileges derived from holding positions in the nomenklatura or in high-level professional associations, not from the ownership of property as in capitalist societies. And those positions, as the purges of the 1930s dramatically underscored, were highly insecure. It is perhaps not surprising then that this Soviet elite developed conservative attitudes, despite its socialist and revolutionary origins. These elites imitated the manners and fashions of the formerly despised bourgeois and aristocratic classes; they honored and sought to acquire the culture associated with prerevolutionary figures in art, music, literature, and dance. In fact, the Stalinist regime as a whole by the mid-1930s was emphasizing order and tradition in many spheres. In education this meant a prescribed curriculum, school uniforms, and emphasis on heroic historical figures in place of the more experimental policies of the 1920s; in family policy it meant tightening up the requirements for divorce, forbidding abortion, and emphasizing traditional gender roles in sharp contrast to the more feminist agenda of the post-1917 decade; in the economic realm it meant abandoning socialist egalitarianism and promoting wage differentials as an incentive for hard work. Stalin's use of the term *intelligentsia,* which generally referred to a well-educated and highly cultured group originating in the nineteenth century, to include this new technical and administrative elite showed the extent to which older values had come to permeate the Soviet regime. It was a way of suggesting that the "new class" deserved its privileges because it had assimilated "culture."[20] Thus, parallel to the vast social and political upheavals of the 1930s—perhaps even because of these upheavals—Soviet society took on, especially at its upper levels, a distinctly conservative tone. That conservatism, long in the making, was among the most difficult obstacles for the Gorbachev reforms in the 1980s to overcome.

If fear born of Stalin's terror and social mobility born of Soviet industrialization contributed to the cohesion of the Soviet regime, so too did its victory in World War II. That victory, despite some twenty to thirty million casualties and immense physical devastation, became a source of great pride for many people from all social classes and seemed to demonstrate the validity and necessity of Stalin's harsh measures in the 1930s. After all, the question went, would we have won the war without those measures? Furthermore, the war added a traditionalist patriotic element to Soviet identity, as Stalin invoked ancient warriors, tsarist generals, and "mother Russia" to sustain his people in that great struggle. In the decades that followed, Soviet leadership nurtured a virtual cult of the war: memorials were everywhere; wedding parties made pilgrimages to them and brides left their bouquets behind; May 9, Victory Day, saw elaborately orchestrated celebrations; veterans were honored and granted modest privileges. Both victim and victor, the Soviet Union had achieved its finest hour through the wise leadership of Stalin and the party and the heroic action of a united people and its armed forces. That was the message of the Great Patriotic War cult. But it was a message that glasnost sharply challenged in the late 1980s, thus eroding yet another prop of the Soviet regime.

In a strange way the Soviet experience in World War II dealt the country a double blow. The physical destruction and loss of life were enormous, but the country's ultimate victory ensured that the process of rebuilding would take place along the same Stalinist lines as before: a centralized command economy, priority to defense industry, suspicious isolation from the West, party domination of society. Unlike Germany and Japan, the Soviet Union received no fresh start after the war, and so the legacies of the Stalin years persisted well beyond the dictator's death in 1953.

Notes

1. Richard Pipes, *Russia Under the Old Regime* (New York: Scribner's, 1974), p. 220.

2. Maureen Perrie, "The Tsar, the Emperor, the Leader: Ivan the Terrible, Peter the Great, and Anatolii Rybakov's Stalin," in *Stalinism: Its Nature and Aftermath,* ed. Nick Lampert and Gabor T. Rittersporn (Armonk, N.Y.: M.E. Sharpe, 1992), pp. 77–97.

3. Geoffrey Hosking, *The Awakening of the Soviet Union* (Cambridge: Harvard University Press, 1990), pp. 19–27.

4. Nicolai N. Petro, *The Rebirth of Russian Democracy* (Cambridge: Harvard University Press, 1995).

5. Richard Pipes, "Birth of an Empire," *New York Times Book Review,* May 25, 1997, p. 13.

6. Richard Stites, *Revolutionary Dreams* (New York: Oxford University Press, 1989).

7. See, for example, Maurice Hindus, *Red Bread* (Bloomington: Indiana University Press, 1988); and John Scott, *Behind the Urals* (Bloomington: Indiana University Press, 1989).

8. For this argument, see Charles H. Fairbanks, Jr., "The Nature of the Beast," *National Interest* (spring 1993), pp. 46–53.

9. C. Smart, "Gorbachev's Lenin: The Myth in Service to Perestroika," *Studies in Comparative Communism* 23:1 (1990), pp. 5–21.

10. Martin Malia, *The Soviet Tragedy* (New York: Free Press, 1994), especially chap. 13.

11. Roman Szporluk, "After Empire: What?" *Daedalus* (summer 1994), pp. 21–40; Hélène Carrère d'Encausse, *The End of the Soviet Empire* (New York: Basic Books, 1993).

12. Martin Malia, "A Fatal Logic," *National Interest* 31 (spring 1993), p. 80.

13. Quoted in Sheila Fitzpatrick, *Stalin's Peasants* (New York: Oxford University Press, 1994), p. 316.

14. Quoted in R.W. Davies, "Economic Aspects of Stalinism," in *The Stalin Phenomenon,* ed. Alec Nove (New York: St. Martin's Press, 1992), p. 41.

15. Loren R. Graham, *The Ghost of the Executed Engineer: Technology and the Fall of the Soviet Union* (Cambridge: Harvard University Press, 1993), p. 90.

16. See, for example, J. Arch Getty and Roberta T. Manning, eds., *Stalin's Terror: New Perspectives* (New York: Cambridge University Press, 1993); and Hans-Henning Schroder, "Upward Social Mobility and Mass Repression: The Communist Party and Soviet Society in the 1930s," in *Stalinism,* eds. Lampert and Rittersporn, pp. 157–83.

17. Hosking, *Awakening of the Soviet Union,* p. 8.

18. Fitzpatrick, *Stalin's Peasants,* pp. 81–82.

19. Sheila Fitzpatrick, *The Cultural Front: Power and Culture in Revolutionary Russia* (Ithaca: Cornell University Press, 1992), pp. 149–82; Schroder, "Upward Social Mobility."

20. Fitzpatrick, *Cultural Front,* pp. 14–15, 218–19.

Chapter 2

Cracks in the Foundation: The Post-Stalin Years

More than three decades passed between Stalin's death in 1953 and Gorbachev's coming to power in 1985. It was the time of Khrushchev's reforms (1954–64), of Brezhnev's "stagnation" (1964–82), and of the short-lived leadership of Yuri Andropov (1983–84) and Konstantin Chernenko (1984–85). For most historians the central issue of those decades has been the extent to which Stalinism persisted in Soviet life and the degree to which it had been eroded. Those who emphasized continuities pointed to the persistence of an official Marxist-Leninist ideology, state control of the economy, Communist Party domination of the state as well as of social and cultural life, sharp restrictions on civil rights enforced by a secret police, and continued Soviet hostility toward the West. The fundamental features of Stalinist totalitarianism, in this view, remained in place.

Others disagreed. The post-Stalinist leadership, they argued, deliberately reversed or modified many earlier policies and practices resulting in the end of terror and purges, high-level criticism of Stalin himself, the release of millions from the Gulag, the easing of restrictions on cultural and intellectual expression, the relaxation of Cold War tensions in détente, new priorities for investment in the economy, and various efforts to reform the system of economic management. And in addition to these policy shifts, slower but even more profound social changes were connected to the country's continued industrial development. Urbanization reduced the rural population to some 35 percent of the total by 1985; rapid growth of higher education created a professional urban "middle class" not so easily manipulated by the party-state apparatus. Did not all this add up to a sharp departure from Stalinism, making the Soviet Union something other than totalitarian?

However one might answer the question, the point of reference was Stalin and Stalinism. It was a comparison looking backward. But the Gorbachev reforms and the subsequent collapse of the Soviet Union have raised new questions about the post-Stalin decades. Historians now look to those years for the origins of the Gorbachev phenomenon, which was almost wholly unexpected in the Soviet Union or abroad. What had happened in the preceding several decades that motivated a reform program of that magnitude and allowed it to be established amid the entrenched power of the party-state apparatus? And how had the apparent solidity of the Soviet regime eroded to the point that just six years of Gorbachev reforms caused it to disintegrate and disappear?

Facing Stalin's Legacy: The Dilemma of Reform

The top leadership of the Soviet Union after 1953 confronted the dilemma of reformers everywhere: how to change the regime without destroying it. On the one hand, that leadership had benefited from the Stalinist system and certainly believed that Soviet socialism, as they understood it, was capable of creating a strong, prosperous, and just nation. Had it not proven itself in the greatest of all modern wars and propelled the country to global power? On the other hand, they recognized that system as a danger to themselves. It had, after all, devoured vast numbers of its own leaders in the 1930s, and a renewal of the purges seemed likely had Stalin's death not intervened. And the leadership was well aware of the country's relative backwardness and many of its economic limitations and inefficiencies. How to address the many problems deriving from the Stalinist legacy while preserving Soviet socialism, the party's political monopoly, the country's superpower status, and their own privileged and powerful positions—that was the Gordian knot confronting Soviet authorities from Khrushchev through Gorbachev. Ultimately, of course, that dilemma proved unsolvable, as the last and most extensive reform initiative brought the entire system to ruin. But those earlier attempts are worth reviewing because they provided precedents, inspiration, lessons, and obstacles for Gorbachev's later efforts.

Khrushchev and De-Stalinization

Most prominent among these earlier reformers was Nikita Khrushchev, (1954–64) whose de-Stalinization efforts dismantled the most repressive aspects of the Stalinist system. Millions of prisoners were released from the Gulag, and millions more, long dead, were formally exonerated for crimes they had never committed. Mass terror and arbitrary arrests ended, while the secret police lost many of their prerogatives and came under party control. The limits of permissible expression in the arts, literature, scholarship, and journalism broadened considerably as a "thaw" in cultural and intellectual life took hold. Driving all of these initiatives was Khrushchev's dramatic Secret Speech, a four-hour oration delivered to a closed meeting of the Twentieth Party Congress in February 1956. There he laid out a devastating, though incomplete, account of Stalin's crimes, particularly those against party members, to an audience of stunned party leaders. The symbolic climax of de-Stalinization came in 1961, when Stalin's body was removed from the mausoleum where it had lain alongside that of Lenin and was reburied under tons of cement outside the Kremlin wall.

What produced this reversal of Stalinist policies and this partial delegitimation of Stalin himself? In part, of course, it reflected the long-standing opposition to Stalin's brutality and excesses by a reformist element in the party that had been cowed into silence by the terror. But the Soviet political elite as a whole recognized that terror, the secret police, and the charismatic authority of one man provided no secure foundation for their continued power. They yearned for a kind of reform that would render their positions secure at last. Thus, they sought to revive the party organization, long neglected by Stalin, together with the cult of Lenin and the mythology of the revolution as bases for their rule. Finally, rebellions in the camps and growing public demands for the release of prisoners represented popular pressure to which de-Stalinization was a response.

The end of terror meant a restoration of the party to political prominence in Soviet life as well as physical security for the elite, a situation from which Khrushchev's rivals and later Khrushchev himself benefited. Now various bureaucratic conflicts and policy disputes could be hammered out within top party circles without the losers fearing the Gulag or the executioner.[1] Artists, writers, and academic specialists perhaps benefited most as the narrow confines of Stalinist orthodoxy were lifted, albeit inconsistently. The whole atmosphere of reform, innovation, and greater freedom inspired a generation of younger, educated people, the so-called children of the Twentieth Party Congress, one of whom is featured in Voices, "A Child of the 'Thaw.'" Among them were many of the leaders and supporters of perestroika, including Gorbachev himself. Khrushchev, many have argued, made Gorbachev possible.

Khrushchev's reforms encompassed not only politics and culture but also the economy. Those reforms illustrated several ways in which the problems of a command economy might be addressed. Since investment decisions were made by political authorities in the Soviet planned economy, adjusting spending priorities was one means of addressing perceived imbalances in the economy. Thus, Khrushchev, while maintaining overall priority for heavy industry, tilted investment toward agriculture. Higher procurement prices would stimulate collective farmers to greater efforts; the opening to cultivation of some 40 million hectares of "virgin lands" in Kazakstan and Siberia would provide much-needed grain; corn, which the Soviet leader obsessively encouraged, would furnish fodder for cattle. Furthermore, housing, long neglected in the Stalin years, almost doubled during Khrushchev's decade in power. And, by relying increasingly on nuclear weapons, he tried to reduce military spending on more expensive conventional forces.

Beyond altering economic priorities, Khrushchev also sought to transform the structure of the economic bureaucracy. The chief problem, in his view, was the enormous power of those ministries responsible for various branches of the economy. Each of them sought to be as self-sufficient as possible and had little inclination to cooperate with one another. Given the persistent difficulties of obtaining reliable supplies and the need to meet their own production targets, this was not entirely unreasonable, but it led to gross inefficiencies. Two enterprises in the same city might produce parts needed by the other, but since they belonged to different ministries, they could be required to ship their products to other distant enterprises in their own ministry rather than to a crosstown factory in another ministry. To remedy such pervasive "departmentalism," in 1957 Khrushchev virtually dismantled

Voices

A Child of the "Thaw"

The Khrushchev "thaw" had a deep impact on the thinking of young professional people, among whom was Tatyana Zaslavskaya, whose sociological research later shaped Gorbachev's perestroika.

The exposure of the "cult of personality of Stalin" created a certain split in the public psyche. The man whom people were accustomed to regard as their friend and benefactor, the architect of victories in both peace and war, had been unexpectedly transformed before their eyes into a criminal who had murdered millions of people. To experience this was not a simple thing. . . . My generation became . . . more critical towards the country's new leadership. For whereas Stalin, who had been put forward as the "genius of all time," had in fact turned out to be a criminal, the people who had taken his place had far more ordinary biographies. . . . There was, therefore, no reason to regard their decisions as the "last word in truth."

An important feature of the "thaw" period was the ending of the Soviet Union's isolation from the capitalist countries. . . . My first trip abroad took place at this time—to Sweden in 1957. It made a very great impression on me; before me was another, a different way of life. . . . [It] shattered the idea I had been given that the working life of people in the West consisted mainly of suffering. We saw that, in fact, the countries of the West had in many instances overtaken us and we had lively discussions about ways of overcoming our weaknesses. . . .

My generation was fortunate—the years of our youth and maturity coincided with a stage of spiritual uplift in society, the memory of which stayed with us in the darkest years of reaction.

From Tatyana Zaslavskaya, *The Second Socialist Revolution* (Bloomington: Indiana University Press, 1990), pp. 28–29, 34.

many of the central planning ministries in Moscow, replacing them with about one hundred regional economic councils *(sovnarkhozy)* to coordinate planning on a regional basis. This was a major administrative shake-up and represented an effort to decentralize the planning process. But it merely replaced the inefficiency of departmentalism with that of localism and seriously disrupted production processes that crossed the boundaries of several sovnarkhozy.

None of Khrushchev's reforms touched the central pillar of the Soviet system—party control over state, economy, society, and culture in the name of Marxist-Leninist ideology. Even his critique of Stalinism was limited, omitting as it did any mention of the brutalities of collectivization and early industrialization and blaming subsequent excesses on Stalin personally, thus exonerating his many collaborators and the party itself. At the time, however, these changes seemed enormous, and they energized reformist thinking and activity all across the vast domain of Soviet policymaking—in administration, law, and foreign policy; in historical institutes, universities, and editorial offices; in family policy and ideology. And in each of these areas reforms proved enormously threatening and provoked spirited conservative resistance. Bureaucrats in central production ministries resented their displacement by the sovnarkhozy; many party officials were upset at Khrushchev's insistence on limiting their terms in office and at dividing the local party organization into agricultural and industrial sections; discussion of prices, markets, cost accounting, and self-financing—born of Khrushchev's economic reforms—seemed to them signs of creeping capitalism; ideological conservatives feared that attacks on Stalin would undermine the legitimacy of the regime in general; and they saw an outbreak of riots in Poland and the anti-Soviet uprising in Hungary in 1956–57 as clear evidence that de-Stalinization threatened the Soviet imperium in Eastern Europe.

Thus, according to historian Stephen Cohen, there emerged "a deep-rooted and persistent political struggle between the forces of reform and conservatism inside Soviet officialdom from 1953 into the 1980s."[2] The central issue was change itself. Was it, as the reformers argued, a means of fulfilling the promise of the revolution and of Lenin's ideals, from which Stalin had led the country astray? Or was change, as the conservatives feared, a threat to the stability and functioning of essentially sound institutions and socialist values that had modernized the country in record time and brought it through the horrors of war to superpower status? Thus, the Khrushchev years established lines of conflict and debate that endured for two decades and reemerged vigorously during the 1980s. But the controversies spawned by Khrushchev's reforms remained largely within official circles and did not engage the larger society as did the Gorbachev experiment of the 1980s.

Turning Back the Clock? The Brezhnev Years

Opposition to Khrushchev's policies and widespread irritation with the impulsive, reckless, and increasingly arbitrary manner in which he pursued them led to his removal from office in 1964. That this political transition occurred peacefully, and with at least the trappings of legality, showed how much things had changed. But the "great reformer" was gone and with him went much that he had initiated. Further attacks on Stalin ended and in textbooks and public media his mountains of crimes were minimized as "violations of Leninist norms" and largely ignored, while an emphasis on his role as industrializer and wartime leader went some distance toward rehabilitating his reputation. A cultural crackdown imposed far narrower limits of acceptable expression and caused anguish among progressive writers, artists, and scholars. Khrushchev's regional economic councils were dismantled, and centralized economic planning through industrial ministries in Moscow resumed. The local party apparatus, which Khrushchev had split into agricultural and industrial branches, resumed its earlier, unified form, and his insistence on fixed terms of office ended.

What replaced Khrushchev's populist and overtly reformist policies was a regime much more conservative in style and tone, no longer given to bold schemes or abrupt departures from established practice. After decades of insecurity from Stalin's terror or Khrushchev's impulsive reorganizations, the nomenklatura elite, many of whom had begun their careers in the 1930s, finally achieved the kind of stability for which they had yearned so long, embodied now in the slogan "trust in cadre." It meant that top party and state officials could ordinarily expect to remain in office for life. This stability led to an aging leadership and a Politburo whose full members averaged more than seventy years of age by 1980. Within that leadership the major bureaucratic and territorial interests competed for budgetary allocations, debated a narrow range of policy options, formed and reformed alliances among themselves, and hammered out a conservative consensus that was presented to the public as the unanimous view of the Politburo. It was, then, a "relatively stable oligarchy," operating collectively, that governed the Soviet Union in the two decades before Gorbachev. Its leader

Voices

Jokes of the Brezhnev Era

A wonderful capacity for humor in difficult circumstances has long helped sustain the people of the Soviet Union. Here are a few of the jokes that focus on the hypocrisies of the Brezhnev era.

Brezhnev's mother visits her son in the Kremlin soon after his coming to power. When she hears about his fine apartment, his luxurious dacha, his expensive cars, and other material comforts, she says, "Leonid, my son, I'm so proud of you, but one thing worries me: What will you do when the communists take over?"

A man was arrested after running through Red Square shouting, "Brezhnev's a fool! Brezhnev's a fool!" After a brief trial, he was sentenced to ten years in jail: five for disturbing the peace and five for revealing a state secret.

During a party meeting, one local official was declaiming on the bright future promised by the next Five-Year Plan. "We'll have more to eat, more cars, better medical facilities, and much improved housing." From the back of the room, a worker shouted, "So much for you. What about us?"

Question: What is a Soviet musical trio?
Answer: A quartet just back from the West.

A man entered a Soviet clinic and insisted on consulting with an ear-and-eye doctor. He was told that no such medical specialty existed. He must see either an eye or an ear doctor. Still he persisted in his demand. An exasperated official finally asked why he wanted such a consultation. "Because," the man replied, "I keep hearing one thing and seeing another."

---

was Leonid Brezhnev (1964–82), but in his position as general secretary of the CPSU, he was constrained by his colleagues' views and interests even more than Khrushchev had been.[3] This was the political system that Gorbachev inherited in 1985.

The ideological expression of this new conservatism in official circles lay in retreat from utopian or revolutionary expectations. While

Khrushchev promised that Soviet citizens would live in communism by 1980, Brezhnev referred to Soviet society as "developed socialism," pushed the transition to communism into the distant future, and projected a practical and businesslike manner. In the daily life of Soviet officialdom, this meant the triumph of *meshchanstvo,* an evocative Russian word that refers to an acquisitive, pretentious, materialistic, social-climbing style of life, far removed from the asceticism and devotion to the common good of traditional revolutionary ideals.[4] Eduard Shevardnadze, Gorbachev's foreign minister, described what was required of the elite: "Sit tight, do your work, and take advantage of the privileges and benefits offered to you. Don't try to yank the fishhook out of your mouth or it will be certain death."[5]

The retreat from reform, however, did not mean a reversion to full Stalinism. There were no more bloody purges and few executions in the repression of political and ideological dissent. Instead, selective trials and imprisonment, exile both internal and abroad, withholding of academic degrees or promotions, "chats" with local prosecutors, dismissals from jobs, and worst of all, confinement in mental hospitals—these were the techniques of repression characteristic of the Brezhnev era. And despite sharp restrictions on the public expression of unorthodox views, academic specialists had some leeway for debate and discussion in their own journals and seminars. Here and there, "oases of open thinking" permitted some original work, even in the social sciences, though creative scholars operated in a constant battle with more conservative opponents.[6]

Nor was economic reform completely abandoned.[7] Brezhnev expanded considerably Khrushchev's effort to refocus investment priorities toward agriculture, largely in huge and environmentally questionable projects in irrigation, fertilizers, and pesticides. In industry, real structural reforms, broadly similar to those later tried under Gorbachev, took shape between 1965 and 1970, associated with Prime Minister Alexei Kosygin. Whereas Khrushchev had tried to decentralize the planning process, the Kosygin reforms attempted to limit the power of now restored central ministries and provide greater freedom and incentives for individual enterprises. It was an effort to energize enterprise managers, encouraging them to act more like entrepreneurs.

It did not work well. The central ministries resisted their loss of power and were able to do so because they themselves wrote the detailed regulations that implemented the reforms. It was a case of the fox guarding the henhouse. But these limited reforms also put the ministries in a real dilemma: they were less able to interfere in enterprise activity, but they were no less responsible for the performance of the enterprises they supervised. Most ministers found it less dangerous to violate the spirit of the reforms and to continue intruding on their enterprises than to risk disappointing their own superiors by failing to produce. Letting go of that detailed supervisory authority challenged the whole culture of Stalinist planning. Furthermore, real efficiency in Soviet industry would inevitably have meant reducing a bloated workforce, but this ran counter to a socialist commitment to full employment and was thought to be politically dangerous. Thus, the Kosygin reforms, though never explicitly repudiated and despite some local successes, faded away in the 1970s, absorbed and emasculated in the vast bureaucratic labyrinth of the Soviet economy. Nonetheless, the discussions that accompanied the reforms injected the notion of somehow combining "the plan" with market incentives, and such ideas percolated quietly in various academic institutes waiting to flower again in the 1980s.

Other, less extensive reforms followed in the 1970s: mergers of enterprises to promote greater efficiency, new incentive schemes, targets that rewarded quality as well as output, the use of computers for more effective planning, experiments with new management techniques. A summary judgment by a leading economic historian on the whole range of post-Stalin economic reforms was that they "involv[ed] enormous administrative upheavals, were sometimes ingenuous and always unsuccessful."[8] Why should this be so? After all, the state had complete control over the economy; the parallel apparatus of the Communist Party was there to monitor compliance with the plan and to resolve problems as they arose. Yet that powerful combination was apparently unable to improve productivity, to stimulate overall technological innovation, to ensure quality, or even to compel competing ministries to cooperate effectively with one another. That question perplexed the Soviet leadership in the Brezhnev era and haunted Gorbachev and his team in the 1980s. Was the Soviet economy unreformable, or had the right formula simply not been found? This "curious powerlessness" of the Soviet leadership requires a closer look at the evolution of the Soviet economy in the post-Stalin years.[9]

From Growth to Stagnation: Explaining Economic Decline

More than anything else, it was the perception of dismal economic performance that drove Gorbachev's reform program. More broadly, the feeling was widespread among the intelligentsia "that society had lost its way, that everything was going wrong, that things could not go on like this for long."[10] Where had this feeling come from? And when had it arisen?

The Soviet economy, after all, did have some achievements to its credit, beyond the simple fact of the country's rapid industrialization and victory in World War II. Practically full employment, low and stable prices for basic goods such as housing, food, books, and transportation, and free medical care and education meant a measure of economic security, even if at quite modest levels. In the uncertain free-for-all of contemporary Russian capitalism, large numbers of people look back on this feature of Soviet economic life with wistful nostalgia.

Furthermore, for twenty-five years after the war, the Soviet economy grew at an enviable rate by world standards—about 5–6 percent per year. And the altered economic priorities of the Khrushchev and Brezhnev years directed some of this growth, finally, to the improvement of Soviet living standards. Millions of families acquired their own apartments, happily abandoning the communal apartments where they had shared a bathroom and kitchen with others. Real income rose substantially and much more rapidly than prices. Consumer goods became more plentiful, and by the early 1980s between 80 and 90 percent of families had a refrigerator, radio, and TV, and about 70 percent had purchased sewing and washing machines, although only 9 percent enjoyed a family car.[11] Consumption of shoes, clothing, meat, and vegetables likewise rose, albeit from very low postwar levels. Finally, the country had some impressive technical achievements—in space and satellite technology, in welding and metallurgy, in gas compressors and turbines, in machine-tool production, and in large-scale fishing operations.

Clearly these achievements had contributed to the sense that the Soviet system was workable, that it was capable of improving material life, and that it was worthy of loyalty, and even pride. Many had reason to believe Khrushchev's confident prediction that the Soviet Union would overtake the United States in production by 1980. Had these trends continued into the 1970s and 1980s, it seems likely that things would have turned out rather differently. But they did not. And herein lies one of the major questions of late Soviet history. Why did an economy that performed credibly in the 1950s and 1960s stagnate in the 1970s and early 1980s to the point that many thoughtful observers saw genuine crisis ahead and felt that bold action was necessary to save the day?

By the 1970s the signs of deteriorating economic performance were accumulating rapidly. Most prominent was a steady and continuing slowdown in rates of annual economic growth, from a respectable 5 percent in the 1960s to 3 percent in the 1970s to 2 percent or less in the early 1980s. The growth of consumption likewise slowed amid periodic shortages, longer lines, and endless complaints about the declining availability and quality of consumer goods. Most Soviet consumers came to depend on the black market, or "second economy," which expanded greatly in the 1970s. Social indicators such as declining life expectancy for males and rising infant mortality rates gave added support to those who saw crisis in the making. Perhaps most embarrassing of all was the growing technological gap between the Soviet Union and the West. In 1987 the USSR had some two hundred thousand microcomputers; the United States more than twenty-five million. Even some of the newly industrializing countries such as Taiwan and South Korea surpassed the USSR in certain areas of technological development. Massive Soviet dependence on grain imports beginning in the 1970s was a further embarrassing sign of economic weakness. What had happened?

We might begin with the Soviet victory in World War II, which legitimated and reinforced the Stalinist system as the country was rebuilding its devastated economy. Yet that economic system was increasingly inadequate to meet new requirements for growth and largely unresponsive to changes in Soviet life. The traditional Soviet approach had focused, in the jargon of economists, on "extensive growth"—adding more land, labor, or capital to achieve increased output. It was a strategy of doing "more of the same." It meant huge projects and massive campaigns, often without careful consideration of costs, either human or environmental. That strategy had worked, after a fashion, because the Soviet Union was rich in resources and had a large labor pool, which it exploited with little mercy. The essential elements of this approach continued in the post-Stalin years.

But the possibilities of this strategy were clearly diminishing by the 1970s. There was little additional arable land to cultivate; a rapidly slowing birthrate in European areas of the country meant fewer workers; and the depletion of easily exploited natural resources forced Soviet planners to look to the North and East, where conditions were difficult and production costs were higher.

The alternative, of course, was a change toward "intensive" growth, emphasizing more efficient use of labor and resources and depending on technological improvements to promote growth. This was the so-called Third Industrial Revolution, of which postwar Japan and West Germany were the exemplars. But a command economy of monopolistic ministries, exercising detailed control over their enterprises, was ill suited to make this transition. It was possible to command the replication of steel mills, based on a known technology, in the 1930s; it was not possible to order into existence a computer industry, based on a new and rapidly evolving technology, in the 1970s.

Many aspects of the Soviet system inhibited its transition to more intensive, cost-effective, high-quality production, despite widespread acknowledgment of the need to do so. The emphasis on meeting annual quantitative targets meant that enterprise managers had little incentive to innovate, if it would mean disrupting production lines. Nor was party supervision able to overcome this reluctance, for local party officials had an equal interest in "their" enterprises meeting targets. At the top, the Politburo appointed industrial ministers, many of whom were guaranteed seats on the party Central Committee, which in turn selected the Politburo. "The bureaucracy absorbed the party," concluded historian Moshe Lewin.[12] Thus, the party was no longer in a position to lead vigorously and to prod the system toward greater effectiveness. Such a closed system of "reciprocal accountability," or "circular flow of power" between party officials and economic bureaucrats, repeatedly decimated reform efforts from the top and created a culture of mutual dependence that minimized risk taking.[13]

So too did an understanding of socialism as state ownership plus party control. Reforms that involved decentralization, market prices, and a weakening of party authority felt like the restoration of a hated capitalism and represented an unacceptable threat to the Soviet elite. That kind of program was in fact adopted in Czechoslovakia in 1968 and precipitated massive Soviet military intervention. But party supervision, no matter how rigorous, provided little stimulus for technological innovation or economic reform.

Other features of the Soviet system likewise contributed to stagnation. The traditional emphasis on heavy industry, modified slightly during the post-Stalin years, created serious imbalances. Neglecting the infrastructure, such as roads and storage, led to enormous wastage and inefficiency in agriculture, which was a drag on the entire economy and required an agricultural workforce far larger than that in other industrialized countries. Neglecting the consumer sector of the economy diminished workers' incentives, for few goods were available to stimulate their desire to earn more money. Enormous investments in the military after 1965, amounting to 15–25 percent of GNP, robbed the civilian economy of investment capital. The magnitude of this drain on the Soviet economy is illustrated by comparable figures for the United States (5–7 percent) and West Germany and Japan (1 percent). Stable retail prices in the face of rising production costs required large state subsidies. It may have been good socialism, but it was poor investment policy, and it led to such absurdities as farmers feeding cheap bread to their animals while selling the more expensive grain. And the isolation of the country from the world economy deprived it of the stimulus of international competition.

The growing complexity of an economy with some fifty thousand enterprises generating more than 24 million separate products arguably overwhelmed the information-processing capacity of a system designed to operate as a single unit directed from the top. Planners simply did not have enough information to set reasonable prices for all these goods or to arrange for adequate supplies to be exchanged among complementary enterprises. Even in the Stalin years, these conditions had led to hoarding of supplies and "storming" at the end of the month or year to meet production quotas. It also often left managers scrambling to obtain supplies by using *tolkachi* (expediters or pushers), who scoured the economy for the necessary items and arranged backdoor transactions. Furthermore, managers often found that an increasingly well-educated workforce was becoming "more difficult to manage" as workers sought a kind of personal autonomy that the system found difficult to accommodate.[14] None of this facilitated the transition to an economy dependent on flexibility, rapid adjustment to new technologies, or the initiative of the workers.

Finally, a changing system of incentives had reduced the old coercive pressures but without really substituting new economic stimuli. The reforms of the post-Stalin years had minimized fear by ending terror, emptying the Gulag, revising production targets downward, promoting "stability in cadre," and winking at widespread corruption and evasion of work responsibilities. But enterprises never went bankrupt for performing poorly, and workers were seldom laid off or fired as the needs of the economy changed.

In the heady years following Soviet successes in space, Khrushchev had boasted about catching up to the United States, and quickly. And in Soviet terms, that had happened, for by 1980 the USSR outproduced the United States in steel, coal, oil, tractors, and various types of machine tools. But "Khrushchev won the wrong race."[15] In the competition that really counted, the criteria for success were quite different: cost-effectiveness, quality of consumer goods, international competitiveness, technological innovation, respect for workers, environmental sensitivity. By all these measures—to say nothing of growth itself—the Soviet Union lost the race, largely because its economy was ill equipped to run it and its political system blocked real reform.

The resulting economic stagnation had serious consequences. It disclosed the rigidity of the Soviet system and hinted at the difficulties that would attend a serious effort at reform. It provoked precisely such an effort in the Gorbachev years as a new generation of Soviet leaders determined to avert what they saw as an impending crisis. And finally, economic stagnation further eroded support for the regime and thus gave that new leadership little room for error and little time to produce meaningful results.

Beneath the Surface: Social Change in the Post-Stalin Years

Beneath the apparently calm surface of the Soviet Union's political conservatism and economic stagnation lay profound social changes, the product of the country's continued industrial development. Within the USSR, however, these changes were obscured by official descriptions of the country as a mature socialist society without "antagonistic" conflict among classes and where national or ethnic loyalties were being transformed into a new Soviet identity. The weaknesses of Soviet social sciences, suspect as "bourgeois," made it difficult to penetrate the fog of official rhetoric. In the West, the understanding of the Soviet

Union as "totalitarian," although challenged in academic circles, still prevailed in public consciousness and projected an image of a passive society thoroughly dominated and indoctrinated by an all-powerful state. Neither description conveyed the reality of Soviet society in the Khrushchev and Brezhnev years.

Understanding those realities, however, is critical to grasping the dynamic transformations of Soviet life in the Gorbachev years and beyond. If economic stagnation motivated Gorbachev's reforms, the social changes of the post-Stalin era provided perestroika and glasnost with millions of active supporters and drove those initiatives further and faster than their leader had ever intended. It was this social momentum, pulsing up from below, that sharply distinguished the Gorbachev era and its reforms from Khrushchev's years of de-Stalinization. From what sources did it derive?

Cities and Universities

It was not until the early 1960s that the Soviet Union crossed the threshold to a dominantly urban society. But by 1985 it was 65 percent urban, and the figure was even higher in the more developed republics of Russia, Latvia, and Ukraine. The continued growth of Soviet industry, although at a slower rate in the 1970s and 1980s, had created a society far different from the predominantly rural peasant country over which Stalin had ruled. Accompanying this urbanization was the tremendous growth of education. As late as 1959 the vast majority of the population had received only a modest elementary education, usually four years of schooling. But over the next twenty-five years, secondary education became required for everyone and higher education expanded tremendously, particularly in scientific and technical fields. Economists, scientists, teachers, doctors, artists, lawyers, but above all engineers poured out of Soviet universities and institutes. By the mid-1980s some 15 million graduates had accumulated in Soviet society, with another 5 million enrolled in institutions of higher education, where they were taught by five hundred thousand professors.[16]

The dual processes of urbanization and educational growth gave rise to a far more differentiated society and one less amenable to control from above than ever before in Soviet history. At the top was the political elite, recruited by Stalin in the 1930s from people with peasant and working-class backgrounds. Not well or broadly educated

(Brezhnev's academic specialty had been the production methods of rolled steel), this generation of the political elite dominated top party and state positions into the 1980s. To those positions they brought the authoritarian, secretive, dogmatic, anti-intellectual, and patriotic values of their Stalinist backgrounds.

Beneath this "political elite" lay the large and growing professional class of experts and specialists trained in the post-Stalin years. This was the "dominant class" in Soviet society, on which the elite depended to run the increasingly complex Soviet economy.[17] Better educated than the political elite, this middle-class, professional, white-collar stratum sought the kind of personal and professional autonomy common in urban settings everywhere. They also sought greater contact with the West, both cultural and professional, and in the process acquired new standards by which to judge their own society. Many such people had been fired with enthusiasm by the fresh winds of de-Stalinization and the cultural "thaw," and were equally disappointed by the more reactionary and restrictive policies of the Brezhnev years.

Thus, important segments of this dominant class developed attitudes and perspectives at odds with official views. But they also acquired economic grievances, as the wage policy of the Brezhnev era distinctly favored the working class. Widespread complaints that bus drivers made more than engineers, that skilled manual workers surpassed teachers, doctors, and researchers, fueled a sense of social injustice quite different from that which drove the revolution of 1917. More and more of these people joined the party, so that by the 1980s more than 30 percent of party members had a higher education, and about one-third of urban males with higher education were party members. They carried their various dissatisfactions and alienation from official values along, and so contributed to the diversity of thought within party circles. Not surprisingly, it was to this dominant class that Gorbachev initially turned for support. Many found in his reforms a means of realizing their own values and their material interests.

By far the largest group in Soviet society, however, was the working class, representing more than 60 percent of the population in the mid-1980s. It too changed substantially in the post-Stalin decades. Skilled and highly skilled workers now far outnumbered the unskilled, just-off-the-farm types of the 1930s, and they were much better educated, most having completed secondary school. More of them were now engaged in the service sector of the economy. And their wages had risen quite considerably owing to a variety of incentive schemes put forward to increase productivity. But the possibility of going on to higher education, and thus to high-prestige professional jobs, had narrowed by the 1970s, as members of high-status families increasingly dominated those opportunities. Thus, the earlier fluidity of Soviet society had hardened somewhat as the Brezhnev era came to an end. Depressing and often depersonalized factories, together with the endemic shortages of the Soviet economy, further limited the incentives for hard work.

At the bottom of the Soviet social hierarchy were the peasants on the collective farms. Substantial investment in agriculture during the Brezhnev era raised rural living standards, and the granting of passports to peasants included them more fully in Soviet life. Still, the rural exodus continued, diminishing the overall proportion of collective farm peasants in the population to less than 15 percent by the mid-1980s and further draining the rural areas of younger and more ambitious people.

Particularly in the urban areas, then, a changing and increasingly assertive society found itself encased in a petrified political system and a stagnating economy. The result was not a social explosion but rather a process by which bits and pieces of that society slowly began to carve out areas of greater autonomy in the interstices or on the margins of official society.

Creating Alternative Space: The Erosion of Totalitarian Society

During the post-Stalin years the relationship between the state and society slowly began to shift. Throughout Soviet history, and much of Russian history before it, the institutions and communities of civil society, those existing independently of the state and able to participate openly in public life, had been weak or nonexistent. The use of the term "totalitarian" to describe the Stalinist regime pointed to the domination of society by the state. But in the three decades between Stalin and Gorbachev the fragile sprouts of a civil society began to take shape. It was quite unlike civil society in the West, where churches, chambers of commerce, trade unions, political parties, youth organizations, newspapers and book publishers, and cultural groups of all kinds had a recognized autonomy. It was rather a matter of informal contacts, ephemeral organizations, underground activity, illegal or semi-legal transactions, changing consciousness, and weakening control by the party-state apparatus. In the absence of private property, none of this had a solid economic foundation, but it represented a slow and modest erosion of totalitarian control and helps to explain both the appearance of the Gorbachev regime and public receptivity to its program.

The most overtly political effort to create alternative space in the Soviet system was the dissident movement, which developed in the Brezhnev era as the possibilities for more open expression of critical views diminished. Its participants, a modest number of intellectuals including highly respected scientists and writers, circulated manuscripts and numerous journals in underground typescript copies (*samizdat*) or smuggled their work abroad to be published in the West. Letters and petitions to state authorities, public defense of arrested colleagues, and occasional small demonstrations were likewise a part of dissident activity.

No common outlook shaped the dissident movement. Marxist historian Roy Medvedev called for the country to return to the purity of its Leninist past; the well-known scientist and creator of the Soviet hydrogen bomb, Andrei Sakharov, evolved toward a more western liberal outlook with a focus on human rights; Aleksandr Solzhenitsyn, whose writings disclosed the horrors of the Gulag and its origins in Leninist practice, represented a Russian nationalist or Slavophile viewpoint. Others wrote on behalf of oppressed nationalities, spoke for women's rights, defended religious believers, or argued for Jewish emigration.

A tiny and divided enterprise with no mass support, the dissident movement made little visible impact on the Soviet system at the time. But it represented what an earlier historian of revolution called the "desertion of the intellectuals," thus diminishing the moral legitimacy of the regime. Here were people willing to write with authenticity, to say simply what they thought, and to cut through that pervasive fog of "doublespeak," half-truths, and outright lies that constituted official ideology. By calling on Soviet authorities to honor their own laws, they exposed the hypocrisy of the regime. By behaving bravely and with great personal integrity, they had an impact on a larger number of sympathetic but less courageous individuals. That Sakharov became a leader of the democratic movement in the late 1980s is a testimony to the impact of earlier dissenters. So too was the energy with which the KGB pursued the dissidents—arresting, harassing, and imprisoning many of them. Though largely crushed by the early 1980s, the dissident movement clearly was a threat to much that the Soviet regime represented.

A much larger number of people, likewise encouraged by the freer atmosphere of the Khrushchev years, fought the creeping neo-Stalinism of the Brezhnev era more quietly and from within their official positions. Particularly within academic institutions, a certain amount of intellectual freedom was possible so long as it did not result in direct challenges to the regime. Thus, some scholars were able to read western literature, to create informal contacts with like-minded colleagues, to explore new disciplines such as sociology, mathematical economics, and political science, and to conduct research on carefully defined topics. But all of this occurred in the face of conservative opposition and with a wary eye on the censor.

The most notable of these "havens of hidden dissent" was *Akademgorodok* (Academic City), located near the Siberian city of Novosibirsk.[18] Established by Khrushchev in 1957, this collection of twenty-two scientific institutes attracted younger, free-thinking scholars who were willing to give up the comforts of European Russia for the greater freedom of this remote site. There, people such as Abel Aganbegyan and Tatyana Zaslavskaya began to develop a critique of Soviet economy and society that later informed Gorbachev's thinking and his early reform program. In 1983 the results of this work came together in Zaslavskaya's "Novosibirsk Report," presented to a closed seminar of 150 scholars and distributed to ranking party officials as well. While framed in Marxist terms, the report was a damning indictment of a system that had reached its limits. It detailed the many ways in which Soviet society and economy had outgrown the highly centralized planning framework, implicitly called for a much greater role for the market, and predicted resistance to such a move from threatened mid-level bureaucrats.[19] So explosive were its contents that after it was leaked to the western press, Soviet authorities attempted to confiscate all copies of the report. In places such as this—and Novosibirsk was not alone—scholars were able to carve from the dogmatism of official ideology some measure of intellectual space, to influence the thinking of some high-level party officials, and, unknowingly, to plant the intellectual seeds of perestroika.

The declining ability of Soviet central institutions to dominate society extended beyond the academic realm.[20] The failure of economic reforms showed that regional party secretaries and enterprise directors had some leverage against their superiors in Moscow. In some Soviet republics, especially in Central Asia and the Caucasus, the republic-level party organization achieved considerable independence from Moscow's control. Most notorious was Uzbekistan, where a pervasive network of patronage and corruption developed under the leadership of Brezhnev crony Sharaf Rashidov, while Moscow turned a blind eye. And even more broadly, a massive construction project permitted many urban families to move out of cramped communal apartments into new single-family flats where they could "shut their own front door," achieve a measure of privacy, and develop a "private glasnost" within a circle of trusted friends.[21]

For such urban dwellers, both economic and cultural alternatives to official Soviet society and values slowly became available. Pervasive shortages and the general inefficiencies of the Soviet economy had created by the Brezhnev era a widespread "second economy"—a vast network of economic transactions operating outside of the official state channels. Some of this was perfectly legal, such as the sale of produce from household plots in farmers' markets or the offering of personal services such as hairdressing or TV repair. But the line was blurry. A person might legitimately offer to repair small appliances, but if he used tools from his job or spare parts from the factory, it was illegal. Thus, much of the second economy made its participants subject to potential arrest.

The second economy took several forms. On the "wholesale" level, enterprise managers might exchange products directly among themselves, lend workers in exchange for necessary goods, hire *shabashniki* (moonlighters) for special construction products, or write off products as rejects while using them to barter for needed supplies. All this was necessary to meet production targets, so supervising party officials, equally eager to reach those quotas, often overlooked the evident illegality.

Far more important for most people was the "retail" second economy. Much of it involved the theft and resale of state property—building materials and gasoline, for example—at much higher prices. Managers and salespeople in state stores were in a position to put aside particularly high-quality goods and sell them under the counter, pocketing the difference in price. Those in charge of waiting lists for high-demand products such as cars, apartments, and appliances easily attracted bribes. The provision of services using state facilities or materials was equally prevalent—chauffeurs who used a government car as a private taxi or repairmen who did private work on the job or with state tools and parts on the weekend. In Moscow during the 1970s, probably 70 percent of spending for repairs went to private individuals, and in Georgia the figure was above 90 percent.[22] Entrepreneurs organized illegal production in private homes and sometimes even within state-owned factories or on collective farms. Home-brewed alcohol, privately produced furs, clothing, tapes and records, hard-to-obtain books—all these and more circulated within the second economy.

Accurate figures are impossible to obtain, but the second economy expanded vastly during the Brezhnev era and a substantial sector of the Soviet economy slipped outside official control. Clearly this process involved official toleration and participation. By allowing people to obtain goods and services the official economy could not provide, the Soviet leadership perhaps took the edge off popular discontent. It was an alternative to real reform, and in the view of some scholars, a quite deliberate policy.

But the price was rampant official corruption. The multiple payoffs, favors, and personal connections among economic managers, some elements of the party apparatus, and large-scale operators in the second economy gave rise to the "mafias" that entrenched themselves first in Georgia, Azerbaijan, and Uzbekistan and later throughout the country. In Azerbaijan, public offices were virtually for sale; the going price for a police chief's job was 50,000 rubles. In Georgia, party boss Vassily Mzhavanadze lived extravagantly and protected private and wholly illegal businesses that produced, among other things, fine clothing in underground factories. Thus, in addition to their official privileges, the top levels of party and state apparatus, extending into Brezhnev's own family, had many opportunities to enrich themselves within the second economy. This of course fueled popular cynicism and justified the petty illegalities of ordinary people: "Of course we steal from them; don't they steal from us on a far larger scale?"

Paralleling the second economy was an alternative cultural arena in which many young people and professionals participated. Like the second economy, it infiltrated official circles even as it encountered official disapproval and repression. Enormously popular bards and poets such as Bulat Okudzhava focused attention on private life—love affairs, scenes from neighborhood streets, nostalgic recollections. It was not political protest, but it ran counter to official values that stressed heroic collective efforts in the public sphere. "By the late 1960s," writes Svetlana Boym, who lived through those years, "privacy began to be seen as the only honorable and uncompromising response to the system of public compromise."[23]

In the 1970s another of these poet-bards, Vladimir Vysotsky, became something of legend, singing about prisoners, convicts, drunks, and common people experiencing the bitter realities of Soviet life. Parodying traditional genres of Soviet music and literature, he expressed the disillusionment with official outlooks that was increasingly widespread in Soviet middle-class circles—not directly anti-Soviet, but distinctly un-Soviet. Amid constant conflict with the authorities, his music spread by samizdat and especially by tapes, recorded at Moscow parties and distributed widely throughout the country. His death in 1980 was an occasion for national mourning.[24]

Writers of Soviet fiction—particularly the better ones outside the official Writers Union—likewise described personal moods and feelings, everyday struggles, and real situations rather than the building of communism associated with "socialist realism." The "village prose" school of writers, for example, celebrated the rootedness of village life (but not of collective farms) and the beauty of the rural landscape and lamented their destruction in the face of mindless change. With deep nostalgia, they looked backward to the "radiant past" rather than forward to communism, and in doing so they called into question collectivization, urban life, and progress itself—all of which were at the heart of official ideology.[25]

In the 1970s, a growing fascination with western popular culture—blue jeans, T-shirts, plastic shopping bags with foreign logos, and above all rock music—also challenged official values. The Beatles, the Rolling Stones, Stevie Wonder, and the Shadows became enormously popular; dozens of Soviet rock bands sprang up and played in cafes and at university parties, sometimes unofficially and sometimes with Komsomol sponsorship. In its individualism, its overt sexuality, and its embrace of the West, rock and roll challenged the official order; it replaced jazz, assimilated after a long struggle into official culture, as the music of social deviance.[26]

The widespread disenchantment with the hypocrisies of official Soviet society, reflected in popular and middlebrow culture, was compounded in the 1970s by a growing perception of economic decline.

Voices

Underground Music

Among the illicit songs of the 1970s was this critique of elite luxury composed by Alexander Galich. In the Gorbachev era it was sung openly on the streets.

Grass is green there
And Stalin's eagles
Eat shish kebab and fine chocolates
Behind seven fences.
Bodyguards and informants
Protect them from the people.
They make us watch films
About factories and collective farms
And at night, they watch imported films
about whores,
And they like Marilyn Monroe.

From Hedrick Smith, *The New Russians* (New York: Avon Books, 1991), p. 108. Used with permission of Hedrick Smith.

That perception was fueled by grandiose and unfulfilled promises, by the obvious failure of many reform efforts, and by comparisons with a more prosperous Eastern Europe, where millions of Soviet tourists visited in the 1960s and 1970s. All this created a growing pessimism among the Soviet middle class about the performance of the Soviet system.[27] It was not directly political; it did not lead to street demonstrations; and it did not consciously embrace or articulate clear alternatives. But the Gorbachev era soon revealed the extent to which popular support for the regime had eroded.

Out of this social and cultural ferment arose new networks of association among Soviet citizens. Informal contacts among scholars and researchers were dubbed "invisible colleges"; hundreds of musical, theatrical, and artistic groups sprang up to perform or exhibit their work, often in out-of-the-way places; organized companies of private tutors responded to the growing demand for extra instruction to pass the entrance exams of prestigious universities and institutes. Writers and scientists organized to protest the environmental damage of Soviet development projects, and they succeeded in reversing or delaying cellulose factories polluting Lake Baikal and the northern rivers diversion project. Here was the beginning of a "public opinion" to which the state had to listen.

Despite this under-the-surface ferment, Soviet society and political life were remarkably stable in the several decades preceding Gorbachev. No overt crisis and no popular demands for dramatic change greeted Gorbachev as he assumed power in 1985. One source of that stability was the memory of the Stalin era. "People feel in their bones that mass terror could once again become a reality," wrote a leading American scholar on Soviet affairs in 1986.[28] And memory was augmented by a pervasive police apparatus and network of informers. The reluctance to have open discussions with foreigners lasted well into the 1980s and testified to the continuing fear of state authorities.

The increased availability of some consumer goods, together with stable state prices and the second economy, made life bearable, though hardly comfortable, for most. Individuals and families wove elaborate networks of contacts and private arrangements to augment the meager provisions available through official channels. The soaring prices of gold, oil, and natural gas, all of which the Soviet Union exported in great quantity, temporarily boosted a declining economy.

Furthermore, there was a core of common belief and loyalty that bound much of the population to the regime. For the older generation it was the legacy of World War II, and for those somewhat younger, the real achievements of the 1950s and 1960s—Sputnik and superpower status. Certain more fundamental values—order, discipline, a paternalistic welfare state, social conservatism—were widely shared across class lines. Studies of Soviet émigrés to the United States, those most likely to oppose the regime, showed widespread appreciation for these features of the Soviet system.

Both Soviet society and the party itself in the post-Stalin years were far more complex and highly textured than images of either "mature socialism" or "totalitarianism" would suggest. Various trends and tendencies planted the seeds for elements of Gorbachev's program. But there were seeds of many kinds, and one of them—ethnic nationalism—later proved the undoing of both the Gorbachev reform program and of the Soviet Union itself.

Making Nations

The nationalist explosion of the late 1980s and the subsequent emergence of fifteen new independent nations from the ashes of the Soviet Union were almost wholly unexpected events, even a few years earlier. Surely such dramatic developments had roots in Soviet history, for they could hardly have sprung full bloom in the six years of the Gorbachev era. One approach to explaining the emergence of anti-Soviet nationalism focuses on Soviet repression, suggesting that long-established nations had been forcibly imprisoned in the Soviet Union and escaped when the opportunity arose. Contemporary nationalism in this view represents the reemergence of deeply rooted cultural identities and long-standing political loyalties. It is the picture that most nationalists themselves present.

Contemporary historical scholarship, however, finds a more complex reality and argues that the various nationalisms that blew the Soviet Union apart emerged largely during the Soviet era and because of Soviet policies and practices. In this view, nationalities have been "constructed identities," not something "natural" or even very old.[29] They drew on the various historical and cultural legacies of more than a hundred separate ethno-linguistic groups the Soviet Union inherited from the Russian Empire: ancient states in Armenia and Georgia, linguistic similarities in particular areas, folk traditions, established religious identities such as Islam in Central Asia and Catholicism in Lithuania, and in some cases the experience of a brief independence in the aftermath of 1917. But the nationalisms of the late 1980s—insistent, largely secular, highly politicized, independence minded, and widely supported—were something quite different from the vaguely recognized ethno-cultural identities of rural village-based societies seventy years earlier. Tracing the emergence of these new national solidarities has become an important task for historians who seek to explain the collapse of the Soviet Union.

The "Flourishing of Nations" in "the Prison of Nations"

The making of modern national identities among the non-Russian peoples had begun only in the nineteenth century among urban intellectuals—linguists, historians, writers, students of folklore. Stimulated by the prestigious nationalisms of Western Europe, they drew on local folk cultures and aspects of their historical experience to create their own "imagined communities"—nations with allegedly deep historical roots.[30] Limited largely to cities in the Caucasus and the western borderlands of the Russian Empire, such conceptions had little resonance in peasant villages, where the vast majority of people lived, and virtually none at all among the Muslim peoples of Central Asia untouched by modern industrial development. Nonetheless, the collapse of tsarism in 1917 provided an opportunity for a variety of urban-based nationalist movements to claim political independence—in Ukraine, Georgia, and the Baltic states, for example—but only briefly. The complex ethnic mixtures of the area, the appeal of socialist ideas, and the military strength of the Bolsheviks meant that most of them were soon absorbed into the new Soviet Union. National consciousness, in short, was only modestly developed when the Soviet Union began.

That state was a strange and in some ways hostile environment for the nurturing of national identities, for it was committed to a resolutely internationalist ideology. Marxism, of course, foresaw the withering away of national consciousness, a remnant of capitalist mentality, as class identity and socialism took hold. And Soviet ideologists looked forward to the "merging" of nations, resulting in the creation of a new "Soviet" identity. Here, in Soviet imagination, was the foundation for a worldwide socialist commonwealth in which the antagonistic nationalisms of an earlier age would be but fading memories.

At the beginning, however, Soviet leaders acknowledged a need to compromise with nationalist sentiments, caused, they believed, by tsarist mistreatment of non-Russian peoples. Lenin in particular was concerned that the imposition of Soviet power should not resurrect memories of Russian chauvinism. Thus, throughout the 1920s and into the early 1930s Soviet policy vigorously promoted the "flourishing of nations," based on the belief that a demonstrated commitment to national equality would erode historic suspicions among non-Russians, gain popular support for the regime, and open the way to an internationalist future.

Known as *korenizatsiya* (nativization), this policy actively encouraged the use of native languages in schools, newspapers, courts, and soviets. The new Soviet regime established school systems using dozens of local languages, many in places where no schools had existed before; it created scripts for previously unwritten languages; it promoted local music, art, folklore, and literature. In the political arena, native officials increasingly replaced Russians in both party and state bureaucracies. In the decade or so after 1922, the number of Ukrainians in the Ukrainian Communist Party grew from 24 percent to 59 percent of the party's membership. In Kazakstan comparable figures were 8 percent and 53 percent.[31] And perhaps most important, the new Soviet Union fixed its internal political-administrative boundaries on territorial units based on nationality. Ultimately there were more than fifty such units: fifteen union republics, twenty autonomous republics, eight autonomous regions, ten autonomous areas—each of which provided an officially recognized homeland for some "national" group.

All this planted the principle of nationality solidly at the core of a self-proclaimed internationalist experiment. It established national elites in the various republics and gave them the trappings of sovereignty (flags, courts, soviets), while maintaining Russian control at the center, where real power resided. The korenizatsiya policy also ensured that millions migrating to the cities in the 1930s were already literate in their native languages, thus giving rise to "national" proletariats with greater immunity to Russification. In Central Asia, korenizatsiya created wholly new territorial-ethnic units—Kazakstan, Uzbekistan, Turkmenistan, Tajikistan, Kirghizia—that provided alternatives both to traditional tribal or clan loyalties and to Islamic religious identity linking people to the larger Muslim world. Enshrining nationality as a principle automatically created "minorities," both in the Union as a whole and in each of its constituent republics. Abkhazians in Georgia, Armenians in the Karabagh region of Azerbaijan, and Chechens in Russia are only three of these smaller peoples whose many grievances escalated into violence in the 1980s and 1990s.

During the Stalin years, korenizatsiya, while never repudiated in theory, was largely abandoned in practice. Believing that collectivization and rapid industrial growth required absolute centralized control, Stalin saw local nationalisms as a potential threat and preferred to rely on a Sovietized Russian elite for controlling the country. Thus, references to the "flourishing of nations" disappeared; thousands of national cadres and intellectuals were purged and often replaced by Russians; Russian-language instruction became compulsory in all schools and fluency in that language became a virtual requirement for successful careers; non-Russian languages now had to be written in the Cyrillic rather than Latin alphabet; rewritten national histories celebrated the contributions Russians (the "elder brother," in Stalin's terms) had made toward the progress of the USSR's other peoples. During World

War II whole peoples—Chechens, Ingushetians, Balkars, Kalmyks, Crimean Tatars, Meskhetians, Volga Germans—were deported because Stalin suspected they might collaborate with the Germans. So too were tens of thousands of Lithuanians, Estonians, and Latvians, whose countries were absorbed into the USSR in 1940 under terms of the Nazi-Soviet Pact.

All this, of course, created lasting ethnic or national resentments. It also disclosed the fundamentally imperial nature of the Soviet state, in which Moscow dictated policy, Russians were the dominant people, and the non-Russian republics were "internal colonies." In a world where "nationalism" was the common language of political life and a country where Stalin actively celebrated the Russian people, it is hardly surprising that other peoples developed their own nationalist response.

Thus, while Stalin's regime prevented the open expression of nationalist sentiment, its own actions fostered the growth of that sentiment. Primary education in national languages continued to nourish national feeling. When internal passports were issued in the 1930s, they identified each citizen's nationality, and this became an acknowledged factor in applying for jobs, university admission, and residence permits. Members of the primary nationality frequently had certain advantages in their own republic. And the massive social upheavals of industrialization, urban migration, and secular education uprooted millions from their traditional village-based identities, threw them together with very different peoples, and created the need for new forms of community. Experience the world over suggests that "modernization" has fostered the growth of more sharply defined national or ethnic identities as people try to sort out the "we/they" question in competitive and culturally diverse urban settings. In particular, some 25 million Russians migrated to other republics, where their more advanced education often landed them better-paying jobs and thus created resentments and sharpened ethnic awareness on both sides. By 1979, Russians represented 21 percent of the population in Ukraine, 28 percent in Estonia, 33 percent in Latvia, and 41 percent in Kazakstan. In more than a dozen other territories, the primary nationality was a minority in its own region.

"Inconspicuous Decolonization" and "the Soviet People"

In the more relaxed atmosphere of the post-Stalin years, growing national consciousness found expression in a variety of ways, some officially approved but many not. The regime continued to crack down on what it regarded as dangerous expressions of national feeling and to promote the creation of a "Soviet people." But by the 1970s Soviet officials and scholars alike acknowledged the reality of national tensions and the failure of their social policies to create this harmonious "Soviet" identity.

One of the clearest expressions of this national consciousness occurred within the official Soviet polity itself. The loosening of central control over the internal affairs of the republics, together with the vast expansion of higher education, consolidated the hold of national elites within the non-Russian republics. Local party leaders promoted their own nationals within party and state bureaucracies. With pervasive links to the "second economy" and extensive networks of patronage and corruption, these republican leaderships evolved into national "mafias" that largely controlled the internal affairs of their republics with minimal intervention from Moscow. According to one scholar, this "inconspicuous . . . decolonization" rendered the Soviet Union increasingly dependent on the loyalty of its non-Russian elite.[32]

Elites in each republic sought support in cultural revivals, led by native intelligentsias, that defended national languages, fostered national literatures, and created national histories, all the while fighting endless battles with the orthodoxies of Soviet ideology. In 1956, for example, the Uzbek party leadership organized a "Congress of the Intelligentsia of Uzbekistan," at which they announced the rehabilitation of Uzbek writers and officials killed by Stalin and urged the assembled intellectuals to combat Soviet images of Central Asian "backwardness."[33] Georgian, Armenian, and Lithuanian historians struggled to depict the independence of their earlier states, while acknowledging their incorporation into the Russian empire as somehow "progressive."

In Ukraine as well, nationalist feelings found expression through official channels, especially during the years between 1963 and 1972 when Petro Shelest was head of the Ukrainian party organization. Reversing the Russification of the Stalin years, Ukrainians came to dominate the political leadership of the republic. Shelest himself articulated Ukrainian economic interests quite openly, and some of his economic officials complained more quietly that their country was being exploited. Ukrainian intellectuals laid out bold demands for resisting Russification and pushed the teaching and the use of the Ukrainian language. The party leadership even protected for a time increasingly radical underground writers. In 1972, however, Moscow cracked down, removed Shelest, and launched a major purge in which perhaps a thousand officials, scholars, and writers lost their jobs. The Soviet leadership was particularly sensitive about Ukrainian nationalism, for it regarded Ukrainians as "little Slavic brothers" whose Russification, together with that of the neighboring Belorussians, would provide a solid Russified Slavic core to the Soviet Union and offset the growing population of Central Asian Muslims. As a major industrial, mining, and grain-producing republic, Ukraine was also of great economic importance to the USSR. Here then was one of the "official nationalisms" tolerated, but within sharp limits, by central Soviet authorities.

National consciousness also found expression in less official ways. Vigorous dissident groups in the republics articulated national themes in their underground writings. Ukrainian poet Vasyl Symonenko perhaps spoke for many others when he declared in verse: "My people exist! My people will always exist! No one can blot out my people."[34] From 1972 until the mid-1980s, the samizdat *Chronicle of the Catholic Church of Lithuania* documented the persecution of the church and illustrated the blending of religion and politics in Lithuanian nationalism.

More public protests occasionally punctured the surface calm of Soviet political life. In 1965, a hundred thousand Armenians demonstrated in Erevan to mark the fiftieth anniversary of their slaughter by the Ottoman Turks, but they simultaneously demanded the return of Armenian lands in the neighboring republic of Azerbaijan. Crimean Tatars and Meskhetians protested publicly and presented numerous petitions to Soviet authorities demanding their return to lands from which Stalin had deported them. Lithuanians by the tens of thousands signed petitions and letters insisting that their rights as Catholics be respected. Jews demanded the right to emigrate, supported by the United States in the context of Cold War rivalries. And in Georgia, a party decision in 1978 to remove Georgian as the official republican language in a new constitution provoked such a widespread outcry that authorities were forced to back down on the issue.

Language, so intimately linked to national identity, was perhaps the most sensitive issue. It was largely through the Russian language that the advocates of assimilation sought to construct the "Soviet people." Thus, in 1958, the Khrushchev regime established the "voluntary principle" in education, which permitted parents in non-Russian republics to send their children to schools in which Russian would be the language of instruction, not merely an additional subject. Since competitive exams for high-prestige universities were held in Russian and since Russian was the "language of success" in most republics, incentives to attend Russian-language schools were great. But to nationalists, such a policy threatened to marginalize their languages, reducing them to domestic and social use.

Again in the 1970s the Brezhnev leadership mounted a major effort to encourage the mastery of Russian as the "second native language" of the Soviet people. It increased the number of hours of Russian-language instruction in schools, required that kindergartens and preschool classes introduce Russian, and that all theses and dissertations be written in that language. Such efforts did increase the number of people fluent in Russian to about 62 percent of the non-Russian population by 1979, but it also provoked widespread resentment and active protest in many republics. Knowledge of the Russian language did not, apparently, diminish national consciousness.

A final expression of national consciousness involved the Russians themselves. In the post-Stalin years a small section of the Russian intelligentsia began to express fears that something uniquely Russian was in danger. For those who defined Russia in cultural or spiritual terms, the Soviet experience had endangered Russian historical monuments, its peasant villages, its landscape and soil, its moral values and family structure, and most of all its churches and Orthodox religious traditions. Some writers came close to defining the entire revolutionary heritage as anti-Russian, since it was based in an alien Marxist ideology. For those who saw the Russian genius embodied in a strong, authoritarian, and imperial state, whether tsarist or Stalinist, the entire de-Stalinization effort was a threat to what they valued, and Soviet federalism was inconsistent with Russian domination.

This spectrum of Russian-nationalist views, often including an anti-Semitic element, emerged with various degrees of militancy in samizdat and émigré writing, in the published works of village prose authors, and even in certain official publications. Russian-nationalist views of a less extreme type clearly had supporters in high party positions, particularly in the Brezhnev years. In 1965, the party authorized an All-Russian Society for the Preservation of Historical and Cultural Monuments, which immediately gained a large membership. Some Russian nationalists developed markedly anti-Semitic and chauvinistic views that foresaw a messianic role for Russia and despised everything non-Russian.

The vast majority of Russians were oblivious to the debates that surged among a small number of writers and scholars. Most identified with the Soviet Union as their "motherland," though they no doubt saw it as a largely Russian achievement. But these currents of Russian-nationalist thought became far more popular and politically significant in the Gorbachev years and played a critical role in the demise of the Soviet Union.

Questions and Controversies: *What Held the Soviet Empire Together?*

Despite the evident growth of nationalist consciousness, the Soviet Union on the eve of Gorbachev's takeover was clearly not about to explode in nationalist fury. While "the Soviet people" remained a distant dream, the state had little trouble containing and managing its national problems. The explosion occurred only *after* glasnost and democratization had decisively weakened the center and permitted the active political mobilization of ethnic and nationalist sentiment.

If the Soviet Union was an empire, it is perhaps more surprising that it lasted so long than that it finally collapsed. After all, the surging force of twentieth-century nationalism had already shattered the Austrian, Ottoman, British, French, Belgian, and Portuguese empires. How had the Soviet empire remained so long immune from such a fate?

One answer is that the Soviet Union was an empire of a unique kind. Russians as a whole derived little clear economic benefit from empire, often compared themselves unfavorably to more prosperous regions such as Georgia or the Baltic republics, and complained about the "burdens" of supporting modern development in the backward republics of Central Asia. Thus, economic exploitation was less prominent in nationalist arguments than in European colonies of Africa and Asia. And unlike other empires, its central integrating institution was an omnipresent political party, long led by a Georgian (Stalin), with an official ideology that denied legitimacy to nationalist claims, and with a membership open to all. The federal structure of the Soviet Union allowed the regime to co-opt and reward handsomely republican elites who were willing to express their nationalist sentiments within prescribed limits. The Soviet regime had indeed inflicted great sufferings on its internal colonies—the destruction of peasant villages, dekulakization, the terror and deportations, the closure of churches, the assault on the environment—but the sufferings of Sovietization were shared in great measure by the dominant Russians.

Furthermore, the coercive capacity of the Soviet state was hardly in doubt, despite the end of Stalinist terror. And the leadership of both the military and the KGB was firmly in Russian hands. In addition, the various non-Russian peoples themselves were largely unable to act in concert with one another. A substantial number of Ukrainians and Belorussians had been effectively Russified; national consciousness was particularly weak in the less developed Central Asian republics where Islam and tribal or clan loyalties retained their hold; and some of the non-Russian peoples were seriously at odds among themselves (Armenians and Azerbaijanis, Georgians and Abkhazians).

Thus, the Soviet Union endured, its political stability not seriously threatened by nationalist upheaval. Other factors described earlier also sustained the Soviet experiment: the long tsarist legacy of autocratic rule and a political culture of deference to strong authority; a real commitment among many people to the socialist idea; possibilities for advancement available in a rapidly industrializing country with widening educational opportunities; pervasive fear born of Stalin's terror; the ever present arm of the party and the secret police; constant propaganda by the regime, and few alternative sources of information; patriotism forged in World War II and reinforced during the Cold War; the prestige of Soviet superpower status; and a measure of economic improvement in the post-Stalin years. But beneath the placid surface, the slow transformation of cultural identity and political loyalty proceeded apace, driven in large measure by the policies and practices of the Soviet regime itself.

The Soviet Union and the World

Finally, the changing Soviet role in the world also helped to shape the subsequent Gorbachev initiatives. In the three decades following World War II, the Soviet Union had emerged as a global superpower able to contest American dominance on the world stage. Its control of Eastern Europe, its achievements in space, its growing role in the Third World, and above all, its enormous military power and nuclear capacity—all had contributed to Soviet international prestige and had persuaded the Brezhnev leadership that the "correlation of forces" was moving in their favor. Thus, the Soviet regime of the early 1970s felt that it could enter a period of détente, or more relaxed relations, with the West from a position of strength. At last, it seemed, the centuries-long quest to catch up with the West was within reach.

That expectation, however, was seriously flawed, for in the decade or so preceding Gorbachev's coming to power, the international position of the Soviet Union deteriorated sharply. At the heart of this process was the economic stagnation described earlier in this chapter. By the 1970s, it was increasingly apparent that, despite the country's military achievements, its economy lagged further and further behind that of the capitalist West in terms of productivity, product quality, computer applications, miniaturization, and general technological development. This was a serious embarrassment for a Communist Party leadership that justified its role in terms of surpassing the capitalist world, and if it were not corrected, it might threaten even the military foundation of Soviet superpower status.

Furthermore, by the early 1980s détente with the West was in tatters. A continued Soviet arms buildup, a more aggressive posture in the Third World, and the invasion of Afghanistan in 1979 had provoked a new round of intense Cold War competition. Ronald Reagan's belligerent "evil empire" rhetoric provided the ideological foundation for a massive American military buildup which presented the Soviet Union with a new arms race it could neither afford nor win. Of particular concern was the American Strategic Defense Initiative (SDI), a high-tech antimissile defense system that the Soviet leadership found both militarily and economically threatening. In addition, active American support for anticommunist forces in Nicaragua, Afghanistan, and Angola increased the economic and political price the USSR had to pay for its Third World involvements. Finally, the "human rights" emphasis in American policy toward the USSR in the 1970s and 1980s both encouraged Soviet dissidents and challenged the legitimacy of the Soviet regime.

Adding to the USSR's international isolation was a deep rift with its supposedly fraternal communist ally, China. That rivalry had led to a military clash over border issues in the Far East in 1969–70, and relations improved little in the decade that followed. The intense hostility between the two great communist states provided an opportunity for their common American enemy to play them off against each other.

Furthermore, China after 1976 embarked on a series of economic reforms known as "market socialism." The dramatic success of these measures provided an embarrassing contrast to the stagnation of the Soviet economy.

Soviet achievements in the international arena had become costly burdens by the early 1980s. Third World involvements in Angola, Ethiopia, and Nicaragua irritated the United States, while producing few benefits for the Soviet Union. Cuba, at one time a promising communist outpost in the western hemisphere, had become a drain on the Soviet economy to the tune of almost $5 billion a year. Poland, the key state in the USSR's Eastern European empire, was seething with discontent, articulated by the Solidarity trade union movement, and was saved from Soviet military intervention only by the imposition of martial law in late 1981. The popularity of Solidarity and its insistence on acting as if Poland were a free country provided a compelling example to those who sought real change in the Soviet Union. Finally, the Soviet invasion of Afghanistan in 1979, undertaken to preserve a friendly communist regime on its southern border, became in Gorbachev's words a "bleeding wound." It was expensive in both money and lives; appalling Soviet casualties and blatant government lies about them hammered home to many the loathsomeness of the country's leadership; and it posed a serious obstacle to relations with the United States, China, and the Islamic world. By the early 1980s, then, the worsening Soviet international position had magnified the country's domestic problems and provided even greater incentive for some change in direction.

Questions and Controversies:
Can Coincidence Explain the Soviet Collapse?

To review briefly, some scholars explain the Soviet collapse by highlighting some essential feature of the Soviet system—a utopian socialist ideology, a multinational empire, or the legacy of a rigid and brutal Stalinist regime. Such an approach suggests the presence of historical "laws" or regularities that decisively shape the outcomes of the historical process. But others, seeking to avoid the charge of inevitability or determinism, have constructed an alternative explanation based on the concept of "conjuncture"—the coming together of a "cluster of interrelated developments" in a unique and often fortuitous fashion. Such an approach, its proponents argue, preserves the complexity, messiness, and unexpectedness of the historical process. It suggests that a major event such as the Soviet collapse represents a unique coincidence of many factors coming together at a particular time rather than the logical working out of a single principle or flaw. And it reminds us of alternative possibilities, of roads not taken, had one or another of these elements not appeared. Thus, it remains faithful to the uncertainty that most participants in the historical drama actually felt as they made choices with little clarity as to what would actually happen.

Scholars seeking to explain the Soviet collapse in these terms generally begin by highlighting a set of connected processes contributing to Soviet weakness, located primarily in the post-Stalin era. In one analysis, historian Alexander Dallin identified six such processes. The first was a "loosening of controls" after Stalin's death, reflected in the end of political terror, the greater degree of personal freedom and security, and the appearance of "cracks" in the system of party-state domination. A second factor was the spread of corruption, which saw virtually everyone from high officials to ordinary workers weaving networks of private connections and the trading of favors outside official channels. A third element, the "erosion of ideology," pointed to declining commitment to Marxism-Leninism, particularly among the elite, and a growing fascination with western ideas and goods. A changing society of more highly urbanized and educated professionals with new expectations for personal privacy and public participation represented a fourth process putting pressure on a rigid Soviet system. Greater exposure to the western world, with its human rights rhetoric and tempting material goods, was a fifth factor undermining the Soviet system, while economic decline and a growing technological gap with the West further weakened and humiliated the country.[35]

Scholars of course endlessly debate the relative importance of particular factors, based in part on their understanding of what drives historical change. Those inclined to see ideas as the primary mover in history focus more on the declining belief in Marxism-Leninism as weakening the regime. Those who understand economic change as fundamental emphasize the stagnation of the Brezhnev era. Had the economy performed more credibly, perhaps the loss of belief would have mattered less. An economically booming communist China, after all, remains intact. Still others view political institutions as the crucial element and highlight the rigidity of an authoritarian Soviet political system unable to adapt as the society it governed changed profoundly.

But none of this, Dallin and others have argued, necessarily spelled doom for the Soviet Union. The country might very well have hobbled along or muddled through for some time to come. No organized movements of workers, peasants, students, or nationalists had arisen to challenge the system. Those establishment intellectuals who were critical of the regime hardly represented a serious political force. The dissident movement was tiny and largely suppressed by the early 1980s. And while the economy was stagnant and falling behind the West, it provided adequately for the population's basic needs.[36] Furthermore, Andropov's reforms in the early 1980s, with their focus on discipline and streamlining the command economy, had some immediate and positive effect. Were it not for his weakened kidneys, which caused his early death, the Soviet Union might have continued well into the next century. In any event, no overt crisis and certainly no imminent collapse greeted Gorbachev upon his advent to the summit of Soviet power.

The appearance of a genuine reformer on the political scene was, in this view, highly improbable, another of those unexpected events that shape the course of history. But that chance event proved decisive. One scholar put it like this: "It was not . . . destabilization that precipitated radical change, but radical change that precipitated destabilization."[37] Gorbachev's policies, by 1989 nothing less than a "revolution from within," inadvertently undermined the Soviet regime in ways that will become clear in the chapters to follow. In this view, then, the Gorbachev reforms represented a "vital link in the chain of destabilization, delegitimation, and disintegration" that brought the Soviet Union to its ruin.[38] Unlike the "fatal flaw" approach, which views the Gorbachev years as but the occasion for an inevitable collapse, this interpretation makes the Gorbachev reform program a primary and independent cause of that collapse. In short, although the patient was chronically ill, it was not the disease that killed him; rather, it was the treatment the doctor prescribed.

Notes

1. Peter Hauslohner, "Politics Before Gorbachev: De-Stalinization and the Roots of Reform," in *Politics, Society, and Nationality: Inside Gorbachev's Russia,* ed. Seweryn Bialer (Boulder: Westview Press, 1989), pp. 40–42.

2. Stephen F. Cohen, *Rethinking the Soviet Experience* (New York: Oxford University Press, 1985), p. 134.

3. Seweryn Bialer, *The Soviet Paradox* (New York: Knopf, 1986), pp. 41–46.

4. For the development of this concept, see Vera Dunham, *In Stalin's Time* (Cambridge: Cambridge University Press, 1976), especially chap. 1 and postscript.

5. Eduard Shevardnadze, *The Future Belongs to Freedom* (New York: Free Press, 1991), p. xiv.

6. Georgi Arbatov, *The System: An Insider's Life in Soviet Politics* (New York: Times Books, 1992), esp. chaps. 4, 7.

7. Thane Gustafson, *Reform in Soviet Politics* (Cambridge: Cambridge University Press, 1981), pp. 4–5.

8. R.W. Davies, "Soviet Economic Reform in Historical Perspective," in *Perestroika: The Historical Perspective,* eds. Catherine Merridale and Chris Ward (London: Edward Arnold, 1991), p. 121.

9. Gustafson, *Refom in Soviet Politics,* p. 143.

10. Tatyana Zaslavskaya, *The Second Socialist Revolution* (Bloomington: Indiana University Press, 1990), p. 45.

11. Gail Lapidus, "Social Trends," in *After Brezhnev,* ed. Robert F. Byrnes (Bloomington: Indiana University Press, 1983), p. 193; Bialer, *Soviet Paradox,* p. 23.

12. Moshe Lewin, "Conclusion," in *Perestroika,* ed. Merridale and Ward, p. 240.

13. Philip G. Roeder, *Red Sunset: The Failure of Soviet Politics* (Princeton: Princeton University Press, 1993).

14. Zaslavskaya, *Second Socialist Revolution,* pp. 49–50.

15. Marshall Goldman, *USSR in Crisis* (New York: W.W. Norton, 1983), p. 33.

16. Moshe Lewin, *The Gorbachev Phenomenon* (Berkeley and Los Angeles: University of California Press, 1988), p. 49.

17. For this distinction between the political elite and the dominant class, see Robert V. Daniels, *The End of the Communist Revolution* (London: Routledge, 1993), pp. 70–71.

18. Hedrick Smith, *The New Russians* (New York: Avon Books, 1991), pp. 8–16.

19. Tatyana Zaslavskaya, "The Novosibirsk Report," *Survey* 28:1 (spring 1984), pp. 88–108.

20. For this argument, see Francis Fukuyama, "The Modernizing Imperative: The USSR as an Ordinary Country," *National Interest* (spring 1993), pp. 13–14.

21. Archie Brown, *The Gorbachev Factor* (New York: Oxford University Press, 1996), pp. 18–19.

22. Dennis O'Hearn, "The Consumer Second Economy," *Soviet Studies* 32:2 (1980), p. 225.

23. Svetlana Boym, *Common Places* (Cambridge: Harvard University Press, 1994), p. 94.

24. Christopher Lazarski, "Vladimir Vysotsky and His Cult," *Russian Review* 51 (January 1992), pp. 58–71; Gerald S. Smith, *Songs to Seven Strings* (Bloomington: Indiana University Press, 1984), pp. 145–180.

25. Kathleen F. Parthé, *Russian Village Prose: The Radiant Past* (Princeton: Princeton University Press, 1992), esp. chap. 1.

26. S. Frederick Starr, *Red and Hot* (New York: Oxford University Press, 1983), pp. 289–315.

27. John Bushnell, "The New Soviet Man Turns Pessimist," *Survey* 24:2 (spring 1979), pp. 1–18.

28. Bialer, *Soviet Paradox,* p. 20.

29. For this view, see Ronald G. Suny, *The Revenge of the Past: Nationalism, Revolution, and the Collapse of the Soviet Union* (Stanford: Stanford University Press, 1993), on which this section draws heavily.

30. The term derives from Benedict Anderson, *Imagined Communities: Reflections on the Origins and Spread of Nationalism* (London: Verso, 1983).

31. Gerhard Simon, *Nationalism and Policy toward the Nationalities in the Soviet Union* (Boulder: Westview Press, 1991), p. 32.

32. Ibid., p. 265.

33. Bohdan Nahaylo and Victor Swoboda, *Soviet Disunion: A History of the Nationalities Problem in the USSR* (New York: Free Press, 1990), pp. 121–22.

34. Ibid., p. 143.

35. Alexander Dallin, "Causes of the Collapse of the USSR," *Post-Soviet Affairs* 8:4 (1992), pp. 279–302.

36. Myron Rush, "Fortune and Fate," *The National Interest* 31 (spring 1993), pp. 19–25. See also Seweryn Bialer, "The Death of Soviet Communism," *Foreign Affairs* 70:5 (winter 1991–92), pp. 166–81.

37. John Gooding, "Perestroika As Revolution from Within," *Russian Review* 51:1 (January 1992), p. 36.

38. Dallin, "Causes of the Collapse," p. 297.

Chapter 3

Reviving Soviet Socialism: The Gorbachev Experiment

Between 1985 and 1991 the central feature of Soviet history was an increasingly far-reaching effort to rescue the country from the accumulated problems of its past. Associated with the leadership of Mikhail Gorbachev, these reforms were designed to revitalize a stagnant economy as well as a Communist Party grown bureaucratic and entrenched, and in so doing to preserve a redefined Soviet "socialism" and the superpower status which the country had so recently acquired. It was, therefore, a fundamentally conservative effort, though one that provoked increasingly ambitious measures and was expressed in the rhetoric of "revolutionary" values.

In the context of Soviet history, however, Gorbachev's proposals were anything but conservative. They began, it is true, with "traditional" communist reform efforts such as cleansing the party of corrupt people, criticizing and reorganizing the state bureaucracy, and reasserting the party's vanguard leadership role. But Gorbachev ultimately went far beyond these measures. Glasnost acknowledged that Soviet society contained diverse and even conflicting interests and provided vast new openings for their expression. Perestroika sought to limit state control over the economy and to open up some space for private economic initiatives. Democratization provided for much greater popular participation in political life and substantially reduced the role of the

Communist Party in Soviet society. And Gorbachev's foreign policy overturned fundamental Soviet assumptions about the world as an arena of hostile competition between two antagonistic camps. In these ways Gorbachev presided over a real transformation of the Soviet system. But in the grandest of ironies, those very reforms seemed to deal the Soviet system a fatal blow. The Soviet experience seemed to verify the old observation that nothing is more dangerous to a bad government than an effort to reform it.

Questions and Controversies: *Debating the Gorbachev Factor*

Since Gorbachev and his reform program have figured so prominently in explaining the Soviet collapse, it is hardly surprising that he should be at the center of academic as well as political controversy. Here we will highlight several of these debates so that you may be alert to them as you consider the Gorbachev era in greater detail in the chapters that follow.

Perhaps the first debate involves understanding how a person of real reformist inclinations could rise to the top of a system that normally filtered out anyone who might pose a threat to it. Was Gorbachev a fluke, an accident of the Soviet system? The Communist Party had long possessed a reformist wing, an "alternative tradition" that saw Leninism and democracy, the plan and the market, as compatible with one other. Though rarely in the ascendancy, adherents of this "soft" communism drew inspiration from the NEP policies of the 1920s and from the de-Stalinization efforts of the Khrushchev era. As a member of the Khrushchev generation, Gorbachev sympathized, discreetly, with this wing of the Communist Party. Furthermore, the social changes of the post-Stalin era saw the rise of a well-educated professional class that provided a constituency for this outlook. And the aging of the party leadership signaled a generational shift by the early 1980s and a widespread recognition that some change was necessary. If Gorbachev's rise to power was surprising, it was hardly an accident.

Still, Gorbachev's evolution from a modest reformer to a "transformer" of the entire Soviet system was remarkable and unprecedented in Soviet history, particularly since he acted *before* widespread popular pressure pushed him in that direction. Why did he do it? To some observers Gorbachev had radical intentions from the beginning, but kept them carefully concealed until political conditions enabled him to act on his original plans. Others argued that he had only vague and modest reforms in mind at the beginning, but learned on the job that the country's problems demanded more extensive changes and that popular pressures required a more radical response.

If Gorbachev's motives have been the focus of much controversy, so too have his personal qualities. To some of his conservative critics, he was an "alarmist," unduly influenced by liberal advisers, who believed that only by quickly closing the technological gap with the West could the USSR remain a great power. Thus, he took unnecessarily radical actions when he could have prolonged the Soviet Union's lifespan by more modest policies aimed at shoring up the command economy and perhaps cutting defense spending. Others have seen Gorbachev as a principled reformer, who believed that the high promise of Soviet socialism could yet be realized by peaceful evolutionary change and who felt, perhaps naively, that new democratic freedoms would bind a grateful population to the regime. Still others have pointed to an overconfidence in his own ability to manipulate the political process and to a degree of popularity in the West that blinded him to more conservative doubters in the leadership. By the end of his tenure, many in the Soviet Union saw him as an indecisive and vacillating figure, whipsawed by conflicting pressures from radicals and conservatives and unable to chart a consistent course for the country.

In raising the question of Gorbachev's motivation and character, we confront the role of individuals and particular actions, as opposed to large impersonal forces and conditions, in shaping the historical process. The Gorbachev phenomenon represents what scholars refer to as "contingency," how the unfolding of the historical process depends on chance, on unpredictable events, on unexpected outcomes. It is a perspective very much at odds with the "fatal flaw" approach described in Chapter 1. Most analysts acknowledge that without Gorbachev's energy and commitment, no reform program of such magnitude would have been undertaken by any other conceivable leader. Should we then agree with the conclusion of economist Vladimir Kontorovich that "the collapse of the Soviet Union was the unintended result of a small number of disastrous decisions by a few individuals"?[1]

A final set of questions about the Gorbachev era asks how, precisely, his reform program contributed to the Soviet collapse. Perhaps the Soviet system was simply unreformable, and any attempt to tinker with its fragile structures would send it spinning into oblivion. Or was it the particular character of the reforms themselves? Certainly Gorbachev was criticized both for moving too slowly and cautiously and for taking unnecessarily drastic and rapid measures. Or should our attention focus less on Gorbachev's policies than on unexpected social responses to them? Such a perspective places the spotlight on those movements of democrats and nationalists that sought to push those reforms in a more radical direction and on the conservative backlash that wanted to restrain reforms and turn the country back to an earlier and perhaps more stable time.

Changing of the Guard

The previous chapter outlined the circumstances that provided incentives and possibilities for new directions in Soviet life. But those social and economic conditions did not automatically dictate the extraordinary and almost wholly unexpected changes that the country experienced after 1985. That required the initiative of a dynamic leadership, willing and able to respond to new conditions.

The man whose name now defines that initiative and the final years of Soviet history, Mikhail Sergeyevich Gorbachev, was born in 1931 in the village of Privolnoye in the rural Stavropol region of southern Russia. His was a peasant family of modest means, though not an ordinary one, for both his father and grandfather had been party members, and the latter had been founder and chairman of the local collective farm. Young Mikhail followed the family's political tradition by becoming active in Komsomol, the party youth organization, and at the remarkably young age of eighteen was a candidate member of the party itself. These political credentials, and his own native intelligence and good academic record, secured his entrance to Moscow State University, the country's premier institution of higher learning. There he studied law, rather than the more common fields of science and engineering, remained active in Komsomol, and became a full member of the Communist Party in 1952.

Returning to Stavropol in 1955 with a degree and a wife, Raisa, Gorbachev entered a career within the party that lasted for the next thirty-six years. He began in the regional Komsomol bureaucracy, transferred to the regular party structure in the early 1960s, and by 1970 had become the first secretary, the number one man, of the provincial party organization. In 1978 he made the leap from the provinces to the "center" with an appointment to the party Secretariat in Moscow, with responsibility for agriculture. Two years later he arrived at the summit of Soviet politics by becoming a full member of the Politburo, the chief policymaking organ of the Communist Party. He was then forty-nine years old, the youngest of the Politburo's fifteen members. Within five years, following the deaths in rapid succession of Brezhnev (1982), Andropov (1984), and Chernenko (1985), Mikhail Gorbachev was named general secretary of the Communist Party.

It was a remarkable career, but one that reflected many of the central features of Soviet history. His family had suffered from Stalinist repression—as both of his grandfathers had been arrested during the 1930s. It was a searing memory that he revealed publicly only in 1990. On the other hand, he had benefited greatly from the opportunities for education and social mobility initially opened up in the Stalin era. His early career coincided with the Khrushchev thaw and marked his break with Stalinism and his political identification with the moderate, reformist wing of the party. Like many other members of the emerging professional class, both within and outside the party, Gorbachev carried the hopes of the Khrushchev years through the "era of stagnation" that followed. Above all, Gorbachev was a creature of the party in which he had spent his entire career. His rapid ascent within the party hierarchy had benefited much from the patronage of several senior leaders who had roots or experience in Stavropol and from his association with many others who visited the popular party health spas in the area. Honest, personable, and hardworking, Gorbachev developed a reputation as an intelligent, open-minded, and innovative party official, though he clearly operated within the prescribed limits of the system. He genuinely believed in the potential of Soviet socialism under proper leadership, and he persisted in his commitment to the party long after many others had abandoned it.

But during his years in Moscow he had seen the party's leadership in its most decrepit, unimaginative, and incompetent phase, particularly during Brezhnev's last years (1978–82) and during the thirteen months of the elderly Konstantin Chernenko's uninspiring tenure (1984–85). While he fully participated in the ritual of extravagant praise accorded these party leaders, he and fellow reformer Eduard Shevardnadze agreed in 1984 that "everything is rotten" and that "it's no longer possible to live this way." If Brezhnev and Chernenko represented what had to be changed, Andropov's fifteen months in power (1982–

Voices

Soviet History in a Single Joke

A widely told joke summed up the USSR's five major political figures, putting Gorbachev's coming to power in a humorous perspective.

The five major figures of Soviet history were on a train together when it suddenly halted in a remote region where the tracks had abruptly stopped. What to do? Lenin was the first to speak, and in his revolutionary enthusiasm he issued a call for a voluntary day of work for local folk to extend the tracks. Stalin objected and ordered the leaders of the railroad ministry shot and the train engineer exiled to Siberia. The always exuberant and impulsively reformist Khrushchev had yet another idea: tear up the tracks behind the train and lay them in front and thus proceed to their destination. Brezhnev's contribution was to order the shades drawn while all the travelers rocked back and forth, pretending to move ahead. Finally it was Gorbachev's turn. The architect of glasnost had the windows thrown wide open and asked everyone to stick their heads out of the train and shout loudly, "There are no tracks! There are no tracks!"

84) provided Gorbachev with a more positive model for many of his own early reforms. Formerly head of the KGB, Yuri Andropov initiated a crackdown on worker indiscipline, started a vigorous anticorruption campaign, replaced a number of Brezhnev cronies with younger and more vigorous men, and more openly acknowledged the country's serious problems. He also commissioned a number of "working groups" to study these problems and brought Gorbachev into close association with this effort. In this way Gorbachev encountered the ideas of the many intellectuals and academics invited to participate in these groups. Some of these people, and certainly their ideas, later became the foundation of Gorbachev's reform efforts. But Andropov's early death and his replacement by the infirm Brezhnev holdover Chernenko put further reform on hold.

The years between Brezhnev's death in November 1982 and Gorbachev's selection as general secretary in March 1985 represent an extended transition in Soviet political life. It was a demographic transition, as the aging Stalin-era leadership died off and was replaced by a generation that had come of age politically in the Khrushchev years. And it was a political transition, as the reformist element of the party, increasingly represented by Gorbachev, assumed leadership. By the time Chernenko died, even some of the old guard, particularly longtime foreign minister Andrei Gromyko, believed that the party needed new, younger, and more vigorous leadership. His support was instrumental in Gorbachev's rapid selection as general secretary, an appointment announced within twenty-four hours of Chernenko's death on March 10, 1985.

Gorbachev's position, however, was hardly one of undisputed control. Real controversies had accompanied each of the three successions between 1982 and 1985, pitting Brezhnev supporters against more reformist-minded members of the party leadership. Thus, Gorbachev's arrival at the summit of the Soviet political system gave him the power of initiative, but his initiatives were constrained by the presence of more conservative Brezhnev-era appointees throughout the party and state bureaucracy, including many at its highest levels. Unlike China's Communist Party apparatus, which had been thoroughly disrupted by the Cultural Revolution, the Soviet Union's party-state bureaucracy was fully intact and quite capable of thwarting the will of the party leadership.

Thus, it is not surprising that among Gorbachev's early priorities was an effort to staff the hierarchy with sympathetic people. Within a year he had engineered the selection to the Politburo of Yegor Ligachev, Nikolai Ryzhkov, Viktor Chebrikov, Boris Yeltsin, and Eduard Shevardnadze—all of them then his supporters—and had secured the retirement of a number of older, more conservative Brezhnev appointees. The party Secretariat was likewise revamped, and the powerful Central Committee experienced a turnover rate of more than 50 percent. While these remarkably extensive personnel changes solidified Gorbachev's own position as party leader, they did not ensure that his policies would be easily enacted or implemented. With a few exceptions, new Politburo members were Andropov men without deep personal loyalty to Gorbachev. Nor were those considered reformers in 1985 of one mind. Within a few years, for example, Ligachev came to oppose major aspects of Gorbachev's program as excessive and threatening to Soviet values, while Yeltsin considered them altogether too slow and modest. Furthermore, new faces in the Central Committee did not necessarily mean new ideas, and conservatives continued to dominate that powerful body. And the vast party-state bureaucracy that managed the economy, education, the media, and cultural expression was far too enormous to be quickly brought under Gorbachev's control. The Gorbachev reform effort unfolded within a political context that contained much reluctance and even outright opposition.

What, then, was the Gorbachev program when he ascended to power in 1985? Clearly, there was no detailed blueprint or set of worked-out policies ready to be proposed. All of that would have to be hammered out amid the conflicting perspectives of various party leaders, the bureaucratic apparatus, and growing popular pressures. It was a political process marked by several sharp turns and many smaller zigzags over the next six years. In that sense no "Gorbachev program" existed in 1985.

But there was a general sense of direction. It was clear, for example, that Gorbachev was highly critical of the immobility, corruption, and stagnation of the Brezhnev era. He was for major change, "a qualitatively new state of society," as he put it. In a speech to a party gathering in December 1984, several months before his selection as general secretary, he made his case in very general terms. "Profound transformation" in both economy and society were necessary, he argued, if the country was to achieve a higher standard of living and enter the new century as a "great and prosperous power." He spoke bluntly about the economic stagnation of recent decades and called for "fundamentally new, truly revolutionary scientific and technical solutions capable of increasing labor productivity many times over." More concretely, he advocated modernizing the machine-tool industry, using economic levers such as prices, profit, and credit, decentralizing economic management, and making individual enterprises responsible for their products. All of this was "restructuring," or in Russian *perestroika,* a term that came to encapsulate the entire Gorbachev reform effort. He touched too on the "improvement of the Soviet political system" through greater participation of working people in the affairs of their own enterprises and "the development of socialist self-government." Finally, he mentioned *glasnost,* openness, as an "integral part of socialist democracy." "Wide, prompt and frank information is evidence of confidence in the people and . . . an effective means of combating bureaucratic distortions."[2]

Here in very embryonic form were many of the major themes that Gorbachev would pursue over the next few years. They arose, not from any popular pressure or street demonstrations, but from a perception among a section of the Soviet elite that crisis was brewing and that the country was in serious straits. Gorbachev's ideas drew heavily on progressive thinking as it had developed in academic research institutes and in more liberal party circles over the past several decades, and they continued many of the emphases of the Andropov regime. They clearly marked his agenda as reformist, but how much so was quite unclear to outsiders and probably to Gorbachev himself. That agenda could be read as the platform of a relatively unthreatening but energetic technocratic modernizer, but there were also hints of something more far-reaching. Such ambiguity, however, defused potential opposition and helped to attract party and popular support for his experiment in revitalizing Soviet socialism during its early years.

Also clear from Gorbachev's early statements was his firm commitment to the larger Soviet system. He repeatedly praised its achievements and asserted his program's continuity with its basic principles. The country had made a "socialist choice" in 1917, Gorbachev argued, and that choice remained inviolable. In frequent references to the importance of "subjective factors," Gorbachev was highlighting the inadequate leadership of the past and affirming the basic soundness of the system itself. And while he recognized party conservatism and bureaucratic stagnation as part of the problem, he also saw the Communist Party as the primary vehicle for renewal in the country; only much later did he accept a multiparty system. Here was a central dilemma in the entire Gorbachev agenda: If the party was an obstacle to reform, could it also be the agent of reform? And if the party had to be weakened or bypassed in the pursuit of reform, what remained to hold the Soviet Union together?

A final element of the Gorbachev phenomenon was the style of its leader. He mixed freely with ordinary people; he spoke directly and without notes; he was often accompanied by his attractive and accomplished wife; he took note of the practical problems of daily life; he was critical of the widely disliked *apparatchiks*. And he was healthy and vigorous. A widely told joke asked about Gorbachev's support in the Kremlin. The answer: He doesn't need support. He can walk unaided! It was a distinct and widely appreciated change from the recent past of sick and senile leaders.

Acceleration: "The Key to All Our Problems"

If the new leader's rhetorical program was broad and general, his concrete actions during the first several years (1985–86) were modest and narrowly focused on restarting economic growth as quickly as possible. To Gorbachev this was "the key to all our problems," both to the looming threat of international decline and to the equally serious inability to provide for the consumer needs of the population. The slogan defining his early program was "acceleration," or *uskorenie,* a term that implied the tightening up of the existing system rather than its fundamental transformation. Given the country's earlier economic achievements, Gorbachev assumed that the Soviet command economy was essentially sound, though it had been allowed to drift due to the laxity, corruption, and inefficiency of the Brezhnev leadership. Thus, it was essential to "activate the human factor"—a more vigorous political leadership, a more responsible industrial management, and a more disciplined workforce. The actual policies or strategies designed to produce "acceleration" were drawn from the grab bag of traditional Soviet reform practices, some already designed or in place, and particularly from those of the Andropov era. They were, however, not noticeably successful in stimulating rapid growth and in fact created additional problems that complicated the more fundamental reforms that followed.

"Acceleration" sought to use the levers of a command economy to achieve higher growth. One obvious possibility was to raise the targets of the 1986–90 Five-Year Plan, then under development. Against the advice of Gosplan (the central planning commission), Gorbachev insisted on substantially higher growth targets in an effort to force more efficiency from the system and greater effort from the workforce. Altered investment priorities favoring machine building, automation, computerization, and robots also became part of the new Five-Year Plan.

Another tempting option in a command economy is reorganization. Thus, Gorbachev, acutely aware of the bloated bureaucracy of economic management, attempted to streamline the system by consolidating a number of smaller planning ministries into several huge "superministries," while reducing their staffs substantially in the process. None of this did much to raise economic growth rates, but it did antagonize many officials, disrupt established bureaucratic relationships, and contribute to mounting economic difficulties. By the late 1980s most of the superministries had been abandoned.

A further, traditionally Soviet, element of uskorenie featured a series of disciplinary campaigns, aimed at specific aspects of the Soviet economy. One of them focused on improving the notoriously poor quality of Soviet production by stationing a small army of independent inspectors at selected enterprises to monitor the quality of their products. Their conscientious review resulted in close to a 20 percent rejection rate and caused a sharp drop in output in certain industries. This, of course, made it impossible for managers to fulfill their targets and workers to get their bonuses, and their resultant opposition led to the gradual abandonment of the effort by 1988.

An even more dramatic campaign involved the effort to curtail widespread drunkenness and alcoholism, an endemic feature of Soviet life that contributed to absenteeism and low productivity at work, to divorce in the home, and to crime and declining life expectancy for men in the larger society. In an effort spearheaded by the puritanical Yegor Ligachev and backed by Gorbachev, the government acted to limit the purchase of alcohol. Production was cut in half, as was the number of shops selling alcohol; sales could occur only between 2:00 and 7:00 P.M. and were forbidden to those under twenty-one; large fines and dismissals penalized drunkenness on the job; and an anti-drinking propaganda effort accompanied these measures.

While the campaign initially reduced alcohol sales substantially, the drop in consumption was soon made up by the rapid growth in moonshining, and a whole series of unexpected and damaging consequences followed. Sugar, used in home brew, virtually disappeared from the stores and had to be rationed across the entire country. State revenues, some 12 percent of which had come from taxes on alcohol, dropped sharply, thus enlarging the state budget deficit and contributing to inflation when the shortfall was covered by printing money. Wine-producing regions of the country were badly hurt when millions of acres of vineyards were destroyed. All of this alienated many people and undermined Gorbachev's support as he became known disparagingly as the "mineral water secretary."[3]

A third campaign sought to eliminate "unearned income," a vague Soviet term that referred to money gained through bribery, extortion, illegal use of state property, and speculation, or the resale of goods bought more cheaply elsewhere. Gorbachev apparently intended to strike a blow for social justice by cracking down on the theft of state property and on those who took advantage of their public position for

This drawing, with "Vodka" on the flag and a caption reading "Bring Back the Brezhnev Era," represents a satirical comment on Gorbachev's anti-alcohol campaign. From Stephen White, *Russia Goes Dry: Alcohol, State and Society* (New York: Cambridge University Press, 1995), p. 149. Reprinted with permission from the author.

private gain. But the local officials responsible for carrying out the campaign turned it into an attack on ordinary people producing legally for farmers' markets, or transporting such products to market in state vehicles for extra money, or renting out rooms or beds to supplement meager incomes. But large-scale illegal activity went largely untouched. Enforcing the campaign appealed to party conservatives, who were hostile to any kind of private economic activity, and to local officials suspicious of what they did not directly control. In any event, the campaign got out of hand and undermined Gorbachev's efforts to promote responsible individual initiative in economic matters.

Why did Gorbachev pursue such traditional and relatively modest reforms in his first two years, particularly since he had so quickly consolidated his personal political base and might have moved more dramatically when his popular support was at its height? After his resignation in 1991, Gorbachev himself expressed regret that he had not moved more decisively during those two years. There was of course opposition even to the limited program he put into place, and he may have felt politically unable to move further. The memory of Khrushchev, ousted by party conservatives who felt threatened by his reforms, was a constant reminder of what could happen. In April of 1985, when several aides presented him with a more far-reaching draft reform program, he eliminated those sections involving political change. "That's for later," he commented. "First we'll have to maneuver."[4]

But it also seems clear that Gorbachev was not fully aware of the depth of the country's crisis or the extent of opposition to substantial change. Later, reflecting on his earlier views, Gorbachev wrote that he and his colleagues genuinely believed that the country's problems "were not in any way connected with any inherent properties of the system" and that they could be resolved "without going outside its original framework."[5] The disappointing experience of uskorenie, however, represented a short course in the limitations of modest reform, and by mid-1986 and early 1987 Gorbachev was moving toward more substantial efforts.

"More Light": The Glasnost Phenomenon

In August of 1986, Gorbachev signaled a deepening of the reform process by arguing that it must encompass "not only the economy but all other sides of social life."[6] Here was a recognition that the roots of Soviet stagnation were deeper and the obstacles to effective action more entrenched than he had first acknowledged. The chief thrust of this new phase of reform entered the world's vocabulary as glasnost. Literally meaning "voicedness" or "speaking up," it has been translated as "openness," "publicity," or "public disclosure." It implied a new level of candor and truthfulness in public life and a new relationship between the state and its citizens. "We want more openness in public affairs in every sphere of life," Gorbachev wrote. "People should know what is good and what is bad too. . . . Truth is the main thing. . . . Let the party know everything. . . . We need glasnost as we need the air."[7]

Official glasnost represented a recognition that a modern economy simply could not operate effectively without a freer flow of information, more public input into decision making, and more initiative at all levels of society. In this sense, glasnost was directly related to economic reform. But, more broadly, the reformist leadership acknowledged that many elements of Soviet society had been thoroughly alienated from the regime by the hypocrisy, censorship, and outright lies of the Brezhnev era. Glasnost was intended to bridge that gulf between the state and society. Restoring a measure of trust between party and people would make party leadership more effective. And finally, glasnost served a political purpose. As Gorbachev recognized more clearly the extent of bureaucratic opposition to his program, he needed allies outside of the official establishment. In this sense, glasnost reached out to the creative and technical intelligentsia and more generally to the professional classes that had long hungered for the intellectual and cultural freedoms that glasnost promised. They, in turn, would be his instrument of pressure on a recalcitrant party and state bureaucracy that he did not wholly control.

While Gorbachev had spoken of glasnost even before his coming to power, little had changed before the nuclear disaster at Chernobyl in April 1986. That catastrophe, and the initial effort to hide or minimize its significance, proved enormously embarrassing to Gorbachev and prompted more decisive measures to implement his glasnost rhetoric. An early signal of this change involved the appointment of new and more liberal editors to a number of major Soviet newspapers and journals. Another was the release from internal exile in December 1986 of the well-known dissident and human rights activist Andrei Sakharov—widely regarded as the conscience of the country. But the veil of party censorship was not lifted once and for all. Rather, it was a trial-and-error process, as statements by Gorbachev and other top leaders calling for frankness and alternative points of view combined with pressures from editors, scholars, and artists to open up one previously taboo topic after another. Over the next few years, glasnost produced a stunning reversal of the stultifying conformity and deceitful optimism of the Brezhnev era. It was among the most far-reaching and consequential of the Gorbachev reforms.

Among the earliest expressions of glasnost was the exposure of many social pathologies once presented solely as the product of capitalism. Crime, prostitution, child abuse, suicide, corruption, homelessness, poverty, declining health standards—all were detailed in reams of statistics, interviews, photographs, journalistic exposés, films, and TV documentaries. The film *Little Vera* not only broke Soviet taboos on nudity and explicit sex but graphically portrayed the alcoholism, violence, and moral bankruptcy of a working-class family to some 40 million Soviet viewers. Newspaper readers learned that the abortion rate in the USSR was the highest in the world, and they discovered something of the humiliating and degrading process of obtaining one. Journalists provided detailed descriptions of the squalor of communal apartments and the attractiveness of prostitution among young women attempting to supplement their meager salaries. TV reporters for the Leningrad program *Fifth Wheel* climbed the walls of a secluded villa to film the luxurious homes of the party elite. Glasnost thus disclosed a range of new social problems, which official ideology had denied, and made clear that older concerns, such as housing and health care, were far from showing steady improvement.

A reexamination of the Soviet past was, if anything, even more devastating than the coverage of current problems. Led by writers and journalists rather than professional historians, this "return of history" sharply challenged the conventional Soviet view of its own past.[8] Brezhnev's love of awards and decorations and the corruption of his family became widely known, and it became possible again to refer to Khrushchev as a courageous reformer. But it was the Stalin question that was the touchstone for historical glasnost. After Gorbachev called for filling in the "blank spots" of Soviet history, revelations about the dictator's crimes virtually poured out of the Soviet media, far more extensively than had been possible in the Khrushchev era: mass graves were uncovered; a former executioner described, on camera, precisely how he shot people; estimates of the number of people "repressed" during the Stalin era jumped into the many millions. A stunning Georgian film, *Repentance,* portrayed a Stalin-like figure with physical characteristics reminiscent of Hitler and Mussolini, thus suggesting the moral equivalence of fascism and communism. Such a view had long been common in the West, but to official Soviet ideology it was heresy of the highest degree. And now it was openly stated. So widely and quickly had Soviet historical understanding been transformed that authorities canceled the 1988 school examinations in history for lack of adequate textbooks on which exams could be based.

Historical figures long vilified were now rehabilitated. Among them was Nikolai Bukharin, spokesman for the New Economic Policy of the 1920s, who had been executed in 1938. For a time Bukharin and the NEP became the focus of much attention as an alternative and humane form of socialism endorsed by Lenin himself that could provide a precedent and pedigree for the reforms of the 1980s. Other rehabilitations followed of both prominent communists and many millions of more ordinary people. Even Leon Trotsky, Stalin's bitterest enemy and long written out of Soviet history, could now be treated as a historical figure, though he was not officially rehabilitated.

The widening boundaries of acceptable discourse touched also on the country's official ideology. The notion of a "single truth" gave way to ideas of a "socialist pluralism" that permitted open political debate while maintaining a socialist framework. "We must treat diversity normally, as the natural state of the world; not with clenched teeth as in the past," argued an article in *Izvestia.*[9] Applied to politics, glasnost implied choice and paved the way to contested elections, competing parties, and the end of Communist Party dominance.

Religion was among the later areas of Soviet life to experience glasnost. As late as November 1986 Gorbachev himself was still calling for "an uncompromising struggle" against religion. But by 1988, with the widely anticipated thousand-year anniversary celebration of the Russian Orthodox Church in sight, the harsh and repressive policies of long Soviet practice began to change. Gorbachev had apparently decided that the Church could be an ally in the struggle against corruption and moral decay in Soviet society, while lending his regime a measure of legitimacy among believers and nationalists. Furthermore, the logic of glasnost could hardly exclude religion. And so, over the next few years, the state returned to the faithful thousands of churches and mosques and gave permission for restorations and new buildings. Anti-religious propaganda largely ceased; the importation of Bibles from the West and the Koran from Saudi Arabia began; and their printing in the USSR was stepped up. During the millennial celebrations, the Bolshoi Theater became the site for a widely televised concert of church music, with Raisa Gorbachev on the platform.

These astonishing changes permitted a genuine religious awakening in the Soviet Union, as attendance at places of worship increased sharply and parish life resumed in many communities. Churches began to organize long-forbidden charitable and educational activities. Clergymen appeared on television, and several were elected to the new Soviet parliament in 1989. The patriarch himself participated in the inauguration of Boris Yeltsin as president of Russia in 1991, thus signaling a wholly new relationship of church and state. Nor was such an awakening restricted to the Russian Orthodox Church. National churches in Lithuania, Armenia, Georgia, and Ukraine found new opportunities for expression and became part of the national awakenings in those republics. So, too, did Islam in Central Asian republics.

During 1987–89, then, glasnost created a contentious, exciting, and sometimes exhausting public life in the major urban centers of the USSR. It transformed deadly dull and wholly predictable newspapers and journals into organs of consuming public interest, sending their subscriptions skyrocketing. It released plays, poems, films, and novels that had been long buried "in the drawer" to a public that virtually devoured them. It permitted the work of disgraced or exiled authors such as Boris Pasternak and Aleksandr Solzhenitsyn to appear in print. It unleashed a torrent of public argument that turned city streets into debating societies. Despite a worsening economic situation, many people echoed the sentiments of the Soviet academic and peace activist who declared, "For me now my country is the most interesting place in the world."[10]

But did glasnost bind a grateful Soviet society to Gorbachev's reformist regime as he had intended? Clearly it fostered a wave of hope, particularly among the intelligentsia and professional groups, that life could now be different and that their country might finally become "normal," which was to say, western. And for several years an energetic Gorbachev, prodding the party toward change and lecturing the country on the virtues of perestroika, enjoyed a wide popularity, particularly in contrast to his decrepit and unimaginative predecessors. It was not long, however, before glasnost slipped beyond the intentions of its originator. Attacks on Stalin turned into criticism of Marx, Lenin, and the revolution itself, discrediting the entire Soviet experience. "Social-

Voices

Experiencing Glasnost

Understanding the sheer novelty of glasnost is no easy task for a western audience accustomed to a wide variety of freely expressed opinion. Here are several Soviet reflections on the startling meaning of glasnost. The first is from poet Alexander Kushner.

Suddenly a clear day, a sudden unexpected ray
Like a tender word in a dark quarrel.
Nowhere, nowhere such a sun,
So longed for amidst the gloom and sleep!
. . . Suddenly, a bright hour in history, so sparing
Of gentle glance and long indulgences.
Suddenly—a loud laugh in an empty square
And a shaft of light, playing tag.

Like an excited boy reads a note from his girl,
That's how we read the papers today
As if time itself
Were airing out cupboards and rooms.
Moscow news [a leading liberal newspaper] . . .
    If you only knew
How tensely Leningrad waits for you.
Oh the rustle of pages, you eclipse the rustle of leaves.
Make noise for God's sake!

From Natalya B. Ivanova, "Poetry in the Age of Perestroika and Glasnost," in *Chronicle of a Revolution,* Abraham Brumberg (New York: Pantheon Books, 1990), pp. 225–26.

(continued)

Experiencing Glasnost *(continued)*

Not everyone saw the new era in such glowing terms. A longtime communist wrote bitterly to the newspaper Pravda:

I cannot be silent! Look at what is going on around us. In Leningrad—the cradle of the revolution—well-fed insolent thugs parade on the streets with swastika armbands.... At an Estonian song contest a half-naked singer cavorts about with a cross round his neck, and this on television! In Armenia there are strikes—people skipping work without any reason. Where is the law? Why is it silent?

From *Pravda,* August 26, 1988, p. 1.
Cited in Geoffrey Hosking, *The Awakening of the Soviet Union*
(Cambridge: Harvard University Press, 1990), p. 1

A more personal and spiritual response to glasnost is revealed as Sergei Zubatov of Novosibirsk describes his encounter with the Bible, long difficult to obtain in the Soviet Union but more available as glasnost took hold.

Now that I have turned the last page of the great book, I cannot get over the feeling of gratitude and joyful shock. Bitter perplexing questions still haunt me: why only now, why so late? Half of my life is already over.... At the age of thirty, I have read the gospels for the first time.

What a treasure they have been hiding from me! Who decided, and on what basis, that this was bad for me—and why?! No, I did not run off to church.... I simply understood that I never was and never will be an atheist.

From *Ogonyok,* October 1989.
Reprinted in Christopher Cerf and Marina Albee, eds., *Small Fires*
(New York: Summit Books, 1990), p. 82

(continued)

Experiencing Glasnost

Finally, the shock of "therapy by truth" comes through in this excerpt from an essay by writer Alexander Tsipko.

No people in the history of mankind was ever enslaved by myths as our people was in the 20th century. We had thought that we had tied our lives to a great truth, only to realize that we entrusted ourselves to an intellectual fantasy which could never be realized. We thought we were pioneers leading the rest of mankind to . . . freedom and spiritual blessing, but realized that our way is the road to nowhere. We thought that building communism in the USSR was the greatest deed of our people, but we were purposefully engaging in self-destruction. We thought that capitalism was a sick old man sentenced to death, but it turned out that capitalism was healthy, powerful. . . . We thought that we were surrounded by people with the same ideals, grateful to us for saving them from capitalist slavery . . . but it turned out that our friends and neighbors were only waiting for a chance to return to their old lives. We thought that our national industry, organized like one big factory . . . was the ultimate achievement of human wisdom, but it all turned out to be an economic absurdity which enslaved the economic and spiritual energies of . . . Russia.

From *Novy Mir* 4 (1990), pp. 173–204.
Cited in Alexander Dalin and Gail W. Lapidus, eds.,
The Soviet System: From Crisis to Collapse
(Boulder: Westview Press, 1995), pp. 283–84.

---

ist pluralism" became simply "pluralism," inviting discussion of noncommunist political alternatives. Non-Russian nationalists could now articulate their grievances openly and even begin to dream of independence. Glasnost, then, gave expression to both anticommunist and anti-Soviet views, which subsequently gained momentum as organized social movements. But those who were appalled or threatened by the new revelations could argue their case in public as well, and so a distinctly conservative movement likewise emerged.

For many people, the impact of glasnost was to erode fatally the sustaining myths of the Soviet regime and to destroy what legitimacy remained to it. It had become painfully obvious that the country was nowhere near surpassing the capitalist world and was in fact falling further behind. And while glasnost exposed the country's many problems in exhausting debate, it had done little to resolve them. It was equally apparent that the historical foundations of Soviet socialism were built on violence and criminality of monstrous proportions. Even the heroic achievements of World War II were tarnished as Stalin's responsibility for the country's early defeats and massive casualties became apparent. Ideological alternatives to Marxism-Leninism were out in the open, as the party's claim to a monopoly on truth lay in tatters. Now that it was possible to say aloud what many had long observed or believed, the ideological glue of the Soviet Union rapidly dissolved.

"What Have We Done?" Democratization and Political Reform

If glasnost was one sign of the deepening of Gorbachev's reform program, another was political reform, or democratization, as Gorbachev dubbed it. By 1988–89, Gorbachev had moved well beyond his early emphasis on revitalizing the existing system of party committees and soviets to a recognition that "we would have to make changes outside the traditional confines of the system, but not outside the confines of socialism."[11] These changes ultimately included contested elections, competing political parties, a more independent legislature, and a much reduced role for the Communist Party. But while moving toward a real transformation of Soviet political life, Gorbachev often invoked the early years of the revolution, when popular participation in the party, soviets, and factory committees had been genuine, before the democratic thrust of 1917 had been perverted by Stalinist dictatorship and bureaucracy. In his own mind, he was acting in the spirit of Lenin.

Democratization served several purposes within the overall reform program. It was necessary to nudge a recalcitrant and entrenched party toward reformist measures by making them accountable to a broader and politically engaged public. The planning for the January 1987 Central Committee meeting, at which Gorbachev hoped to introduce far-reaching measures of political and economic reform, illustrated the problem. So great was the opposition to some of these measures that the gathering was postponed three times. When it finally did convene, Gorbachev hammered home his critique of senior party officials, "who abused their authority, suppressed criticism, sought [personal] gain, and . . . who viewed initiative and activism of people as something little short of a natural calamity." Democratization was essential to replace or reeducate such people. Without it, Gorbachev said flatly, "perestroika will fail."[12]

Democratization was also necessary for mobilizing society for the tasks of perestroika. The heavy hand of an unaccountable party-state bureaucracy—an "ossified system of government," in Gorbachev's words—had everywhere stifled popular initiative. Particularly in the soviets, from the local to the national level, where hundreds of thousands of citizens served, representatives were nominated by party authorities, were elected on single-candidate ballots, and rubber-stamped party decisions with almost no discussion or debate. Here was the deeper root of Soviet stagnation, and the solution was "profound democratization"—in the workplace, in the soviets, and in the party itself. This, according to Gorbachev in January 1987, was the party's "most urgent task."

Little concrete action occurred before the special Party Conference called for June 1988. But in the several years preceding the conference important developments took place in the realm of ideas that prepared the way for the policy changes that followed. Glasnost permitted new political ideas, previously dismissed as "bourgeois," to circulate. One was "socialist pluralism," an idea that legitimized diversity of opinion as opposed to the concept of a single "party line." Another was the notion of a "law-governed state," which put the spotlight on the arbitrary and unrestrained power of various individuals and institutions within the Soviet political system. And a third was "checks and balances," which represented yet another means of limiting the power of the Soviet executive. Gorbachev personally endorsed these ideas, all of which drew heavily on western political thinking, and attempted quite deliberately to stretch the concept of socialism to incorporate them. It was a way of reassuring nervous party leaders that they could embrace new ideas while remaining faithful to the core of Soviet socialism.

Providing that reassurance was no easy task. Gorbachev personally met with almost all of the three hundred members of the Central Committee, charming them at his dacha while trying to persuade them to adopt measures that stood to limit their own power. He encouraged discussion of electoral reform in the media and urged a few local soviets to experiment with multicandidate elections.

A final element of preparation for political reform lay in formulating concrete proposals for the Party Conference to consider. That task fell to a small cadre of Gorbachev aides: Alexander Yakovlev, Anatoly Lukyanov, Georgi Shakhnazarov, Anatoly Chernayev, and a few others. Meeting in a dacha outside Moscow in March 1988, they argued for days on end, debating various forms of government and in the process inventing a unique form of Soviet democracy. It was this small group of Gorbachev and his inner circle, a minority even within the leadership, that initiated the democratization process, well before widespread popular pressure had surfaced.

That process finally took shape in late June 1988 at the Nineteenth Party Conference, a special all-Union gathering of party representatives, called specifically to consider the question of political reform. The meeting itself modeled the new democratic spirit. Extended debate and disagreement among delegates, much of it televised, replaced the previous unanimity of closed party meetings. Members of the Politburo were criticized by name. Devastating disclosures about the country's social and economic conditions punctuated the debates. Boris Yeltsin, dismissed from the Politburo the year before for his impatient radicalism, blasted party privileges and the paralysis of reform, while the more conservative Yegor Ligachev responded in an equally heated defense. It was high political drama of a kind not witnessed before in the Soviet Union. Throughout, Gorbachev presided, improvised, intervened, and generally dominated the proceedings.

The substantive heart of the conference lay in its adoption, virtually intact, of Gorbachev's proposals for major political change. When formally adopted by the Supreme Soviet in December 1988, they became the law of the land and gave the country a markedly different political system. The most radically democratizing feature of the new system involved electoral reform. The right to nominate candidates for public office was extended to meetings of five hundred or more voters, with no limit to the number of candidates put forward. Thus, the country abandoned decades of single-candidate balloting in favor of competitive elections. Furthermore, contrary to Soviet practice, all voters would now mark their ballots secretly in a voting booth. The major institutional innovation was the creation of a new parliament to replace the old Supreme Soviet, which met for only a few days a year to give formal legal approval to party proposals. The new body was a complicated, two-tier affair consisting of a large, popularly elected Congress of People's Deputies with 2,250 members, which in turn selected from its members a smaller Supreme Soviet of 542 deputies. That body, unlike the old Supreme Soviet, would stay in session most of the year as the country's major legislative organ. It would be a real, working parliament whose elected chairman (Gorbachev) was the effective head of state. In Gorbachev's defense of the system, it was a return to the early Bolshevik slogan, "All power to the soviets."

All this represented a quite dramatic departure from previous Soviet practice and was thus threatening to those who enjoyed power under the old system. A variety of provisions sought to reassure them and gain their support for the new arrangements. While groups of voters could nominate candidates, local election commissions, often dominated by party officials, had the authority to approve those candidates before they could appear on the ballot. Furthermore, of the 2,250 deputies in the Congress, some 750, or fully one-third, would be chosen by a variety of "public organizations," including the Communist Party and the trade unions, with one hundred selections each. This allowed top party leaders to secure uncontested seats in the Congress. The other 1,500 would be elected in national or republican territorial constituencies. In addition, the Supreme Soviet would be chosen indirectly by the Congress rather than by direct popular election. And while there would be competitive elections, there would be no competing parties, as the Communist Party was still the only legal party in the country. Political reform was therefore a compromise between the impulse to democratize and the desire to maintain the leading role of the party and attract the support of its leading members for perestroika.

Perhaps the most important moment of the Nineteenth Party Conference came at the very end, when Gorbachev asked the weary delegates to endorse a specific date for the first election to the new Congress of People's Deputies: spring of 1989. They did so unanimously and thus turned pious declarations of principle into imminent reality. Leaving the hall, some of them could be heard murmuring, "What have we done?"[13]

The answer to that question emerged as the first real election campaign since 1918 unfolded. Despite a complicated nomination process that often allowed local party officials to shape the outcome, determined groups of citizens forced more independent and democratically minded candidates on the ballot in many places. Particularly in major cities, candidates faced sharp grilling from voters' groups about their views and their records. It was wholly unprecedented in Soviet history. In the end, 74 percent of the territorial constituencies featured two or more candidates, though by no means all of these were ardent democrats.

The results of the elections, in which 90 percent of eligible voters participated, were impressive in many ways. The vast majority of newly elected deputies (some 87 percent) were party members, though subsequent debate gave lie to any notion of party unanimity. There were fewer workers, collective farmers, and women than in earlier Supreme Soviets and far more white-collar professionals, academics, and cultural figures. Committed democrats and reformers were a small but vocal and active minority. Among their number were such well-known figures as Boris Yeltsin and Andrei Sakharov. The most dramatic outcome of the election concerned those who lost. The mayors of Moscow and Kiev, a whole slate of Leningrad party leaders, thirty-eight regional and district party secretaries, the prime minister of Latvia—all of them major party leaders—were decisively rejected at the polls. Some lost despite running unopposed, as more than half of the voters scratched their names from the ballot! Particularly for the upper echelon of party leaders, it was a "symbolic humiliation that cut deep."[14] The party, declared Soviet prime minister Nikolai Ryzhkov, had lost the election.[15]

The next act in the drama of Soviet political transformation came as the Congress of People's Deputies and then the Supreme Soviet actually met and deliberated. The entire first session of the Congress, two weeks in late May and early June of 1989, was televised live to an audience of a hundred million or more. By all accounts the country was transfixed as long-standing taboos were shattered and real political debate, long hidden within closed party meetings, now sprang to life before the cameras. In an early speech, Sakharov called for a contested election for chairman of the congress, and he walked out in protest when Gorbachev was the only candidate. Another deputy, champion weightlifter Yuri Vlasov, decried the continuing status and power of the KGB despite its murderous past. It was an unprecedented attack on a central pillar of the Soviet state. Another called for Lenin to be removed from his mausoleum and reburied as an ordinary mortal. Nor were conservative forces silenced. Speaker after speaker lambasted

Sakharov, now the focal point of reformist sentiment, for insulting Soviet military forces as he attacked the war in Afghanistan. The Congress thus became a national forum for genuine political debate, with most of the country watching. "On the day the Congress opened," wrote Boris Yeltsin, "they were one sort of people; on the day that it closed they were different people."[16]

But the Congress also created a different government. The Congress and Supreme Soviet subsequently rejected a number of government ministerial appointees and sharply questioned others; it launched its own investigative commissions on a number of sensitive issues; and it established an elaborate structure of committees for undertaking its legislative business. Groups of like-minded deputies soon established caucuses or blocs within the parliament. The Inter-Regional Group represented the most radical reformist deputies, while the Soyuz (Unity) bloc spoke for the conservative/patriotic faction. Beset by hordes of journalists, a number of deputies emerged as new political figures and TV celebrities. Clearly a new arena of political power was emerging within the Soviet state. As chairman of the new body, Gorbachev now had a base of power outside the party structure.

What then was happening to the party in the midst of this democratizing process? As if to symbolize the party's diminished status, when the Congress convened, the Politburo did not sit on the stage as it had before but in a special section reserved for dignitaries off to the side of the hall. Furthermore, Gorbachev, as head of the party, told communist deputies that they were not bound by party discipline but were free to speak and vote as individuals representing their constituencies. And some of these deputies—all of them communists—lined up with sharply opposing factions or blocs. Party unity, perhaps the central communist virtue for decades, was obviously and publicly in shambles.

In addition to these external shocks, the party also had to confront the internal reforms Gorbachev pushed as an integral part of perestroika. If the party was to retain its "leading role" in the new circumstances, it must, Gorbachev argued, "reconstruct itself faster than society."[17] But progress was slow. In 1989, when 74 percent of Congress deputies were elected competitively, only 8.6 percent of local party secretaries had been chosen in that way.

Perhaps even more important, there was widespread agreement that the party should withdraw from detailed supervision of the economy and other public bodies and focus its attention on broad policy positions and a loose coordinating function. In the fall of 1988 Gorbachev acted on this understanding and reduced the Central Committee Secretariat from twenty to nine departments, cutting about 30 percent of its staff in the process. And local party committees were told to stop meddling in the economic affairs of their regions. Here was an effort to end the cozy relationship of party authorities and economic ministries, to foster greater self-regulation in the economy, and to transfer responsibility for economic oversight from the party to the new parliament. Since so much of the party's function had involved economic management, this represented a sharp reduction in its role in Soviet life, at least at the central level.

There was more to come. In early 1990 the party finally lost its constitutionally guaranteed role as the "leading and guiding" element in Soviet political life when Article Six of the Constitution was formally rescinded. Radical deputies, led by Sakharov, had earlier called for the abolition of Article Six, but Gorbachev resisted. Then, in December 1989, Sakharov's death resulted in an outpouring of support for democratic reform that persuaded Gorbachev and party authorities to accept the inevitable, albeit reluctantly. Thus, the Soviet Union, for seven decades a single-party state, now officially opened the door to the creation of other political parties.

Accompanying the end of Article Six was the creation of an executive presidency with very substantial powers. The diminution of party authority, a growing economic crisis, the strength of nationalist forces, and the inability of a divided parliament to provide effective leadership all contributed to support for this new office. Gorbachev was elected to it, but by the parliament, not by popular vote. Democrats sharply criticized this procedure, and it no doubt cost Gorbachev a measure of public legitimacy. But it also meant that Gorbachev rested even more of his authority on this new state office rather than on his party position. Now the presidency, rather than the Politburo, was the focal point of Soviet government. Nonetheless, he rejected the advice of many democratic reformers to give up his party leadership altogether, fearing that conservative forces would take over the party and use it against perestroika. Thus, Gorbachev remained identified with the Communist Party as its standing in the country plummeted.

All this produced confusion and eroded confidence within the party itself. Gorbachev bravely promised that the party could retain a respected and leading role in the country, but now that role would have to be earned within a competitive electoral environment. How could the CPSU, with a seventy-year monopoly on political power, make the transition from a vanguard to a parliamentary party within a few years? The party had resources of money, publishing houses, newspapers, and an immense network of connections, but the nomenklatura system of appointments had been undermined by the new prerogatives of the parliament. And the party's public standing, now tracked regularly by polls, fell precipitously. By mid-1990, only 14 percent "completely trusted" the party, while 38 percent had "absolutely no confidence" in it.[18] Little wonder then that the party's membership began to fall. Almost a quarter of the party's members resigned in the last eighteen months of the country's existence.

Between 1987 and 1990, Gorbachev had engineered something close to a political miracle. Competitive elections, a real working parliament, the end of the party's political monopoly, and the creation of a powerful executive presidency—all had occurred within a few years, with the party's reluctant consent, and without a violent backlash. How had it happened? One answer, ironically enough, lies in the tradition of party discipline and in the deference and respect accorded the general secretary. Not a few anxious party leaders went along with Gorbachev's reforms, despite their reservations, from force of this communist habit. Then, too, there was the "conceptual ambiguity" of Gorbachev's reforms; it was not clear precisely what democratization really meant, nor how seriously it would be taken. Particularly at the beginning, almost everyone recognized the need for some change, and Gorbachev consistently articulated his reforms within a socialist framework, even if that socialism had been much watered down. This was an important factor in a political system where ideological correctness counted for much. Furthermore, Gorbachev proved extraordinarily skillful in making sufficient compromises to keep the old guard on board, as he demonstrated in crafting the package of electoral reforms for the Nineteenth Party Conference. And finally, Gorbachev's genuine popularity in the country, at least up to mid-1989, and the considerable growth of a democratic movement urging even more radical policies, provided leverage for democratization.

But at the same time those victories for political reform bypassed, diminished, divided, and demoralized the Communist Party. Here, clearly, is one of the central elements in the collapse of the Soviet Union. Gorbachev felt compelled to attack and weaken the party in order to implement his reform program, but in doing so he fatally undermined the single institution that had bound the country together.

Toward the Market? Perestroika and the Soviet Economy

Glasnost and democratization were intended in large measure to support the centerpiece of Gorbachev's reform program, perestroika, or economic restructuring. Following the disappointments of early efforts to promote more rapid growth, Gorbachev moved to deepen the specifically economic features of his program, as well as those in the cultural and political domains. By 1987, the many deficiencies and outrages of the administrative-command economy had been thoroughly detailed by reform-minded economists, journalists, and lawyers, and numerous suggestions for new approaches circulated. Gorbachev's own thinking, or what he felt able to say in public, evolved considerably during his years in office. At the beginning it was still politically taboo to even use the word "market" in a favorable way. Within a few years, however, Gorbachev was speaking about a "socialist market," a "regulated market," a "mixed economy," and by 1990, was contemplating a full transition to a market economy.

Putting any such ideas into practice, however, encountered sharp opposition at every turn.[19] The network of economic ministries that supervised productive enterprises objected to the diminution of their authority that any reform would entail. Their ability to circumvent the implementation, if not the adoption, of various policy initiatives had largely swallowed up the Kosygin reforms of the late 1960s, and they limited the effectiveness of Gorbachev's efforts as well. Likewise, the party apparat had reasons to resist serious economic reform. Some objected in principle to measures that seemed to restore a despised capitalism. Others found the pace of market reforms too rapid and pleaded for more time. And regional and local party officials, who had long played an important role in troubleshooting amid the irrationalities of the system, were reluctant to surrender a function that brought them local power and prestige. The vast majority of them paid only lip service to perestroika and continued to intervene actively in local economic matters. Popular opposition, particularly among working-class people, was also a factor. Unlike democratization and glasnost, which extended the theoretical rights of Soviet citizens, market reforms seemed to threaten long-established rights to job security, low prices, and a livable wage. Centuries of experience in peasant communes and decades under communism had generated deeply held egalitarian and collectivist values and engendered widespread suspicion and hostility toward individual wealth. To many people the very notion of private property suggested greed and selfishness.

Such opposition meant inevitable compromise as reform policies were formulated and further dilution as they were implemented throughout the labyrinth of the party-state bureaucracy. In part, as a consequence of such opposition, perestroika was the least successful of Gorbachev's major reforms. Its dismal failure transformed the stagnant economy of 1985 into an economy in crisis and sharp decline by 1990, exacerbating all of the country's other problems.

The most broadly conceived element of perestroika, articulated in the Law on State Enterprises in mid-1987, sought to free the actual productive units—the enterprises—of the Soviet economy from the heavy hand of central government ministries, which had traditionally planned virtually every detail of their activities, including products, wages, prices, customers, and suppliers. Freed from this minute regulation, so the argument went, enterprises would behave more like private firms, seeking profits, becoming self-financing, and responding creatively to consumer demand, even while operating within a state-owned and socialist system. Accordingly, enterprises were granted the authority to construct their own plans, to determine within limits what they would produce, to set the wages for their employees and the prices for at least a portion of their output, and to contract directly with suppliers and customers for a certain fraction of their production. And as part of the democratization process, workers were to elect the managers of their enterprises. All this was, at least on paper, a significant departure from Soviet practice.

The law was clearly a compromise, as the central planning function was reduced but by no means eliminated. Instead of the Plan's mandatory output targets, central ministries would now issue nonbinding guidelines, but they largely retained control of supplies and investment. Their most powerful lever was the ability to issue mandatory "state orders" for essential products. Initially state orders would comprise 70–85 percent of enterprise output, and for the balance enterprises could produce what they wanted, sell it on the open market, and use the income as they pleased. Here was the incentive for newly aggressive managers. And within a few years, the law promised, the percentage of state orders would diminish significantly, leaving enterprises free to determine independently the bulk of their productive capacity.

It did not, however, work as planned. As the law went into effect in 1988, it was opposed or watered down in practice, and it gave rise to unexpected behavior that merely worsened the economic situation. Central authorities, always reluctant to grant wide autonomy to enterprises, used state orders and their control of supplies to maintain their dominant position. In mid-1989 the director of the huge Uralmash industrial complex complained that, "one way or another, they decide ninety-five percent of our output, and we decide only five percent."[20] And many enterprise managers, wholly inexperienced as entrepreneurs, welcomed and even sought out state orders that relieved them of responsibility for finding suppliers and customers. In those enterprises that could choose their own product mix more freely, managers naturally opted to produce high-priced, profitable goods, thus contributing to shortages of cheaper but less profitable goods such as children's clothing, matches, soap, and toothpaste. And elected managers, eager to win favor with their workers, granted substantial wage increases that added to growing inflationary pressures.

But Gorbachev's reforms did weaken the power of central ministries. Their ability to provide detailed regulation or support of enterprises diminished as the staff of these ministries dropped by 46 percent (from 1.6 million to 871,000) between 1986 and 1989.[21] And the party's control of the ministries had been curtailed as well when Gorbachev in August of 1988 eliminated most of the Central Committee departments charged with economic oversight. Thus, Soviet enterprises, and their local party officials, were increasingly on their own. But there was no functioning market system to replace the discredited and partially dismantled planning system. Neither the institutions of the market—credit, a banking system, contract law, wholesalers, free prices—nor the values of the market—competition, risk taking, personal responsibility—had substantially developed in the few years of the Gorbachev era. Thus, perestroika created a kind of limbo economy, in which neither the Plan nor the market worked effectively.

Perestroika sought not only to decentralize decision making in the dominant state sector of the economy but also to open up some space for small-scale private enterprise. Since this was ideologically threatening to communists and conjured up visions of creeping capitalism,

Gorbachev frequently invoked the experience of the New Economic Policy of the 1920s, when Lenin himself had opted for a measure of private enterprise within a primarily socialist economy. In the delicate political environment of the Gorbachev era, language was important, so when the legislation authorizing such activity was enacted in May 1988, it was called the Law on Cooperatives.[22] That law recognized small-scale businesses of full-time worker-owners as a basic unit of the economy, legally equal to state enterprises, able to hire workers on contract, and permitted to sell their goods or services for whatever price they could get. In a sharp reversal of Soviet tradition, the law stated that all activities not specifically prohibited were permitted. The hope was that cooperatives would help to saturate the immense consumer market and in the process provide competition and stimulus to the state sector. It was a major breakthrough and the single most radical element of economic restructuring.

The cooperative movement grew dramatically—from 8,000 businesses employing 88,000 people in late 1987 to 245,300 businesses with 6 million employees in early 1991. Restaurants and catering, apartment repair, tailoring, construction, software design—these and many other activities found a place in the burgeoning cooperative movement. Most co-ops were small, with an average of twenty-five employees, but wages were far higher than in the state sector, as were the prices they charged. But co-ops were closely linked to the state sector, both because they often fulfilled state orders and because they were dependent on state authorities for facilities, supplies, and credit.

While the co-op movement was the product of official initiative, its very visibility placed it at the center of both official and popular opposition to perestroika (see Voices, "Defending Cooperatives"). For some it was an ideological offense against socialism. For others it threatened to drain labor and resources from the state sector. Local officials found the independence of co-ops annoying. And in the minds of many ordinary people, the high prices were an outrage and the sudden wealth of co-op members suggested criminal activity. As a result, various authorities in the far-flung Soviet bureaucracy attempted to restrict these new businesses. Laws and regulations narrowed the scope of permitted activity, outlawing, for example, the manufacturing of wine and vodka, publishing ventures, and certain kinds of medical services. The disdain for private business held by many local officials led to frequent bureaucratic roadblocks to registering co-ops and to the arbitrary closing

Voices

Defending Cooperatives

In this letter to the editor of Ogonyok, *the chairman of a Moscow cooperative defends these new businesses and speculates about the sources of so much popular hostility against them.*

Are you seriously convinced that it is the *cooperatives* that are to blame for the empty shelves in the stores? The same cooperatives whose share of the goods produced in the country totals 1 percent? And are you convinced that it is *we* who have corrupted young people whose involvement in crime . . . is growing? Perhaps the cooperatives are the most convenient target today for people who are looking for an answer to the age-old Russian question: who is to blame? At one time they blamed the aristocrats, then the intelligentsia, the peasants, the "cosmopolitans," the dissidents, the Jews and foreigners. . . . Interesting—if cooperatives did not exist, whom would you blame? . . . [P]eople were told for decades that being rich was immoral, that commerce and stealing were the same thing, that wearing out the seat of your pants and receiving your little kopeks was a worthy activity, but earning a good living was shameful. People were psychologically unprepared for the cooperative phenomenon; what kind of attitude could you expect?

From Christopher Cerf and Marina Albee, eds., *Small Fires*
(New York: Summit Books, 1990), p. 52.

of many others. And high tax rates, sometimes exceeding 75 percent of profits, further hampered the new businesses. Thus, co-ops became an entering and beleaguered wedge of private enterprise in a socialist Soviet Union, but in the Gorbachev era they made only a modest dent in the state-run economy.

Even more restricted than the growth of cooperatives was the development of private farming. Despite the sorry state of Soviet agriculture, with its endemic shortages and enormous waste, Soviet economic reform did not follow the Chinese model, in which rapid decollectivization of agriculture was a priority that brought considerable prosperity to the countryside. Gorbachev pushed the idea of long-term lease holding, in which a family or a group of farmers would receive land, livestock, and buildings in a contractual arrangement with a collective or state farm, with a right to market their produce and keep their earnings above an agreed-upon rent. Despite legal approval for various forms of agricultural leasing, only a very modest number of such farms actually appeared during the Gorbachev era. By April 1992, some one hundred thousand private farms had been registered in Russia, but they accounted for less than 2 percent of agricultural land. Furthermore, a distinct minority of these farmers came from the collective and state farms; most, in fact, were urban residents who took up private farming to supplement their incomes.[23]

How can we explain this apparent unresponsiveness to private farming? In the first place, there was massive political resistance from a small army of rural party officials, collective and state-farm chairmen, and their administrative and technical staffs, who had a vested interest in the existing system. The rapid growth of private farming might cost them their jobs. At the top of the Soviet hierarchy there was at best ambivalence about private farming. Gorbachev himself, while supporting the market and leasing, proclaimed his strong opposition to full private ownership of land with the right to sell. And Yegor Ligachev, the party official in charge of agriculture, argued that small-scale farming ran counter to world trends and that the problem was insufficient resources devoted to collectivized agriculture. Many feared that only corrupt officials, the "mafia," and foreigners would be financially able to take advantage of private agricultural opportunities, thus dooming the majority of rural residents to ruin.

Finally, and perhaps most important, few Soviet collective or state-farm workers themselves—only 10 percent according to polls—were inclined to seriously consider a plunge into private farming.[24] Soviet agriculture had, after all, been collectivized for sixty years. Its practitioners had become specialized agricultural workers with no direct experience or memory of what private farming meant. Furthermore, most of the energetic younger people had long ago fled to the cities, leaving an older, conservative, and primarily female labor force behind in the villages. And since the 1960s most collective farmers had become salaried employees whose wages and social benefits had substantially improved. They were reluctant to forgo this newly won security for the vagaries of commercial farming.

Even for those who might be interested, the practical obstacles were daunting. Would a collective farm grant a private farmer some of its best land or the use of its best machinery? How could credit be arranged? How might products be transported to market? Were the legal foundations of private farming really solid? Could the government be trusted to keep its word? And what of the neighbors, most of whom treated private farmers, especially successful ones, with suspicious hostility and sometimes even violence? With reform facing such an array of problems, the Gorbachev era ended with Soviet agriculture largely unreformed. No spurt of rural prosperity emerged, as it had in China, to jump-start a stagnant economy.

A final arena of perestroika involved the country's international economic relationships. An effort to increase and decentralize foreign trade represented one element. Formerly a single ministry controlled all foreign trade, but now a variety of branch ministries, individual enterprises, and regional governments were authorized to trade directly with foreign companies. But the bureaucratic infighting that accompanied this decentralization limited its effectiveness, as foreigners found it difficult to identify officials who could make binding decisions. Soviet foreign trade thus remained limited to about 6 percent of national income, compared with 20 percent or more in most western countries.

More symbolically significant was the authorization for foreign firms to participate with Soviet enterprises in "joint ventures." Intended to attract foreign capital and technology into the stagnant Soviet economy, joint ventures raised ideological hackles and prompted among some officials fears of foreign capitalist penetration. They need not have worried. The Soviet market did not prove widely attractive to foreign investors, and by January 1990 only 1,274 joint ventures had been registered and only 307 were actually operating. Clearly the Soviet economy would not be rescued through its involvement in the world market.

By 1990, the Soviet economy was in a clear crisis (described more fully in Chapter 4), with massive shortages, rising prices, and the growing threat of unemployment. The central planning mechanism had been weakened before a functioning market had emerged to replace it. And no great stimulus had emerged from small businesses, private farming, or foreign trade and investment. Perestroika, clearly, had failed.

Questions and Controversies: *What Went Wrong with Reform?*

To some observers, judging the Soviet system unreformable and the patient too far gone to respond to any treatment at all, the entire Gorbachev program was doomed from the start. Other critics and scholars, instead of focusing on Gorbachev's reform program as a whole, have pointed to various policy errors or strategic mistakes within it. The implication of such second-guessing has been to affirm the possibility of reform in general, while blaming its failure, and the country's subsequent collapse, on specific shortcomings in the process. On the economic front, critics have scored Gorbachev for neglecting agricultural reform and for failing to dismantle the system of collective farms. Others noted that his policy of raising wages and increasing social benefits, while ignoring the importance of balanced budgets, allowed inflation to get out of control and thus undermined the entire effort. And rather than focusing solely on economic change, as the Chinese reformers did, Gorbachev pushed a destabilizing democratization and glasnost at the same time. Might a more sequenced approach, delaying political change until a market economy took hold, have prevented the Soviet Union's disintegration? But without the pressure of glasnost and democratization, could substantial economic reforms have been implemented at all?

Gorbachev's alleged political errors have been subject to even more damning criticism. He ousted Boris Yeltsin from the leadership team in 1987, instead of using his radicalism to bring pressure on the conservative party establishment. He declined to stand for election as president and was instead selected by the Soviet parliament, thus depriving himself of popular legitimacy. Nor would he agree to split the Communist Party and align himself with its progressive faction. Instead he retained his role as general secretary and tried to keep even the most conservative members within the party, while its standing in the country sharply declined. In late 1990 and early 1991, he treated democrats with scorn and hostility, thus alienating his most natural base of support, as he turned increasingly to the conservatives. And he was distressingly slow to grant the republics genuine autonomy.

Yet could he have moved faster, further, and more decisively without being ousted from power as Khrushchev had been? Here is the heart of Gorbachev's defense of his policies: "In some abstract sense, it is probably right that I moved too slowly, but I did not have the luxury of living in the abstract. I lived in the world of harsh political reality. . . . I simply did not have a free hand and should not be judged as if I had."[25] In this defense Gorbachev points to a fundamental contradiction in the entire reform process: given the history of the USSR, the Communist Party was the only organization through which reform could have been introduced; but those reforms asked the party to surrender its privileged status and to take on wholly new tasks. Perhaps it was asking too much.

"A Consensus of All Mankind": New Thinking in Soviet Foreign Policy

While domestic issues occupied the central place in Soviet reform efforts, they were closely linked in Gorbachev's thinking to changes in Soviet foreign policy. The hostile and confrontational relationship with the United States that prevailed when Gorbachev assumed power in 1985, together with the country's more general international isolation, provided a clearly inhospitable environment for perestroika. It drained resources and attention, badly needed in the civilian economy, into an already bloated defense establishment; it complicated Soviet access to the world economy and to western technology; it gave added political clout to a military-industrial complex likely to resist reforms that diminished its budget and status; it created a general sense of fear and embattled insecurity that was hardly conducive to reform. The continuation of such intense Cold War hostilities, in short, seemed incompatible with an increasingly ambitious domestic agenda.

Gorbachev was able to act more decisively and earlier in the foreign policy arena than in domestic policy in part because it was less bureaucratically complex. The major player was the foreign minister, and in mid-1985 Gorbachev appointed his close friend and political ally, Eduard Shevardnadze, to this position. Two years later Gorbachev replaced the conservative Marshal Sergei Sokolov as minister of defense when a young German pilot managed to evade Soviet air defenses and land his small airplane in the center of Moscow near the Kremlin itself. Together with a team of a half dozen personally chosen aides, Gorbachev was able to make dramatic changes in Soviet foreign policy, both conceptually and in practice, that played a major role in bringing the Cold War to its surprising and altogether unexpected conclusion.

An essential, and genuinely revolutionary, part of that process lay in Gorbachev's willingness to confront the core assumptions or worldview that underpinned traditional Soviet foreign policy.[26] In his own writings and speeches and in the work of international specialists from government, party, and academic circles, there soon emerged a sharp critique of past practice and a novel approach to foreign policy issues that became known as the "new political thinking." At its heart lay a challenge to the traditional Soviet view of two social systems, socialism and capitalism, locked in permanent conflict and ending only in the global victory of socialism. While Khrushchev's doctrine of "peaceful coexistence" had earlier suggested that war between these two camps was no longer inevitable, the notion of a ceaseless "class struggle" in the international arena persisted. Now Gorbachev set that view aside. Technological and social change, he argued, and particularly the advent of nuclear weapons, had created a single interconnected and interdependent world. Thus, the solution of "common human problems" such as environmental pollution, poverty, famine, and avoiding nuclear war should take precedence over class conflict. "Further world progress is now possible," he declared to the United Nations in late 1988, "only through a search for a consensus of all mankind."[27] It was a stunning reversal of communist thinking, which had long held that progress came through conflict, not consensus, and that the world's proletariat rather than "all mankind" was its agent.

Much else followed from this fundamental revision in official Soviet thinking. It meant that while socialism was a real contribution to world culture, the Soviet Union, as Gorbachev admitted, had much to learn from the earlier achievements of human civilization, including the rule of law and market-based exchange. It led also to a strikingly different conception of national security. "Security," Gorbachev wrote, "is indivisible. It is either equal security for all or none at all."[28] This meant acknowledging that Soviet behavior had at times been threatening to other nations and that this had undermined Soviet security itself. Furthermore, in the nuclear age, security could not be defined primarily in military terms, but had to incorporate economic, environmental, and political dimensions as well. The implication for Soviet military policy was summed up in the notion of "reasonable sufficiency" in defense, rather than trying to match the West weapon for weapon.

It also meant abandoning the Marxist illusion of some final communist victory and acknowledging the long-term durability of capitalism. This in turn diminished the role of the Third World in Soviet foreign policy. Asia, Africa, the Middle East, and Latin America were no longer seen as arenas for heroic "national liberation struggles," but rather as a drain on Soviet resources and a source of regional conflicts.

Accepting diversity as legitimate and natural rather than postulating a "single truth" now came to characterize Gorbachev's presentation of the Soviet role in the world. This led directly to his emphatic and repeated articulation of "freedom of choice" as a new principle of Soviet foreign policy. At the UN General Assembly, Gorbachev flatly stated that "force and the threat of force can no longer be and should not be instruments of foreign policy."[29] Thus, the country that had forcibly imposed communist regimes in Eastern Europe and repeatedly intervened to sustain them now implicitly abandoned its right to do so.

This conceptual revolution in Soviet thinking did not represent a sudden surge of humane idealism but rather new understanding of Soviet national interests. Some have seen it as an effort to put the best possible face on the country's decline as a global superpower. But whatever its precise motivation, new thinking also produced new actions that went a long way toward ending that fundamental global divide that began with the Russian Revolution.

One expression of that divide, and surely the most dangerous, was the arms race, especially in nuclear weapons. Eager to curtail the American SDI program, soon after coming to power Gorbachev announced a unilateral moratorium on nuclear testing in the USSR, and in early 1986 he outlined a plan to rid the world of nuclear weapons by the year 2000. Practical results followed in 1987, when the United States and the Soviet Union agreed for the first time to eliminate and destroy an entire class of weapons, the intermediate and short-range nuclear weapons based in Eastern and Western Europe. Furthermore, Gorbachev accepted disproportionately deep cuts in his own forces. By 1991 the two sides had agreed to substantial cuts in their strategic intercontinental weapons as well. While major Soviet concessions facilitated these agreements, Gorbachev had found in the American president Ronald Reagan a negotiating partner whose strong anticommunist credentials were matched by his antinuclear sentiments.[30] It was this combination that enabled a striking reversal of an arms race that had lasted for more than forty years. Nor were the reductions limited to nuclear weapons. In his December 1988 speech to the United Nations, Gorbachev announced sharp and unilateral cuts in Soviet conventional forces and followed up with substantial cuts in Soviet military spending.

It was in Eastern Europe, where the Cold War had begun more than forty years earlier, that the most dramatic consequences of "new thinking" unfolded. Since communist rule there had been in large measure imposed from outside, it had developed only shallow domestic roots. Dismal economic performance, particularly in comparison with Western Europe, furthered weakened those regimes. But it was Gorbachev's ascent to power and his "freedom to choose" rhetoric that stimulated the massive upheavals of 1989 that brought about the collapse of communist governments all across the region. Several years earlier Gorbachev had told Eastern European party leaders not to count on Soviet military intervention, and now, when push came to shove, no help was forthcoming, despite the presence of substantial Soviet forces in the region. Almost overnight, Soviet political gains realized after World War II vanished. The subsequent reunification of Germany, and within the NATO alliance, restored to a potentially powerful position the nation that had twice invaded Soviet territory in the twentieth century. And it had happened with Gorbachev's active involvement and consent. Thus, the long-standing division of Europe was substantially overcome, giving some substance to Gorbachev's description of the continent as "our common home."

The Third World as well had been an active arena of Cold War rivalries, and there too Gorbachev's "new thinking" sought to reduce tensions. Soviet withdrawal from its long and bloody intervention in Afghanistan removed a major source of late–Cold War hostilities and improved Soviet relations with China and the Islamic world as well. Soviet diplomats, at times in tandem with their American counterparts, worked to resolve regional conflicts in the Middle East, Angola, Cambodia, and Nicaragua. Soviet economic aid to its Cuban ally diminished. References to support for national liberation movements ceased. Gorbachev even gave political, though not military, backing to the American-led invasion of Iraq in 1991 despite a Soviet "friendship treaty" with that country. In these ways, Gorbachev tried to distance the USSR from Third World conflicts and to limit Soviet stakes in that region's poorer and more troubled countries.

If "new thinking" helped to reduce international tensions and to bring the Cold War to a close, did those policies support and enable domestic perestroika as Gorbachev had hoped? In some ways they clearly did. Gorbachev's growing international prestige, symbolized by his Nobel Peace Prize in 1990, strengthened his political position at home, at least for a time. The reduction of Cold War fears was likewise widely popular in the Soviet Union itself, where virtually every family had known personal tragedy during World War II. This too added to public support for perestroika. The importance of human rights in western perceptions of the Soviet Union provided added incentive for enlarging personal freedoms and the rule of law at home, so that Soviet diplomats could defend their country's record abroad. And Gorbachev's ability to begin force reductions and military spending cuts in 1989 would have been politically impossible without the earlier successes in reducing Cold War tensions.

In other ways, however, "new thinking" worked against Gorbachev's domestic reforms. His rhetorical emphasis on "freedom of choice" and Soviet willingness to accept the collapse of communism in Eastern Europe certainly stimulated and encouraged national groups within the Soviet Union, particularly the Baltic states, in their desire for independence. Especially in 1990 and 1991, they came to view Gorbachev's reluctance to grant them the same freedom of choice as a hypocritical double standard, and it enraged them.

At the same time, Gorbachev's foreign policy began to energize an increasingly vociferous opposition to perestroika from some party conservatives, military officers, and KGB officials.[31] They objected to the apparent acceptance of western universalist values and the general opening up to western culture and economic penetration that "new thinking" seemed to imply. They resented Gorbachev's diminished emphasis on military security and believed that his arms control concession had been excessive. But most of all, they felt deeply about the loss of Eastern Europe and German reunification. The Soviet Union, it appeared to them, had surrendered, with little in return, a security buffer for which the Red Army and the Soviet people had paid in rivers of blood during World War II. To Gorbachev's more extreme critics, it was little short of treason. Such objections in principle were only reinforced by the drastic decline in living standards many military families suffered as Soviet forces pulled out of Eastern Europe and returned home to live in miserable circumstances.

Questions and Controversies:
Did Western Pressure Push the Soviet Union Over the Brink?

Most analysis of the Soviet collapse focuses on matters internal to the country and argues that its demise was self-induced. But was the end of the Soviet Union conditioned by external pressures as well? Did the outside world significantly contribute to the Soviet collapse? One answer to this question, argued passionately by American Cold War "hawks," held that newly aggressive Reagan administration policies in the early 1980s won the Cold War for the West and in the process drove a weakening Soviet Union to ruin. According to one account, the Reagan team, spearheaded by CIA director William Casey, formulated an explicit "secret strategy" to exacerbate Soviet weaknesses and undermine Soviet power: a costly high-tech military buildup, intended to bankrupt the Soviet Union; economic warfare by opposing Soviet oil and gas sales to Western Europe and by lowering, in cooperation with Saudia Arabia, the world price of oil, thus denying the USSR badly needed foreign currency from one of its major exports; financial assistance to Solidarity in Poland and military assistance, including Stinger antiaircraft missiles, to the Afghan resistance movement; and a challenge to the USSR's moral legitimacy by declaring it an "evil empire."[32] In this view, the country did not simply self-destruct; it was defeated.

How should we evaluate such an argument? On the one hand, a number of Soviet-era leaders have themselves stated that American policies "accelerated" the country's decline and were a "catalyst" for its collapse.[33] And few observers would doubt that Soviet military spending, running at some 15–25 percent of a GNP roughly half the size of the American economy, contributed to its economic stagnation. Furthermore, Gorbachev made no secret of his desire for a less hostile international environment generally and for sharp limits on the American SDI project in particular. Only such conditions, he argued, would allow him to reshape the budgetary priorities of the USSR and promote real reform. And a drop in world oil prices in the mid-1980s surely damaged Gorbachev's economic reforms by sharply reducing the country's hard currency earnings.

But critics of hard-line American policies, sometimes dubbed Cold War "doves," have sharply contested such a self-congratulatory analysis.[34] Those policies, they note, had produced only Soviet intransigence before Gorbachev's arrival on the political scene. Thus, the credit for ending the Cold War should go to Gorbachev rather than Reagan. Furthermore, they argue that American refusal to restrict its SDI project and the rush toward German reunification strengthened conservative forces in the Soviet Union and undermined Gorbachev's position. Such policies, coupled with the growing penetration of western culture, gave credence to conservative arguments that Gorbachev had "sold out," compromised the country's independence, and opened it to western decadence. A more accommodating policy might have helped both Gorbachev and a democratizing Soviet Union to survive and thus avoided the ethnic conflicts and threats of nuclear proliferation that accompanied its collapse. And the doves simply disagree about the relative importance of American policies in explaining the Soviet collapse. At most, those policies represented an added strain on the Soviet economy, but the country's internal weaknesses were far more important. Thus the debate about the Soviet collapse remains thoroughly entangled with the long controversy over American foreign policy during the Cold War.

Still another point of view holds that the West conditioned the Soviet collapse less through direct pressures from governments than by simply providing an alternative and more successful model of modern society. Both political leaders and educated citizens in the USSR increasingly saw their country's technological development, its standard of living, and its international standing in the mirror of superior western achievements. That highly unflattering comparison both eroded the legitimacy of the Soviet system in their eyes and prompted Gorbachev's vigorous efforts to rectify the situation. He called repeatedly for the Soviet economy to match "world standards," which were in fact western standards.[35] Those who retained a commitment to socialism now referred to Swedish or Austrian models as they abandoned Leninism. Comparisons operated as well in cultural matters. Particularly for younger people, the attractions of western popular culture—TV, movies, rock and roll, jeans, and T-shirts—and its permissive lifestyle "seduced the communist world far more effectively than ideological sermons by anticommunist activists."[36]

All of these comparisons, of course, derived from the greater knowledge of the West made possible by increased travel, tourism, and exchanges, as well as by information obtained from European and American radio services such as the BBC, Voice of America, and Radio Free Europe. In 1950 only 2 percent of Soviet citizens had shortwave radios, but by 1980 at least half of the population could tune into these broadcasts.[37] Soviet isolation was breaking down.

Beyond the West, other foreign involvement may have contributed to the Soviet collapse as well. One was the war in Afghanistan.[38] Originating in 1979 as an effort to stabilize a recently imposed pro-Soviet regime, that war became the USSR's Vietnam, a "bleeding wound" in Gorbachev's words, until the Soviet withdrawal in 1988–89. It shredded the Soviet Union's propaganda image as a "peace-loving" country and drew bitter criticism not only from the West but also from the Third World and even from many other communist parties. That criticism contributed to the international isolation of the Soviet Union that Gorbachev set out to overcome. Even more important, failure to overwhelm the Afghan resistance devastated the proud image of the Soviet military. Mounting casualties, numbering some twenty thousand to fifty thousand killed, sowed doubts about the Soviet regime in the minds of many people, despite the absence of an overt antiwar movement. Widespread drug abuse and the physical and psychological traumas suffered by many Soviet veterans also brought the costs of that conflict home.

Events in the communist world and elsewhere as well echoed in the Soviet Union during its final decade. China's vigorous reforms predated Gorbachev's efforts by six years and far surpassed Soviet policies in their economic success. China in fact became a model that Gorbachev's critics used to good effect. Free-market advocates pointed to China's decollectivization of agriculture, while conservatives focused attention on China's ability to retain party control of the reform process. The Chile of General Augusto Pinochet, who combined free-market policies with a highly authoritarian political system, also surfaced in discussions about alternatives to Gorbachev's approach.

But outside of the western world and Afghanistan, the most consequential international developments occurred in Eastern Europe, where communist regimes everywhere dissolved during 1989. Soviet policies under Gorbachev had both stimulated and permitted that disintegration, but once it was accomplished, the collapse of communism there had a deep impact on the Soviet Union itself. It encouraged and emboldened nationalists in the "inner empire." Why could Lithuanians and Georgians not achieve what Poland and Czechoslovakia had? And it infuriated conservatives who saw treachery and betrayal in the loss of the "outer empire."

Thus, the international environment in which the Soviet Union operated in the 1980s, while not itself decisive in causing the country's collapse, contributed to three internal processes that fundamentally undermined the Soviet system: the declining legitimacy of the communist regime in the eyes of its own citizens and leaders; the increasingly apparent need for serious reform; and the sharpening divisions within Soviet society as the reform process unfolded.

Notes

1. Vladimir Kontorovich, "The Economic Fallacy," *National Interest* 31 (spring 1993), pp. 43–44.

2. For an extended summary of this speech, see Robert G. Kaiser, *Why Gorbachev Happened* (New York: Simon and Schuster, 1991), pp. 75–80.

3. Stephen White, *Russia Goes Dry: Alcohol, State, and Society* (Cambridge: Cambridge University Press, 1996).

4. Jack F. Matlock, Jr., *Autopsy on an Empire* (New York: Random House, 1995), p. 57.

5. Mikhail Gorbachev, *Memoirs* (New York: Doubleday, 1995), p. 250.

6. *Pravda,* August 2, 1986, pp. 1–2.

7. Mikhail Gorbachev, *Perestroika: New Thinking for Our Country and the World* (New York: Harper and Row, 1987), pp. 61–64.

8. David Remnick, *Lenin's Tomb* (New York: Random House, 1993), chap. 4.

9. Quoted in Andrei Melville and Gail W. Lapidus, *The Glasnost Papers* (Boulder: Westview Press, 1990), p. 24.

10. Ibid., p. 1.

11. Gorbachev interview with BBC World Service Radio, February 17, 1995. Cited in Donald Murray, *A Democracy of Despots* (Boulder: Westview Press, 1996), p. 4.

12. Quotes from this paragraph and the next derive from *Pravda,* January 28–29, 1987.

13. Murray, *Democracy of Despots,* p. 31.

14. John Miller, *Mikhail Gorbachev and the End of Soviet Power* (New York: St. Martin's Press, 1993), p. 115.

15. Murray, *Democracy of Despots,* p. 40.

16. Boris Yeltsin, *Against the Grain* (London: Summit Books, 1990), p. 245.

17. *Pravda,* June 10, 1989, pp. 1–2.

18. Stephen White, *After Gorbachev* (New York: Cambridge University Press, 1993), p. 254.

19. This paragraph draws on Archie Brown, *The Gorbachev Factor* (New York: Oxford University Press, 1996), pp. 132–33, 137.

20. Hedrick Smith, *The New Russians* (New York: Avon Books, 1991), p. 252.

21. Anders Aslund, *Gorbachev's Struggle for Economic Reform* (Ithaca: Cornell University Press, 1991), p. 196.

22. On the cooperative movement, see Anthony Jones and William Moskoff, *Ko-ops: The Rebirth of Entrepreneurship in the Soviet Union* (Bloomington: Indiana University Press, 1991).

23. Mark Selden, "Russia, China, and the Transformation of Collective Agriculture," *Contention* 3: 3 (spring 1994), pp. 76, 81.

24. Ibid., p. 81.

25. Matlock, *Autopsy on an Empire,* p. 659.

26. Robert Legvold, "The Revolution in Soviet Foreign Policy," *Foreign Affairs: America and the World* (1988–89), pp. 83–98.

27. Mikhail Gorbachev, Address at the Forty-third UN General Assembly Session, December 7, 1988. Reprinted in Alexander Dallin and Gail W. Lapidus, *The Soviet System: From Crisis to Collapse* (Boulder: Westview Press, 1995), pp. 442–54.

28. Gorbachev, *Perestroika,* p. 128.

29. Gorbachev, Address at the General Assembly, December 7, 1988.

30. For this argument, see Daniel Deudney and John Ikenberry, "Who Won the Cold War?" *Foreign Policy,* 87 (summer 1992), pp. 123–38.

31. Bruce Parrot, "Soviet National Security under Gorbachev," *Problems of Communism* (November–December 1988), pp. 1–36; Alex Pravda, "Linkages between Soviet Domestic and Foreign Policy under Gorbachev," in *Perestroika: Soviet Domestic and Foreign Policies,* eds. T. Hasegawa and A. Pravda (London: Sage Publications, 1990), pp. 1–24.

32. Peter Schweizer, *Victory* (New York: Atlantic Monthly Press, 1994).

33. Ibid., p. xi.

34. See, for example, Raymond Garthoff, *The Great Transition* (Washington D.C.: Brookings Institution, 1994).

35. For this argument, see Fred Halliday, "A Singular Collapse: The Soviet Union, Market Pressure, and Inter-State Competition," *Contention* 1:2 (winter 1992), pp. 121–41.

36. Deudney and Ikenberry, "Who Won the Cold War?" pp. 123–38.

37. Walter Laqueur, *The Dream That Failed* (New York: Oxford University Press, 1994), p. 62.

38. Anthony Arnold, *The Fateful Pebble: Afghanistan's Role in the Fall of the Soviet Empire* (Novato, Calif.: Presidio Press, 1993).

Chapter 4

Unintended Consequences: Economic Crisis and Social Awakening

After five years of the Gorbachev reform effort, the Soviet Union had changed substantially. New freedom to express diverse and critical views, a much diminished role for the Communist Party, genuine elections and a real parliament, an opening for private enterprise, no more bombastic rhetoric about building communism, an end to the Cold War and Soviet domination of Eastern Europe—was the Soviet Union, some have asked, still a communist state? But none of these changes went uncontested. And while the Gorbachev experiment deliberately activated Soviet society, in the process it brought that society's deepening fissures to the surface.

Here was the grand irony of the Gorbachev reform program: its immediate outcomes were at such variance with its intentions. Designed to revive Soviet socialism, that program opened the door to its further discrediting. Intended to renew economic growth, the policies of perestroika drove the economy toward collapse. Aimed at rejuvenating the Communist Party, democratization undermined and challenged the party at every turn. Expected to preserve and strengthen the Union, Gorbachev's reforms stimulated nationalist pressures that blew it apart. Hoping to enhance the Soviet Union's global posture, Gorbachev presided over the loss of its superpower status. If ever we needed a lesson in the limited ability of leadership groups to shape the historical process, the Gorbachev era provides a compelling example.

Nothing to Buy: The Unraveling of the Soviet Economy

Among the most consequential and bitter disappointments of the Gorbachev reform program was its almost total economic failure. That failure was rooted in the long-term imbalances and irrationalities of the Soviet economy detailed in Chapter 2, but it was perestroika, the attempted cure, that turned mere stagnation into outright decline. For some, that cure was too little too late, while for others it was too much too soon. But whatever its precise origins, by 1989–90 economic crisis was a central topic of Soviet discourse—in the media, among intellectuals, around kitchen tables, and in the endless lines that were the lot of ordinary citizens.[1]

Central to this economic crisis was the growing shortage of both agricultural and consumer goods.[2] The scarcity of food was certainly the most maddening. Milk, meat, cheese, sugar, fruits and vegetables, sometimes even bread, potatoes, and vodka, became difficult to find in state stores. It was not a question of famine, starvation, or even outright hunger, but rather one of pervasive shortages, vast uncertainty as to when and where particular items might be found, and the aggravating need to hunt endlessly for necessary goods and to wait in line for hours on end to get them. Consumer goods such as soap, laundry powder, cosmetics, and toothpaste likewise vanished from store shelves. An acute shortage of cigarettes in the summer of 1990 prompted threats of strikes in various cities and provoked riots in Leningrad. By 1991, of eleven hundred kinds of consumer goods only twenty were regularly available throughout the country. Rationing coupons, not used since the privations of World War II, reappeared in many places.

At the heart of the shortage problem lay the unraveling of the tightly integrated Soviet economy, as individual enterprises and municipal and regional governments gained power at the expense of central authorities. The reforms of perestroika had granted enterprise managers more autonomy and had limited the prerogatives of industrial ministries. And party oversight, which had frequently enabled an inefficient command economy to function, was now reduced. Thus, industrial and agricultural producers increasingly failed to make required deliveries to central stocks or to their prescribed customers. Instead they sought to preserve scarce goods for their own regions, to negotiate alternative deals at higher prices, or to barter for goods unavailable through state channels. Enterprises unable to obtain regular supplies simply could not maintain planned levels of production. A clothing factory in Ivanovo, for example, had to substantially curtail its production of popular denim suits in 1990 when its supply of cloth dropped from 120,000 meters to only 20,000 meters.[3] As these breaches of contracted deliveries rippled through the economy, growth rates, once a proud Soviet boast, moved into the negative column. Output was actually shrinking. National income produced during 1991 was some 20 percent less than for the previous year,[4] a greater drop than the United States had experienced during the Great Depression.

Efforts to cope with a contracting economy only made shortages worse. For individuals and families, this meant hoarding. Consumers snatched up whatever they could buy whenever it was available, knowing all too well that it was unlikely to be there tomorrow and would cost more if it was. Kitchen cabinets loaded with sugar, soap, or flour, of course, only meant even greater shortages in the future. Corresponding action on the part of city and republican governments meant rationing—or "public hoarding"—in an effort to protect scarce supplies for their own regions. When the Moscow city government in May 1990 attempted to limit the purchase of certain food products to city residents, angry neighboring cities and regions retaliated by holding back deliveries of milk and meat to the capital. Kyrgyzstan acted to prevent the sale of vegetables to parts of Russia, and Georgia limited the export of its citrus fruits. It was economic warfare, and it soon spread throughout the entire country. In large measure the Soviet Union had ceased to exist as an integrated economic space well before it collapsed politically.

Another kind of economic warfare also contributed to shortages—that between the industrial and agricultural bureaucracies. Soviet food production had long depended on mobilizing students and urban workers, especially at harvest time. But as industrial enterprises obtained more freedom of action, they increasingly refused to provide this much-resented labor. In many places, this "urban boycott" meant a marked decline in agricultural output.

Accompanying the shortages was an equally dismaying increase in

Voices

Economic Crisis and Soviet Humor

An elderly man from the provinces, visiting Moscow for the first time in many years, enters a meat store and asks for two kilos of meat. "We're out of meat," the clerk tells him. So the man opens a small notebook and writes, "no meat." Much the same experience awaits him in each of the other stores he visits, and each time he dutifully notes the results: "no eggs"; "no cigarettes"; "no cheese"; and even, "no bread." Soon he is approached by a burly official in a leather overcoat who demands to know what he is doing. Perhaps he is collecting information for foreign governments to embarrass the Soviet state. But the man explains that he is merely keeping a diary so he can tell his wife what he has seen in the capital. "Well," grunts the official, "forty years ago you would have been shot for that!" Once more the man takes out his pen and jots in his notebook, "no bullets."

Two men, waiting in a long line for vodka, become exasperated and begin to curse Gorbachev, blaming his policies for this enormous waste of their time. One of them decides to shoot the Soviet leader and takes off for the Kremlin, asking the other to hold his place in line. Three hours later, he returns to find his place in the vodka line not much closer to the counter. "Well, did you shoot the bastard?" his friend asks. "No," he replies in a resigned voice, "the line was too long."

retail prices. According to Soviet estimates, annual inflation rates grew as follows: 7.3 percent in 1987; 8.4 percent in 1988; 10.5 percent in 1989; 53.6 percent in 1990; 650–700 percent in 1991.[5] In the last two years of the Gorbachev era, these devastating price increases were a central element of the country's economic crisis. Where had they come from?

The Soviet Union's controlled and often artificially low prices, coupled with pervasive shortages, meant that the economy already possessed considerable inflationary pressures and that any loosening of controls would send prices skyward. Perestroika accomplished that loosening of controls in several ways. Individual enterprises could now set some of their own prices, and co-ops were free to determine their prices as well. Furthermore, substantial wage increases, far in excess of gains in productivity, put more rubles into the pockets of consumers and thus fueled inflation. So too did the antialcohol campaign, which reduced spending on alcohol only to leverage other prices upward. In the face of the state's obvious inability to supply necessary goods, a rapidly mushrooming black market, in which prices ran three to five times those of state stores, provided an outlet for these inflationary pressures. But the state itself, seeking to bring the economy gradually into equilibrium, also raised official prices and freed some prices altogether, especially in a dramatic price reform in April 1991, which had the effect of roughly doubling consumer prices virtually overnight.

A further contribution to galloping inflation lay in rapidly growing deficits in the government's budget, amounting to 20–30 percent of GDP by 1991, which were covered in substantial measure simply by printing money.[6] That deficit resulted from state expenditures that were not matched by state revenues. On the expenditure side, subsidies to unprofitable enterprises continued to grow, as did grain imports in 1988–89; Gorbachev considerably increased the importation of expensive machine tools; both the Chernobyl explosion in 1986 and the Armenian earthquake in 1988 called for massive, unexpected spending; increases in state wages, pensions, children's benefits, and other social spending, all designed to protect the population from inflation, represented an added burden on the treasury; and interest charges mounted on a rapidly growing foreign debt. All of this had to be paid for. On the revenue side, the loss of taxes from the sale of alcohol and the declining world market price of oil, a major Soviet export, cut sharply into the government's income. So, too, did the growing power of the republics, which withheld substantial portions of tax revenues due to the central government. In the first quarter of 1991, the Soviet state had collected only 36 percent of planned revenues.

A third element of the economic crisis was unemployment, particularly painful in a society in which the guarantee of a job had been among the regime's most solemn promises and one that had been largely honored. When the government finally admitted to a measure of unemployment in 1988, figures varied widely about the extent of the problem, but most estimates were in the 2-to-4-million range by 1991. Even these estimates represent a surprisingly modest level of joblessness—certainly less than in most developed capitalist societies. But it was the fear of unemployment as the Soviet economy moved toward the market model that proved so unsettling to so many people. Soviet workers were well aware of the inefficiency of their enterprises and could well imagine that their jobs might disappear in a new, market-oriented system. In fact, in a large survey conducted in mid-1991, some 46 percent felt at risk of losing their jobs in the transition to the market.[7]

By 1990, then, the Soviet economic crisis had produced an embittered and angry population, most of whom saw themselves as victims of perestroika rather than its beneficiaries. By the time Gorbachev received the Nobel Prize in 1990, an award that symbolized his massive international prestige, he had substantially lost the support of his own people. That crisis also engendered a search for an explanation for all of this suffering and disappointment. Who was to blame: the Communist Party elite, the mafia, the new businessmen of the cooperatives, western capitalists, Gorbachev and his allies, the democracy movement? A certain nostalgia for the stability and predictability of the Brezhnev era, and even for the strong hand of Stalin, likewise surfaced amid the growing desperation of the late Soviet era.

A far more impoverished society took shape during this economic crisis. However the official poverty line was defined, many more people lived below it in 1991 than had in 1985. Particularly vulnerable to impoverishment were pensioners, women, the disabled, and large families, especially in Central Asia. Substantial segments of the population spent upward of 60, 70, or even 80 percent of their income on food, leaving little for other purchases. For the first time in Soviet history, private charities and soup kitchens began to operate as the "safety net," for the Soviet welfare state lay in tatters.

But beyond impoverishment, the quality of life was also eroding. Crime was on the rise, and city streets once widely regarded as safe, even after dark, now became markedly less so. Prostitution and pornography, once viewed as capitalist decadence, now made an increasingly open appearance in major cities. The "mafia," shadowy networks of criminal businesses and protection rackets often in league with local authorities, emerged in tandem with the new economic freedoms. A small elite of "new Russians" paraded their recently acquired private wealth in the face of mass impoverishment. All of this registered in a pattern of steadily declining birthrates, at least in Russia, since

1988. Russians, it seemed, were too discouraged to reproduce, and since 1992 the death rate has exceeded the birthrate.[8] Almost alone in the contemporary world, the country's population has been declining. It was within these grim circumstances—both economic and social—that still other unintended consequences took shape.

Democratic Awakenings: Anticommunism in the Communist Heartland

The Gorbachev reforms not only occasioned the collapse of the Soviet economy; they also provoked and permitted a remarkable "awakening" of Soviet society. To some extent, of course, this had been the stated intention of the Gorbachev program—to activate the "human factor" and to stimulate popular engagement with the tasks of perestroika. By 1989–90, however, that process had slipped well beyond the control of the regime and had moved in directions largely unanticipated and unwanted by Gorbachev and his colleagues.

No single voice emerged to represent this awakening of Soviet society. A democratic awakening spoke for those who sought a "normal" western society with its civil liberties and political competition. A labor awakening articulated the grievances of workers—especially miners—unable to find satisfaction or even expression in the workers' state. A cascade of national awakenings sought autonomy and then independence for subject peoples. An environmental awakening pointed to the vast ecological damage wrought by Soviet industrialization. A religious awakening sought to fill the spiritual void of a discredited socialist and atheistic worldview. Throughout Soviet history, from Lenin to Gorbachev, the Communist Party leadership had sought to mobilize society for its own grand purposes. Now various elements of Soviet society were mobilizing themselves, and for purposes that were increasingly at odds with those of the country's leadership.

Among the most significant developments of the Gorbachev era was the rapid proliferation of "unofficial" groups, organizations, and associations. Common and unremarkable in the West, all such groups had been forbidden in the Soviet Union, where trade unions, youth and women's groups, professional associations, and even peace organizations had been created by the Communist Party and operated under its supervision. To be sure, as Soviet totalitarianism eroded in the post-Stalin decades, a number of so-called informal groups had emerged to pursue their interests in culture, religion, education, sports, environment, and human rights. But they were illegal, persecuted, and often repressed. In the freer atmosphere of glasnost and perestroika, however, such organizations mushroomed to an estimated ninety thousand by 1990. Some of them disappeared after an ephemeral existence; others split along lines of personal or ideological conflict; many coalesced, at least for a time, in larger umbrella organizations. In these informal groups, according to one study, "Soviet society has emerged as a viable counterweight to the state."[9] This enormously important process of "perestroika from below" represented the undoing of a Stalinist social order that had long cast the party as the only legitimately active agent in society.

It began slowly. Between 1985 and 1987 circles of like-minded friends and associates, particularly in the major cities, created a wide variety of clubs devoted to music, dance, sports, karate, and yoga. At the same time, a number of discussion or study groups focused their attention on more public or even political issues such as combating alcoholism, protecting historical monuments, and preserving the environment. The Moscow-based Club for Social Initiative, for example, sought to move from mere discussion to action by helping to create a theater studio, a computer club, a home for the disabled, and by investigating police brutality against a group of hippies. In Leningrad several informal groups joined together in an unsuccessful effort to save a historic hotel from demolition.

Initially such groups, which still had no legal standing, actively supported Gorbachev's perestroika and operated within its framework. In return, the reformist Soviet leadership praised their initiatives and viewed them as a useful pressure against entrenched conservative elements. But this positive relationship did not last long. In August of 1987 an "informational meeting and dialogue" brought together in Moscow representatives of some fifty informal political groups. It soon became clear that some of them had moved well beyond Soviet-style socialism or even beyond any socialism at all. More orthodox participants tried for a time to prevent those with "anti-Soviet" or "anti-constitutional" views from speaking. In the end they agreed to disagree and went their separate ways. But this split, and similar conflicts within other informal groups, marked the emergence of a more clearly defined "democratic" movement, distinct from reform communism, which increasingly rejected Marxism-Leninism to embrace western political and economic values.

This democratic awakening radicalized rapidly in 1988 as new organizations with a variety of approaches took shape.[10] One of the most important was Memorial, which focused on the recovery of Soviet history and particularly on the construction of a monument to Stalin's victims.[11] Despite opposition by authorities and internal conflicts, Memorial organized a "week of conscience" in late 1988 and constructed a "wall of memory" in Moscow, where thousands of photographs of people repressed under Stalin provided an evocative reminder of a past long denied. By early 1989 Memorial had 180 branches across the country and some 20,000 members, including many leading scholars and cultural figures. More directly political and confrontational was the Democratic Union, a small, self-described opposition party that launched street demonstrations, sought to practice nonviolent resistance, proclaimed in favor of a fully democratic parliamentary regime, and refused to work within Soviet institutions. Other informal groups were more willing to operate within the system and worked to select progressive delegates to the Nineteenth Party Conference in 1988.

Various efforts to bring the mushrooming number of informal groups together within an all-Union opposition movement completely failed, since democratic movements in the non-Russian republics were increasingly focused on national autonomy or independence. Thus, we will consider those efforts later in this chapter as national awakenings. But even within the Russian Republic, efforts to achieve a united "popular front" of democratic forces repeatedly failed. The country was huge, and no overriding issue of ethnicity or independence provided the emotional basis for unity. Thus, ideological differences and conflicts among leaders surfaced repeatedly to keep the Russian democratic awakening organizationally fragmented.

Perhaps the most important stimulus to the democratic awakening lay in the elections of March 1989 to the Congress of People's Deputies and subsequent elections to republican, city, and local legislatures. While parties other than the CPSU were still forbidden, many of the democratic "informals" geared up to promote progressive candidates and campaigned actively for them. In the process their self-confidence grew; they became radicalized, and in some cases they joined together in umbrella organizations to coordinate their activities. Young activists, prominent scholars, cultural figures, former dissidents and human rights campaigners, disillusioned communists, and maverick politicians such as Boris Yeltsin found themselves working together despite some suspicions of one another. In their independent publications (some six hundred of them by 1989), in street demonstrations that attracted tens and sometimes hundreds of thousands, and in frequent conferences and congresses, the Russian democratic movement brought its message to a growing public.[12] That message was increasingly anticommunist, calling for the repeal of Article Six, multiparty democracy, private property, and sharp curbs on the KGB. And at least until 1990, most Russian democratic groups sought to bring this democracy to the Soviet Union as a whole rather than to its separate republics as independent states.

Success in these elections, substantial though by no means overwhelming, gave the democratic movement a new outlet and a new arena of activity in the revived legislative organs of the Soviet Union and the Russian Republic. In the Soviet Congress of People's Deputies a loose coalition of several hundred democratic deputies congealed as the Inter-Regional Group, with the name chosen to emphasize its nationwide reach. While the Inter-Regional Group had only a modest impact on legislation, it was able to push the political agenda of the Congress and the country in a more radical direction, particularly in advocating the repeal of Article Six. The leading member of the Inter-Regional Group, and the spiritual leader of the democratic movement generally, was Andrei Sakharov, the prominent physicist and longtime human rights activist who had been exiled to the provincial city of Gorky for years. His moral clarity and saintly reputation attracted many to the democratic movement; his ideas largely constituted its program; his death in December 1989 gave the movement its martyr; and his funeral service became a political rally with thousands of mourners carrying signs calling for the repeal of Article Six. The emotional and political momentum of these events persuaded Gorbachev and the Congress to act, and in March 1990 the Communist Party's political monopoly in the Soviet Union came to an end. It was a signal achievement of the democratic movement.

Democrats likewise found a platform in the city soviets of Moscow and Leningrad, where their candidates captured the majority of seats in the elections of 1990 and where democratic mayors Gavriil Popov and Anatoly Sobchak, respectively, became prominent movement leaders. Likewise, in the newly elected Russian parliament (like its Soviet counterpart, also called a Congress of People's Deputies), about 25 percent of the deputies were affiliated with the democratic movement.

There Boris Yeltsin emerged, narrowly, as the chairman of the Congress. A further arena for democrats emerged within the Communist Party itself. In January of 1990, a conference of 455 delegates representing 175 party clubs and organizations from 102 cities established the Democratic Platform within the CPSU. Its clear intention was to turn the CPSU into a social democratic party operating within a multiparty parliamentary framework, and failing that, to withdraw from the Communist Party altogether and create a formal opposition.

With the repeal of Article Six, the thousands of informal groups were now joined by a number of competing political parties, all seeking to contest the still dominant position of the Communist Party.[13] The Social Democratic Party modeled its program on similar parties in Western Europe. The Republican Party of Russia had a very similar outlook but was composed of people who had only recently broken away from the CPSU. The Movement for Democratic Reform was created in the summer of 1991 by nine leading reformers, including former Politburo members Alexander Yakovlev and Eduard Shevardnadze. The Democratic Party of Russia, led by the charismatic Nikolai Travkin, became the largest of the new parties, with twenty-five thousand to fifty thousand members. Somewhat more conservative in political outlook were the Russian Christian Democratic Movement and the Constitutional Democratic Party. There were dozens more, both at the all-Union level and within the Russian Republic. Most of the major parties and many individuals joined together in a very loose coalition, called the Democratic Russia Movement, aimed at fostering cooperation among progressive groups and thus competing more effectively with the Communist Party.

By 1990–91, then, the democratic movement had become an important force within the Soviet Union, effectively ending decades of political silence and creating a legal opposition for the first time in Soviet history. It had seized the political initiative from Gorbachev and increasingly set the agenda for the country. Furthermore, it had transformed that agenda from communist "reform" to outright democracy. By 1991 some of the leaders of that movement were in fact warning their followers against an excessive anticommunism! In the process the democratic movement had triggered a growing conservative backlash, which led ultimately to the August 1991 coup. In articulating publicly an alternative social order and in demonstrating widespread popular support for it, the democratic movement undermined the Soviet system.

But the democratic movement itself did not overthrow that system. Nor did it create an effective multiparty alternative to the CPSU. Its separate parties and organizations remained small, ranging in membership from a few hundred to tens of thousands, and they gave rise to no unified opposition such as Solidarity had created in Poland. And those democrats elected to various legislative bodies proved generally ineffective as lawmakers.

Some of these weaknesses grew out of the sheer novelty of democracy after seven decades of Communist Party domination.[14] Because these new organizations were so intent on establishing their own unique identities, they were consumed with procedural details and long-winded discussions of general principles, making it difficult for them to unite with other groups despite very similar outlooks. Their "hyperdemocratic" structure—little hierarchy or internal discipline and large, unwieldy leadership bodies—grew out of a desire to break decisively with the highly centralized Bolshevik tradition, but it gave rise to long meetings filled with speech making and to ineffective organizations. The coming of major elections *before* alternative parties were legalized, robbed those new parties of a chance to discipline themselves through electoral activity. It also meant that the democrats who were elected, even with the assistance of informal organizations, did not represent particular parties. They were on their own. This freelance feature of legislative politics contributed to its ineffectiveness. Furthermore, there were some real divisions among the democrats: Was mass demonstration or organizational work the preferred strategy? How much autonomy, if any, should individual organizations give up when they entered umbrella groups such as Democratic Russia? Was the goal of the democratic movement a noncommunist Soviet Union or a series of separate and independent republics? Should democrats cooperate with reformers already in authority or vigorously confront the entire system? These questions were the occasion for endless discussion and serious internal conflict.

Unlike parties and movements in more established democracies, those in the late Soviet Union faced a hostile rather than a neutral state. Despite its enfeeblement, the Soviet state still had powerful resources at its disposal and was not hesitant to use them, particularly as the democratic movement openly advocated replacing, not just reforming, the existing system. It could delay the official registration of informal groups. Paper for informal publications and access to printing presses and meeting places could be hard to find. KGB infiltration and disruption of meetings was frequent, and the suspicion of it was universal among democrats. Furthermore, elements of the party-state apparatus created or encouraged "puppet" organizations alongside authentic autonomous groups and then publicized them widely in the official press. One such group was the Liberal Democratic Party, led by the eccentric demagogue Vladimir Zhirinovsky, which later became a major political force in its own right, preaching a highly nationalist and quasi-fascist message. Thus, Russia's democratic awakening was understandably more effective in acting against the Soviet system than in actually creating a viable alternative to it.

Labor Awakenings: Working-Class Protest in the Workers' State

Paralleling Russia's democratic awakening was the emergence of an independent working-class movement, expressing itself in a series of dramatic strikes, especially in the mining industry, between 1989 and 1991. This labor awakening challenged the very core of the country's ideology, for the revolution of 1917 had been made in the name of the working class, and the interests of that class presumably were identical with those of the state itself. Workers thus had no need of an independent voice in the workers' state. Official trade unions, firmly under the control of the party and the enterprise in which they were located, had little involvement with questions of pay or working conditions, and nothing like collective bargaining existed. Instead, unions encouraged workers to fulfill the enterprise plan and distributed a variety of benefits such as housing, health care, and vacations. And the few strikes that had occurred outside this structure of control during the Soviet regime had been harshly suppressed.

Thus, the eruption of large-scale strikes in 1989, and the articulation of worker demands through independent organizations, demonstrated the hollowness of official claims about working-class harmony. Those strikes, and the anti-Soviet views they later expressed, were also surprising because workers had benefited considerably during the Brezhnev era as both wages and living standards rose. Reformers generally had viewed the working class as apathetic and often counted it among the conservative opponents of perestroika.

The events of 1989, however, proved these expectations wrong. The freer atmosphere of the Gorbachev era had already stimulated the formation of various workers' clubs or discussion groups. The Law on State Enterprises, which called for a measure of worker participation in management affairs, had generated some opportunity and enthusiasm for greater worker activism. And the growth of a democratic movement, together with the elections of March 1989, demonstrated the possibility of independent organizing without fear of serious repercussions.

It was in the coalfields of Russia, Ukraine, and Kazakstan that these conditions first gave rise to a vigorous and independent labor movement. Appalling health, safety, and housing conditions had long been a part of miners' lives, as had a deep resentment that the state used them to dig as much coal as possible with little regard for their welfare. The deteriorating economy of the late Soviet era exacerbated their problems as bonuses were cut back, supplies were even more difficult to obtain, and rumors of threatened mine closings circulated. Even soap had become a scarce commodity. "Can you imagine," demanded one outraged worker, "what it's like for a miner without soap?"[15] And so in July of 1989 a local strike in the Kuznetsk region of Siberia triggered massive walkouts in most Soviet coalfields that idled close to a half million miners for a two-week period.

The organizational basis of the miners' movement lay in a multitude of "strike committees," established at the enterprise, city, and regional levels and led generally by small groups of activists, many of whom were party members. Their demands were primarily economic: higher wages and pensions, longer vacations, better housing and medical services, no more compulsory Sunday work, more food in the cafeterias and stores, meat and sausage in the mines, improved work clothing, and soap! They also insisted on greater independence for their mines from the dictates of the central government, believing, perhaps naively, that if they could freely sell their coal at market prices, they would be able to finance improvements in the mines.

Faced with this unprecedented protest, the government made substantial concessions and promises on economic issues, which persuaded the miners to return to work by the end of July. And legislation in October 1989 actually legalized strikes for the first time in Soviet history, though with many restrictions. Despite these concessions, many of the strike committees persisted and in some cases led to the formation of alternative, independent trade unions that rivaled their official counterparts.[16] And, during 1990, the strike movement stimu-

Voices

The Miners Speak

The coal miners of the Donbass region of Ukraine articulate here the grievances that led to their 1989 strikes. The first selection comes from an interview with a father and son.

To get this one glass [of vodka] you have to reach into your pocket and shake well because it costs 15 rubles. That is five times more than before. . . . Let's talk about razor blades—there is nothing to shave with. And detergent! How can Gennady's wife stand in line if she has to work? A few days ago . . . I saw a hundred people standing in line for soap. How can we approve of him [Gorbachev] after he got us to such a point. . . ?

How are our quotas determined? My father had his quota—five tons—but I have to extract eight tons. . . . That's why we're fighting. So that the quotas are not hiked up.

The following excerpts from an official trade union meeting in August 1989 show the kind of questions that union leaders received from rank-and-file delegates.

Delegate 2: Your role should have been to defend us, not the mine administration. The second question is: where was your conscience when you bought an imported refrigerator. We . . . only found out two or three days ago that they had been sold. . . .

Delegate 3: How many people can go to our resort . . . ? And . . . why do we get only two or three trips per section, and how did it happen that total strangers are spending time at our resort . . . ?

Delegate 4: Why did [you] get the title of Honorary Miner of the Ukraine and receive the full Miner's Glory award? For what . . . ? We've got people working for over thirty years, tunnel cutters and coal producers, without getting a single award, forget titles. Explain this, please.

Delegate 5: [H]ow many times did you get trips to the resorts . . . ?

From Lewis Siegelbaum and Daniel J. Walkowitz,
Workers of the Donbass Speak
(Albany: SUNY Press, 1995), pp. 27–28, 101–2.

lated labor action well beyond the coal industry, as health workers, teachers, journalists, ship workers, textile workers, bauxite miners, and others either struck briefly or more often merely threatened to do so. Generally the government accommodated their wage demands as well.

In March and April 1991, the miners, bitterly disappointed with the unwillingness or inability of the state to fulfill the promises of 1989, renewed their strikes. Now their insistence on wage increases to match inflation was combined with overtly political demands, calling for the resignation of Gorbachev and his government. Leaders of the miners' movement had by now sided clearly with the mounting democratic forces headed by Boris Yeltsin, and many of them were calling openly for a transition to a market economy. It was only the intervention of Yeltsin and the transfer of Russian mines to the control of the Russian government that persuaded the miners to end their strike. As they did so, yet another series of strikes broke out in Minsk, the capital of the normally stable and quiet Belorussian Republic, over government-engineered price increases.

The labor awakening these strikes represented had a major impact on the final years of the Soviet Union. Loss of production and highly inflationary wage concessions greatly exacerbated the economic deterioration of the country generally, and paralyzed serious economic reform for fear of triggering even more massive actions by the workers. Politically, the workers' movement represented an important new ally for Russia's democrats, who were struggling with increasingly assertive conservative forces. And perhaps most important, the labor awakening created a new relationship between the working class and the state that had long claimed to represent it. By 1991 disillusionment with socialism and the Soviet regime, particularly among miners, was almost total, and their capacity for independent action had been unexpectedly demonstrated. They demanded and got not only hefty wage increases but also the transfer of the mines to the jurisdiction of the Russian, Ukrainian, and Kazak republics, further weakening the central government in the process. No longer "supplicants" before an all-powerful state, significant segments of the working class had become an "independent power group" that negotiated with that state from a position of new strength.[17]

The miners' strikes of 1989 and 1991 stimulated hope among some reformers that a broad-based workers' movement might become the foundation of Russian democracy, playing a role similar to that of

Poland's Solidarity.[18] It did not happen. Widespread strikes remained limited to the mining industry, and even there labor activity was fragmented and largely uncoordinated. Elsewhere, walkouts were very brief and highly localized in a single factory or shop. Most workers' groups, strike committees, and independent unions had very small memberships, focused largely on individual workplaces, and found it difficult to create larger umbrella bodies. The labor awakening, then, gave rise to no mass movement or working-class organizations that could independently and consistently articulate labor's demands in the political arena.

After decades of repression, it was probably unrealistic to expect a powerful and coordinated labor movement to emerge within a few years. Furthermore, Soviet industrial policy had long provided a wide range of goods and services—housing, consumer goods, health and child care, vacations—through the enterprises and official trade union organizations. This meant that workers were dependent on their enterprises for far more than wages alone, and this dependence increased as enterprises gained greater autonomy from the central ministries and as the economy collapsed around them. And the energy that might have gone into labor organizing was drained away in several directions. Official trade unions, now somewhat revived and purged of their older and most conservative leaders, beckoned to some workers. Labor leaders, recognizing the weakness and divisions of their movements, looked increasingly to the more established democratic political organizations for political, legal, and financial support and, in doing so, got caught up in political rivalries and lost touch to some extent with their rank and file. Party conservatives appealed for worker support on the grounds that radical economic reform would have a devastating impact on the working class. The very weakness of the state, and its willingness to concede quickly to workers' economic demands, gave the labor movement no solid target against which to rally support.

Russia's labor awakening placed industrial workers in an awkward position. They had come to despise the Soviet system, including its reformist leadership, for leading them into an economic dead end. And their actions had helped to weaken that regime and would play a role in its collapse. But workers found it difficult to embrace fully a market economy that had already sent prices skyrocketing and would, they feared, eliminate both the subsidies on which many of their industries depended and the job security and social services that gave their lives a measure of stability. Threading their way between the rock of a discredited socialism and the hard place of a threatening capitalism was no easy task.

National Awakenings: The Empire Strikes Back

If the democratic and labor awakenings challenged the distinctly "communist" elements of the Soviet Union, the various national awakenings that exploded in the late 1980s called into question the continuation of any Soviet state at all. Those national awakenings—Lithuanian, Ukrainian, Georgian, Kazak, Russian, and many others—surprised virtually everyone with the speed and intensity of their eruption. Unlike glasnost, perestroika, and democratization, which Gorbachev had initiated, the national issue forced itself onto the political agenda of the late Soviet Union against the expectations and the wishes of its leadership. More than anything else, those movements of national assertion were responsible for the political disintegration of the Soviet Union.

Chapter 2 showed how contradictory Soviet policies over many decades had created or strengthened national consciousness despite the internationalism of official Soviet ideology. On the one hand, Soviet policy both recognized and encouraged national cultures and provided a modest autonomy for their political and cultural elites. Each non-Russian republic had its own party organization, supreme soviet, ministries, universities, and academy of sciences. On the other hand, the restrictive centralization of the Soviet system and its domination by Russians and the Russian language sharply limited their prerogatives and offended their sensibilities. So, too, did massive Russian migration into many of the non-Russian republics. Still, no crisis of nationalism threatened the Soviet peace in 1985 when Gorbachev ascended to the leadership of the country. By late 1990, however, every one of the country's fifteen union republics had declared its "sovereignty," and in some cases its independence, as had many of the smaller autonomous republics as well. What had happened? How had Gorbachev's reform program produced or permitted an outcome so completely at odds with its intentions?

In retrospect, it seems clear that Gorbachev and his colleagues seriously underestimated the strength of existing nationalist sentiment and certainly did not foresee how virtually every one of their reform policies would catalyze nationalist movements even further. Glasnost, for example, gave rise in the peripheral republics, as in Russia itself, to a multitude of informal groups. By 1988, many of these groups had come together within their respective republics into "popular fronts," claiming to support the Gorbachev reform program. Led by members of the cultural and academic elite, these organizations soon took advantage of the new freedoms to articulate publicly a variety of nationalist themes.[19] One of them was history. The impulse to recover and reassert earlier national histories was a common thread in the nationalist discourses of the late 1980s. So too was a reinterpretation of Soviet history. Stalinism, for example, was portrayed not simply as political oppression but rather as national repression and, particularly for those peoples uprooted and removed during World War II, an attempt at national annihilation. Protecting national languages and cultures against the onslaught of Russification was a second theme now openly discussed. Ukrainians and Belorussians deplored the paucity of national-language schools, while Central Asians and Moldavians protested the requirement to write their languages in the Cyrillic script.

Environmental issues likewise became a prominent element in nationalist debate. Soviet industrial practice had long paid scant attention to environmental outcomes. The Chernobyl disaster in 1986, which scattered radioactive fallout over parts of Ukraine and Belorussia, only heightened awareness of these issues. A substantial number of the informal groups that sprang up after 1985 focused their attention on the multiple environmental disasters Soviet industrialization had spawned. Massive use of fertilizers and pesticides that exhausted the soil and showed up in mothers' milk; industrial pollution of rivers, lakes, and seas, which contaminated drinking water; the shrinkage of the Aral Sea owing to massive irrigation to support an almost exclusive emphasis on cotton growing; air pollution in certain cities that resulted in rising rates of birth defects and infant mortality—all of this provided grist for the mill of cultural and environmental protest in the republics. They argued that centralized decision making in Moscow treated them as colonies to be exploited and was responsible for these environmental outrages. The implication was clear and was increasingly asserted: only a new union with a much weaker center and greater republican autonomy could ensure the recovery of national histories, the flourishing of national cultures, and the protection of national environments.

Perestroika and democratization likewise contributed to national awakenings. The weakening control of central economic ministries and the collapsing economy persuaded the leadership of many republics to act independently. Thus, they withheld tax revenues from Moscow; they refused to ship contracted goods to other republics; they prevented non-natives from shopping in their cities. And multicandidate elections for parliamentary bodies at both the central and republican levels provided an incentive for ambitious politicians to seek support on nationalist grounds. In some cases—the Baltic states, Georgia, and Armenia, for example—candidates supported by the local "popular front" organization made a strong showing in these elections and diminished considerably the standing of republican communist parties. But not a few communist leaders, seeking a new basis of legitimacy, themselves became ardent nationalists. As competitive local elections rather than appointment by Moscow became the route to power, such "nomenklatura nationalism" flourished. And Gorbachev's repeated declaration of "freedom of choice" as the basis of his new foreign policy and the success of Eastern European states in breaking away from Soviet control only added fuel to nationalist fires. By 1990 these newly assertive nationalisms had produced a "war of laws," as union republics refused to honor Soviet laws unless they were endorsed by republican legislatures.

Gorbachev's anticorruption drive also acted as a catalyst for nationalist movements. Long-established and highly corrupt party "mafias" in the Central Asian and Caucasian republics, many of which had achieved a degree of independence from Moscow, seemed to Gorbachev both a barrier to reform and a threat to Soviet unity. But public exposure of such corruption in the Moscow media and the ousting of corrupt officials triggered much resentment in the affected republics. Many were deeply offended by the apparent condemnation of entire peoples for the offenses of a few, and by the implication that only Russians could set matters aright. The removal in late 1986 of Dinmukhamed Kunaev, the head of the Communist Party of Kazakstan and himself an ethnic Kazak, and his replacement by a Russian triggered riots involving perhaps 10,000 people in the central square of the republic's capital Alma-Ata. Shouting, "Kazakstan for the Kazaks," the demonstrators were dispersed only with army troops and tanks. It was the first open demonstration of what would soon become a flood of nationalist demands.

Gorbachev's personnel policies in Moscow only exacerbated the problem. By 1987 there were few representatives of the Central Asian or Caucasian republics left in top leadership circles which were dominated by Russians or other Slavs. With no defenders in the central apparatus, many in the southern republics perceived the anticorruption campaign as a further effort to assert Russian domination and to deny them even the limited autonomy and representation they had achieved in the Brezhnev era.

Despite the common outcome of political independence, there was no single path to national awakening in the Soviet Union. Rather, the interaction of Gorbachev's reforms with the particular circumstances of each republic produced a variety of distinct awakenings in the Baltic republics, in Ukraine, in the Caucasus, in Central Asia, and in Russia itself.

Baltic Awakenings

Lithuania, Latvia, and Estonia consistently led the way to national awakening and served as a model and inspiration to other Soviet republics. This unique role derived from their distinctive place within the USSR. With strong German, Polish, and Swedish influence dating from medieval times, and practicing Roman Catholic or Lutheran rather than Orthodox Christianity, the Baltic republics had long been the most European region of the Soviet Union. For many Russians, visiting these republics meant "going West," culturally as well as geographically. Furthermore, they enjoyed perhaps the highest standard of living in the country, certainly higher than many parts of Russia, and they hosted some of the USSR's most advanced industries.

But what set off the Baltic republics most clearly was the manner and timing of their incorporation into the Soviet Union. Long a part of the Russian Empire, the Baltic states had achieved independence following the revolution of 1917 and proudly maintained that status for two decades. Then in 1939, in a secret protocol to the infamous Nazi-Soviet Pact, Hitler and Stalin had agreed that the Baltic region lay within the Soviet sphere of influence. Acting on that agreement, the Soviet Union in 1940 forcibly annexed the Baltic states and subsequently subjected them to a brutal process of Sovietization, including the deportation of hundreds of thousands of citizens and the migration to the Baltic states of large numbers of Russians. The memory of independence and the forcible Soviet takeover thus provided a unique moral and political basis for Baltic nationalism. The consistent refusal of the United States to recognize the legality of their incorporation into the USSR added international support.

The initial focus of Baltic assertion during the Gorbachev era, however, involved environmental issues. In 1986–87 dissidents, scientists, and cultural activists launched successful campaigns to halt or delay construction of a massive hydroelectric power station in Latvia, extension of phosphorite mining in Estonia, and building an additional nuclear reactor in Lithuania. Ostensibly nonpolitical and concerned with ecological damage, these environmental protests also gave voice to the fear of further Russian immigration that such projects would surely stimulate. Latvians were already a minority in their own republic, where Russians held many of the best jobs and, adding insult to injury, were generally unwilling even to learn the local language. Opposition to these projects also reflected resentment about Baltic subordination to Moscow in economic matters. "Have those who sit in various Moscow planning institutes been but once to the places they so nonchalantly propose to obliterate?" wrote one furious Latvian.[20] The success of these efforts provided some confidence that things had really changed and that public protest might be effective, even in the political arena.

The following years, 1988–90, saw the radicalization of Baltic nationalisms, culminating in the Lithuanian declaration of independence in March of 1990. Central to that process was the formation during 1988 in each of the Baltic republics of a "popular front," an umbrella organization that brought together scattered informal groups on a platform of demanding greater sovereignty in culture, language, legislation, economic decision making, and control over immigration. Their central symbolic demand, however, was for the simple acknowledgment of the secret agreement with Hitler that had brought the Baltic states illegally into the Soviet Union. A series of increasingly large public demonstrations, timed to coincide with significant historical anniversaries surrounding Baltic independence, dramatized the issue. They climaxed on August 23, 1989, the fiftieth anniversary of the Nazi-Soviet Pact, in a "human chain" that stretched 370 miles and connected the three Baltic capitals. More than a million persons joined hands and passed the word "freedom" along the chain. A few months later the recently elected Soviet Congress of People's Deputies finally admitted the existence of the secret documents, long denied by the Soviet government, and declared them illegal and invalid. It was a

Gathering signatures for a petition on behalf of a Lithuanian soldier wrongly imprisoned by Soviet authorities was an element of Lithuanian national protest in the late 1980s. Photograph from the author's collection.

signal triumph for Baltic nationalism, for it undercut the moral and legal basis for the Baltic states' incorporation into the USSR.

The growth of Baltic nationalism was further reflected in and stimulated by the national elections of 1989 and the republic elections of 1990, in which candidates supported by the "popular fronts" won substantial victories. The growing pressure of these movements and their obviously widespread support persuaded local Communist Party organizations to embrace major elements of their programs and to enact them into law through the republics' supreme soviets. Thus, highly conservative party leaders were removed, and the Lithuanian Communist Party officially severed its relationship with the CPSU. Flags, anthems, and coats of arms from the previously independent states made a joyful appearance at public demonstrations and processions. Indigenous languages were declared to be official state languages, while in Estonia all residents were given four years in which to learn Estonian, and all signs in Russian came down. A Lithuanian law limited automatic citizenship to those who had been citizens of the prewar republic and their descendants. All three republics declared "sovereignty," a vague term that implied the primacy of local over Soviet law and represented a claim to autonomy, though still within a Soviet framework.

All of this proved immensely threatening to significant sections of the Russian minority in each of the republics. Many were angry about the need to learn the local language, feared losing their jobs and homes, and were increasingly concerned about discrimination. Invoking the "friendship of peoples" and Soviet internationalism, they presented themselves as a persecuted minority rather than an outpost of Russian imperialism—as they were often seen by local people. And they, too, organized, demonstrated, and appealed to Moscow for support. Such actions, of course, only heightened Baltic determination to win free of Soviet and Russian control.

By early 1990 talk of outright independence was widespread. In January of that year, Gorbachev himself visited Lithuania, where nationalist demands were then most far-reaching, in an extraordinary but futile effort to dampen its demands for independence. Separation, he argued, would force an unprepared country to operate in the world market and thus impoverish its citizens; Lithuania would have to pay compensation for Soviet property; Soviet military bases represented a further problem. And the USSR, he insisted, was becoming a "true federation" whose laws would include the possibility of legal secession. He virtually begged them to wait.

But the momentum of national awakening had gone too far to be halted by argument or threat. When Sajudis, the Lithuanian popular front, swept the republic's elections in early March of 1990, the country's newly elected Supreme Soviet voted immediately and almost unanimously for complete independence. It changed the country's name to the Republic of Lithuania and legally freed its citizens from service in the Soviet army. Estonia and Latvia followed suit, though with somewhat less stringent declarations of independence. With Lithuania's action, the Baltic national awakening was complete, and it posed an enormous challenge to Gorbachev's regime. The final struggle was under way.

Ukrainian Awakenings

If national awakenings in the Baltic republics set the process of Soviet disintegration in motion, the Ukrainian awakening sealed the country's fate. Days after the August 1991 coup, the Ukrainian parliament declared independence from the USSR, and on December 1 of that year Ukrainian citizens overwhelmingly confirmed that decision when more than 90 percent of them voted for independence in a national referendum. With a population of 51.5 million people, Ukraine was the second largest republic in the Soviet Union and possessed some of the country's richest agricultural land and much of its most advanced industry. Its unwillingness to remain within even a reformed and decentralized Union spelled the end of the USSR. Ukrainian defection also represented a rejection that many Russians found extraordinarily difficult to accept, for they had long viewed Ukrainians, speaking a closely related eastern Slavic language, as near-Russians or "little brothers." Thus, Ukraine's size, wealth, and Slavic character gave it a distinctive place among Soviet republics and a unique path to national awakening.

As in the Baltic republics, the new freedoms of the Gorbachev era gave rise to numerous informal groups and organizations, led by former dissidents recently released from prison and by intellectuals and cultural activists associated with the Writers Union of Ukraine. They articulated, now in a public fashion, many of the themes that Ukrainian dissidents had long expressed from underground: the crimes of the Stalin years, especially the famine of the early 1930s; the threat to

Voices

Ukrainians: Not Little Russians

To Ukrainian poet, translator, and critic Mykola Ryabchuk, the chief task of the Ukrainian national movement was to throw off a colonial mentality, "little Russianism," imposed by centuries of Russian domination. In a 1989 interview, he spells out the meaning of this concept.

For 300 years, Ukrainians—a separate Slavic people with its own ancient culture, language, and traditions distinct from those of all other Slavic nations—had a certain stereotype of their status thrust upon them. . . . The essence of this distortion was the idea that they were not a separate nation. . . . It boils down to the following: the Ukrainian language is a dialect of Russian; the real heir of Kievan Rus—the ancient culture of old Rus—is actually Russia; and Ukraine is some sort of misunderstanding. . . . This causes an inferiority complex, which for me is what Little Russianism is. . . . Ukrainians, in becoming Little Russians, actually assume such a consciousness and take on this image; they grow into it. . . . If the Ukrainians themselves do not know and study their history, if they deny their language, if they themselves do not know their own writers. . . , then it is not strange that other nations know nothing of this as well. . . . Why should anyone know about some provincial culture, some provincial language, second-rate and not genuine? Many people in the world . . . are not even aware of the existence of this nation of 50 million people in the middle of Europe.

From Roman Solchanyk, *Ukraine: From Chernobyl to Sovereignty: A Collection of Interviews* (New York: St. Martin's Press, 1992), pp. 19–20, 23.

Ukrainian language and culture posed by Russification; the demand for religious freedom and the legalization of the Catholic and Ukrainian Orthodox churches; and the multiple environmental tragedies spawned by Ukrainian industrialization, now given dramatic new impetus by the Chernobyl disaster.

But the course of national awakening in Ukraine differed substantially from that of the Baltic republics. For example, opposition forces were slower to coalesce into a united "popular front." Such an organization, known as RUKH in Ukraine, took shape only in September 1989, about a year after similar developments in the Baltics. Furthermore, RUKH's platform, calling for "democratization and a humane society" in a sovereign Ukraine based on a new Union Treaty, was rather more modest than the demands of the Baltic popular fronts. And popular support for opposition groups proved far less widespread than in the Baltic states. In the March 1990 republican elections, candidates solidly opposed to the communist regime won only 25–30 percent of the seats in the new Ukrainian Supreme Council, while Baltic popular front organizations had achieved substantial majorities in their parliaments. Even a year later, in a referendum called by Gorbachev, some 70 to 80 percent of Ukrainian voters opted for remaining within some sort of reformed Union at a time when the Baltic republics were declaring themselves completely independent.

This distinctive pattern of Ukrainian national awakening reflected unique elements of Ukrainian history. The country was, of course, far larger and more diverse than the small, relatively homogeneous Baltic republics. Particularly important was the difference between the western region, containing about 18 percent of the country's population, and the rest of Ukraine. Long living under Austrian or Polish rule and belonging to the Ukrainian Catholic Church, western Ukrainians had been incorporated into the Soviet Union only in 1939 and had launched a military opposition to that incorporation that lasted into the 1950s. Thus, they became far more ardent nationalists than their counterparts in the rest of the republic, who had been for several centuries part of the Russian Empire and then the Soviet Union. That experience had brought to Ukraine a large number of Russians, about 21 percent of the republic's population by 1989, and had concentrated them in the heavily industrialized eastern region of the country. The cultural and linguistic similarities between Ukraine and Russia and the policies of both tsarist and Soviet governments had resulted in a substantial Russification of Ukraine, with perhaps 40 percent of the population feeling themselves culturally Russian rather than Ukrainian.[21] And Ukraine, unlike the Baltic republics, had no tradition of independent statehood in modern times, except for a few years following the revolution of 1917. Thus, Ukraine lacked the sharply etched focus on restoring a well-remembered independence that was so important in the Baltics.

A further obstacle lay in the continuation of a highly repressive communist regime in Ukraine under the leadership of Volodymyr Shcherbitsky, in power there since 1972. Such hard-line Communist Party leaders had usually been removed elsewhere and replaced by those more in tune with perestroika. But Gorbachev evidently felt that stability in the critical Ukrainian Republic was more important than pushing reform there, and so the conservative Shcherbitsky, giving only lip service to perestroika, remained in power until the fall of 1989. As a result, the Communist Party of the Ukraine (CPU), some three million strong, continued to dominate Ukrainian public life and actively used its control of the media, police, and legal-administrative channels to make life difficult for the budding opposition. Whereas the communist parties of the Baltic states had early embraced the programs of the popular fronts, no such "national communism" appeared in Ukraine until 1991.

Nonetheless, the formation of RUKH and the success of some opposition candidates in the March 1990 election had put the Ukrainian government and the CPU on the defensive. So too did the creation in January 1990 of a "human chain," modeled on the Baltic example, that stretched for three hundred miles between western Ukraine and the capital in Kiev. It was intended to demonstrate RUKH's ability to bring various regions and diverse groups together. The outbreak of the miners' strike in 1989 also brought pressure to bear on the conservative communist establishment in Ukraine. But for the mostly Russian-speaking miners of eastern Ukraine, concerned primarily about economic and social issues, it was difficult to find a common language with the RUKH leadership, led by writers, intellectuals, and western Ukrainians who were more engaged with national, cultural, and political matters.[22] Thus, even by 1990 RUKH and the nationalist opposition were unable to dominate Ukrainian public life in the way that the Baltic popular fronts had done for several years.

By early 1991, however, the Soviet Union was obviously unraveling. The economy was in crisis; Gorbachev was trying to negotiate a new Union Treaty with greater powers for the republics; and the Ukrainian parliament had decided to establish an elected presidential form of government for the republic. Under these conditions, the leadership of the CPU increasingly embraced the nationalist cause in a belated effort to maintain the party's position.[23] Leonid Kravchuk, formerly the ideology chief of the CPU and now head of the Supreme Council, emerged as the exemplar of Ukrainian national communism.

As a candidate for the Ukrainian presidency, he adopted many of the policies, symbols, and rhetoric long articulated by RUKH and nationalist Ukrainians. It was the August coup attempt that finally pushed Kravchuk and the CPU, after some initial hesitation, to endorse complete independence for Ukraine, as the Supreme Council voted 346 to 1 to break decisively with the USSR. But unlike the Baltic republics, where nationality and even citizenship were frequently defined in ethno-linguistic terms, the new alliance of nationalists and communists in Ukraine spoke carefully in terms of territory. Everyone living in Ukraine, regardless of national background, linguistic preference, or religious tradition, was to be regarded as Ukrainian. Consequently, many Russian speakers actively supported Ukrainian independence, and no large-scale Russian-based "inter-front" organizations surfaced in Ukraine as they had in the Baltic states.

Thus, the prolonged gulf between the slowly emerging forces of Ukrainian nationalism and the CPU was finally overcome. On December 1, 1991, the country elected Kravchuk, previously a ranking communist, as its first president and confirmed by a vote of 90 percent the decision for independent statehood. Ukraine's national awakening, slower and more tentative than those of the Baltic states, had been finally achieved—with the Soviet Union the chief casualty of that process.

Caucasian Awakenings

Between the Caspian and Black seas lay the small Soviet republics of Armenia, Azerbaijan, and Georgia, together making up only 5.4 percent of the Soviet population. Their distinct peoples, each aware of a long historical tradition, possessed many of the same grievances that animated national awakenings in Ukraine and the Baltic republics. They too had experienced serious environmental damage in the course of Soviet industrialization, with Yerevan, the capital of Armenia, ranking among the most polluted cities in the entire country. They too feared for their languages and cultures in the face of Soviet-borne Russification. Mass Georgian demonstrations in 1978 had forced the Soviet government to back off its efforts to reduce the status of the Georgian language. And they too were governed by repressive communist parties, often corrupt and always subordinate to Moscow, even if local elites had achieved a measure of autonomy. All this had fostered dissident activism in the Brezhnev era and was the focus of many newly permitted "informal" organizations in the early Gorbachev period.

But what distinguished the national awakenings in the Caucasus from those of the Ukraine and the Baltic republics was the extent to which they were propelled by conflict *among* the various peoples of the region and by the widespread bloodshed that characterized those conflicts. The most protracted of these struggles centered on Armenia, an ancient Christian land and long among the most loyal of Soviet republics. Armenian nationalism had historically been directed more against the Turks of the Ottoman Empire, where many Armenians lived, than against the Russians, for it was the Turks who had unleashed against them pogroms of genocidal proportions early in the twentieth century. Armenians had come to view the Russian Empire and then the Soviet Union as their "Christian" protector against the Muslim Turks.

But their incorporation in the early 1920s into the Soviet Union as a republic carried with it not only protection but also an enduring grievance, for about 130,000 Armenians, living in an area called Nagorno-Karabagh (Mountainous Karabagh), had been placed within the neighboring republic of Azerbaijan as an autonomous region. There they were cut off from the Armenian Republic and felt culturally and economically threatened by the Muslim Azerbaijanis who formed the vast majority of that republic's population. Repeated requests to Moscow to transfer Nagorno-Karabagh to Armenian control had been refused, but the advent of perestroika, with its emphasis on democracy and reexamining past injustices, seemed to present a unique opportunity to reopen the case. In early 1988, some eighty thousand Karabagh Armenians, practically the entire adult population, signed a petition requesting the redrawing of boundaries. Its rejection by the Soviet government triggered large-scale demonstrations in Karabagh and in Armenia itself under the slogan, "One people, one republic." To Armenians the Karabagh issue represented nothing less than a "test of perestroika" and its democratic principles, and they invoked the Leninist idea of self-determination to support their case.

To Azerbaijanis, however, it was a test of a different kind, one of Soviet constitutionality and the territorial integrity of their republic. A Muslim people culturally and linguistically linked to Turkey, Azerbaijanis had never enjoyed a state of their own and had come to a sense of nationality within a distinct territory only as a Soviet republic.

Thus, Armenian demands over Karabagh enraged them, activated long-held resentments against the more prosperous Armenians, and led, at the end of February 1988, to two days of bitter anti-Armenian violence in the Azerbaijani city of Sumgait.[24]

Thus, the fuse was lit. What followed was an escalating pattern of conflict, intermittent violence, and an apparently intractable dilemma, which neither the Soviet government nor the post-Soviet states have been able to resolve. Violence on both sides produced tales of horror and streams of refugees. Popular front organizations in both republics took up the issue of Karabagh and in the process challenged the declining authority of their respective Communist Parties. Gorbachev and the Soviet government tried to promote compromise, leaving Karabagh under Azerbaijani jurisdiction but with greater autonomy; they tried repression, arresting activists on both sides and ordering in early 1990 a virtual invasion of Azerbaijan to protect its Armenian residents from escalating violence; and they tried ruling Karabagh directly from Moscow.

Nothing worked. The Karabagh issue relentlessly drove the national awakenings of Armenia and Azerbaijan. Initially directed largely against one another, by the late 1980s these awakenings turned both republics sharply against the central Soviet state. Neither was satisfied and both felt betrayed by Gorbachev's response to the Karabagh crisis. Thus, as the Soviet state weakened, it had few supporters in Armenia or Azerbaijan.

Something similar was taking place in Georgia. But there, interethnic conflict occurred within a single republic rather than between two republics. A number of small ethnic minorities—Abkhazians, Azerbaijanis, Ossetians—demanded some special status or transfer to the Russian Republic, each drawing on long-standing grievances against Georgians that could now be more freely expressed. Such demands only intensified the nationalist determination of the Georgian majority to defend its territorial integrity. Many suspected that Russians in the Soviet leadership were using these demands as a pretext for intervention in Georgian affairs and for preventing Georgian independence.[25] When Soviet authorities violently crushed peaceful demonstrations for independence in the Georgian capital of Tbilisi in April 1989, Georgian sentiment solidified in favor of complete independence. And when the Soviet Union finally collapsed in 1991, Georgia refused to participate in the Commonwealth of Independent States that replaced it. But the "micronationalisms" that had so provoked Georgian nation-

alism persisted in the post-Soviet era and soon thrust independent Georgia into a bitter civil war.

Central Asian Awakenings

The largest non-Russian region of the Soviet Union was Central Asia, consisting of the Kazak, Uzbek, Turkmen, Kyrgyz, and Tajik republics. With Islam as a common religion, their peoples also shared a Turkic ethno-linguistic heritage, with the exception of the Tajiks, whose cultural connections lay with Persia, or contemporary Iran. They had been incorporated into the Russian Empire only in the second half of the nineteenth century and were defined as distinct administrative units or republics only in the 1920s and 1930s under Soviet control.

Despite their profound cultural differences from the more European regions of the Soviet Union, national awakenings in the Central Asian republics were much weaker and less highly developed than elsewhere in the country. Whatever the reasons for this paradox, it was not for lack of grievances. Central Asia was clearly the least economically developed region of the Soviet Union; its population growth rates were substantially higher and its poverty and unemployment problems far worse than in the rest of the country. More than half of the Uzbeks and Tajiks, for example, earned incomes below the official Soviet poverty line, while only 6.3 percent of Russians did so.[26] And infant mortality rates approached those of poorer Third World countries. Furthermore, the imposition of a single-crop, cotton-growing economy on large parts of Central Asia during the Stalin years had created a highly dependent, almost colonial relationship with the more developed regions of the Soviet Union. It had also contributed to environmental disaster, reflected particularly in the drastic shrinking of the Aral Sea, the salinization of adjacent farmland, and in widespread chemical pollution of the soil and water. Substantial Russian immigration, amounting by 1989 to 38 percent of the population in Kazakstan and 21 percent in Kyrgyzstan, only added to the sense of colonial control, especially as the immigrants dominated skilled-labor jobs, showed little interest in learning local languages, and often looked down on local people as primitive or backward.

Glasnost did provide opportunity for the expression of these and other grievances, largely in urban areas and by writers and other intellectuals. There were anti-Russian protests and demonstrations against

nuclear testing in Kazakstan; an Uzbek popular front organization called Birlik pushed for official recognition of Uzbek as the state language of the republic and protested "cotton monoculture"; Turkmen scholars challenged the official line that their area had "voluntarily joined" the Russian Empire and openly celebrated the military resistance which their ancestors had made against Russian imperialism; Central Asian journalists published shocking exposés about historical, economic, and environmental issues.

But none of this gave rise to the kind of mass political mobilization and widespread demands for independence that characterized Baltic, Ukrainian, or Caucasian nationalism. Popular front organizations formed in only a few places, and nowhere did they gain anything close to the degree of popular support that they did elsewhere. And while each of these republics declared its "sovereignty" during 1990, they clearly did not see this as a step toward complete independence. Even after the August 1991 coup, as the USSR was clearly disintegrating, the Central Asian republics remained the chief advocates of preserving some kind of union. They accepted independence with considerable reluctance. How can we account for the more limited development of nationalist, pro-independence sentiment in Central Asia despite sharp cultural differences with the Soviet heartland and deep grievances against it?

One answer perhaps lies in the relatively shallow historical roots of national identity in Central Asia. No historical states corresponded to the novel administrative units the Soviet government created in the 1920s and 1930s. Larger Islamic loyalties or highly localized identities based on clan, region, or tribe were then far more compelling than anything resembling national or ethnic allegiance. And while substantial social changes accompanied the Soviet experience in Central Asia, they had produced far less urbanized societies than elsewhere. In the late 1980s some 60–65 percent of the indigenous population still worked in agricultural jobs, a figure at least double that for the rest of the country. This meant that far more people lived in rural areas where "traditional" identities persisted rather than in cities where national or ethnic identities most often took shape.

Furthermore, Communist Party leadership in Central Asia had become deeply entrenched and intertwined with patronage networks based on kinship and clan ties. Members of the intelligentsia were far more closely tied to this power structure than elsewhere, and no dissident movement had emerged during the Brezhnev era. When Gorba-

chev attacked Central Asian "corruption," these local communist leaders and their intellectual spokesmen could represent themselves as victims of Russian persecution and defenders of local autonomy. These leaders also recognized quite clearly how deeply their economies were connected to that of the USSR as a whole, how unprepared they were to go it alone on the world market, and how much they needed the skilled Russian workers who lived among them. Thus, they acted to suppress the more radical expressions of nationalist sentiment, while making concessions on issues of language and religion. The Uzbek government, for example, actively undermined the Birlik popular front organization, but it made Uzbek the official state language, opened a number of mosques, and began to print the Koran in the Uzbek language. And, finally, the creation of various Islamic parties provided an alternative focus for political organization that drained at least some support from more directly nationalist groups.

If Central Asian nationalisms displayed reluctance about outright independence, they found expression—often accompanied by violence—in bitter conflicts with displaced minorities and immigrant groups.[27] Perhaps the most serious violence took place in the Uzbek Republic in 1989, when Uzbek young people in a number of towns attacked Meskhetians, a Muslim people from Georgia who had been deported by Stalin in 1944. About one hundred people were killed, a thousand wounded, and some thirty-four thousand Meskhetians forced to flee. A similar, though less deadly, pattern of antiforeigner violence erupted in the Kazak city of Novy Uzhen against immigrants from the Caucasus. And in Kyrgyzstan, mere rumors that refugees from the civil war in Azerbaijan would be resettled in their area prompted mass demonstrations against such a possibility. Armenian immigrants in the Tajik and Turkmen republics faced a similar sentiment: "no new immigrants." All of this took place in the context of rapidly growing populations unable to find adequate employment or housing in their own areas. If such backwardness made independence impractical, it also fostered hostility toward vulnerable minorities who were increasingly defined as unwelcome foreigners.

Russian Awakenings

No less than the other peoples of the Soviet Union, Russians experienced a national awakening during the Gorbachev era as growing numbers among them came to feel that they too required autonomy or independence from the Soviet Union in order to flourish, perhaps even to survive, as a people. Here was a remarkable and quite rapid transformation of Russian national identity, for traditionally that identity had been imperial. Russians had created the tsarist empire, and they were clearly the dominant people in the Soviet Union. Polls showed that 70 percent or more of Russians in the early 1980s considered the Soviet Union as their "motherland," while the vast majority of Georgians or Uzbeks, for example, identified primarily with their own republic.[28] The very structure of the Soviet state reinforced Russian identification with the Union, for Russia, alone among the republics, lacked its own capital, its own branch of the Academy of Sciences, its own Communist Party, its own TV and radio station. Russians were to find expression through all-Union rather than republic-based institutions. Finally, the presence of some twenty-five million Russians in the various non-Russian republics further cemented their connection to the Union.[29]

In many ways, the Gorbachev era undermined the previously firm association between Russia and the Soviet Union and pushed Russian national identity in an increasingly separatist direction. Most important perhaps was the sharply anti-Russian character of many peripheral nationalisms that exploded in the late 1980s. The return of large numbers of Russian refugees from many non-Russian republics, bearing stories of discrimination and persecution, triggered widespread anger at the "ingratitude" of Baltic, Caucasian, or Central Asian peoples. Raised to believe that they had sacrificed for the benefit of these peoples, Russians now were made to feel like foreigners in those republics.

Furthermore, glasnost made it possible to discuss publicly what many Russians had long believed: that some of the Baltic and Caucasian republics enjoyed a higher standard of living than Russia itself and that population growth in the Muslim republics far exceeded that in Russia. The multiple historical revelations of the Gorbachev era likewise inflamed nationalist thinking. The destruction of traditional rural life, the assault on the church, the damage to the environment, the emigration of so many Russian intellectuals, the prevalence of alcoholism and divorce—all of this provided nationalist writers with compelling evidence that the Soviet experience had badly damaged Russia and Russian culture. And the explosion of the black market, frequently dominated by merchants from the Caucasian republics, embittered many Russians against what they saw as price gouging and criminal elements from the Soviet south, as the excerpt in Voices, "Russian Nationalism from Below" (page 168), illustrates.

In response to these conditions, an awareness of distinctly Russian concerns grew rapidly in public life after 1987. A variety of new informal organizations focused attention on Russian or Slavic nationalist themes. These included, among many others, an Association of Russian Artists; the Foundation for Slavic Literature and Culture; a group of scholars devoted to producing a Russian encyclopedia; a Leningrad organization promoting the social role of the Orthodox Church. Writers and intellectuals articulated various Russian national concerns: the preservation of the Russian environment; the restoration of the Russian church; the recovery of Russian history; the promotion of Russian patriotism; and the protection of Russian culture from westernizing influences and insidious Jewish or Masonic conspiracies. A distinctly separatist note was sounded at the first session of the Soviet Congress of People's Deputies in 1989. There the conservative nationalist writer Valentin Rasputin, commenting on growing anti-Russian sentiment in various republics, suggested jokingly, "Perhaps it is Russia which should leave the Union, since you accuse her of all your misfortunes."[30] The following year the famous exiled dissident Aleksandr Solzhenitsyn published a pamphlet, greeted by widespread acclaim, advocating the secession of Slavic-speaking regions of the Soviet Union. "The time has come for an uncompromising choice," he declared, "between an empire of which we ourselves are the primary victims and the spiritual and physical salvation of our own people."[31] By 1990 a variety of polls showed a widespread willingness among Russians to accept the loss of empire and an overwhelming unwillingness to use force to preserve it. In just a few years a remarkable shift in Russian national identity had taken place.

That shift soon registered in the political arena, as groups and individuals all across the political spectrum sought to accommodate and take advantage of Russian nationalism. Gorbachev named a universally respected moderate nationalist, Dmitri Ligachev, as president of the Fund for Soviet Culture, and village prose writer Sergei Zalygin as editor of the prestigious journal *Novy Mir*. He also gave visible support to the millennial celebration of Christianity in Russia and thus presented himself as a defender of Russian religion. And he incorporated some fairly extreme representatives of the Russian national movement, including Valentin Rasputin, into his advisory Presidential Council.

Voices

Russian Nationalism from Below

Russian nationalism found expressions not only in the declarations of writers and intellectuals but in the experience of ordinary people as well. Here are two illustrations drawn from letters to the editor of Ogonyok *magazine in 1989.*

Just go to any market [in Moscow]. Behind the counter you find rude, greasy, ugly faces with telltale southern suntans. . . . No doubt we need markets, but the traders in them should be our people, Russians. They don't have that money-grubbing quality that is so characteristic of Armenians and Georgians. . . . We need to . . . cleanse Moscow of all this filth.

For almost two years now, we've been living in constant fear for our lives. . . . We are Russians living in the capital of Azerbaijan, Baku . . . where two once brotherly peoples [Armenians and Azeris] are now enemies to the death. There are two in this fight, but apparently a third is to blame. . . . That's why the most dumped-on, insulted people is we—the Russians. . . .

At every turn you hear, "Go back to that Russia of yours!" . . . They don't want us here on Azerbaijani soil. . . . Everywhere you go, it's the "oppression by the Russians." . . .

The Azerbaijanis are chasing us out. Why should they live calmly in Russia? Look how many of them have settled all over Moscow!

From Christopher Cerf and Marina Albee, eds., *Small Fires* (New York: Summit Books, 1990), pp. 211, 231–32.

Thus, Gorbachev sought to harness Russian nationalism in service to perestroika and legitimized it in the process.

By 1989–90, liberal democratic forces, previously concerned more with reform than nationality, began to argue their case in nationalist terms. Boris Yeltsin, by now the emerging leader of the democratic movement, successfully ran for president of the Russian parliament in 1990 on a platform of "total sovereignty." Real reform, he argued, included a more rapid movement toward a market economy and restoring the moral authority of the church, and both required greater independence for Russia from the timid all-Soviet policies of Gorbachev. Russia, in short, could better enter the new world of democracy and capitalism on its own. The Russian parliament moved clearly in that direction in mid-1990 when it declared "sovereignty." That action reflected the extent to which Russian national identity had already changed from an imperial to a separatist posture, and it vastly weakened the Soviet Union's chances of survival as a viable, united state. Its largest republic and its dominant people had begun to withdraw.

The more traditional imperial version of Russian nationalism did not, however, disappear from the political arena. In fact it gained new life as groups opposing perestroika and fearing the breakup of the USSR embraced it. Such sentiments found expression in an odd political alliance between extreme elements of the Russian patriotic movement and conservative elements of the Soviet political elite, particularly in the military, police, party, and state bureaucracies. What they had in common was an "imperial geography" that saw Russia and the Soviet Union as essentially the same political unit.[32] Some Russians living in the peripheral republics, though by no means all of them, likewise supported an imperial version of Russian nationalism. In the waning years of the Soviet Union, however, such views had very modest public support in Russia generally, as the elections of 1989–90 showed. But it was people with "empire-saving" ideas who launched the August 1991 coup in a vain effort to preserve the Soviet Union, and their own privileges, from the separatist nationalism that increasingly dominated both Russia and the non-Russian republics.

The Russian national awakening, then, was unusual in the political diversity it encompassed. Russian democrats increasingly embraced Russian nationalism; Gorbachev and political centrists tried to accommodate it; conservative opponents of reform appropriated its language;

anti-Semitic and chauvinistic extremists on the far right wing of late Soviet politics likewise claimed to be defending Russia from assorted enemies.[33]

The Russian national awakening also differed from all the others in the absence of a clear or single target. That awakening was torn between those who defined Russia as an imperial state under attack and those who saw it as a unique society and culture that could prosper only in separation from the USSR. That conflict in turn reflected the ambiguous position of Russians in the Soviet Union. They were the chief builders of that Union and were responsible for many of its atrocities. Yet they were among its victims as well. It was an ambiguity resolved in favor of separatist nationalism in late 1991, but the loss of empire was a profound trauma and produced many reverberations of Russian imperial thinking in the years that followed the Soviet collapse.

While the economic disaster of the late 1980s and the multiple awakenings of Soviet society had deep roots in Soviet history, the Gorbachev reforms had catalyzed them and had provided both opportunity and stimulus for their expression. Those wholly unintended consequences of Gorbachev's efforts to revive Soviet socialism seriously undermined that effort, and set the stage for the final act of the Soviet drama.

Questions and Controversies: *Who Acts in History—Great Men, Elites, or the Masses?*

For some scholars, the great emphasis on Gorbachev and other leading political figures has overplayed the decisive role of "great men" in historical change and has obscured the significance of more ordinary people and social movements in the Soviet drama. One such scholar, for example, has argued that "Gorbachev was an instrument rather than the source of change."[34] In this view, Gorbachev acted, at least initially, with the consent and on behalf of a large section of the Soviet elite, intent on preserving a deteriorating system through modest changes. A related argument suggests that Gorbachev was the more or less inevitable product of social changes—urbanization, professionalization, education—that created "irresistible pressures for democratization." Thus the "impersonal forces of history," not the actions of an individual, become the decisive motor of change, and the significance of Gorbachev's personal role is thereby diminished.[35]

Furthermore, once Gorbachev's reforms had "uncorked" Soviet society, mass movements of nationalists, of democrats, and of mine workers exerted enormous pressure on political leaders, both on the streets and in the voting booths. Party functionaries in many republics who rapidly became nationalist spokesmen represented one sign of this impact. A widespread outcry against the use of violence in Georgia, Azerbaijan, and Lithuania no doubt weakened the resolve of conservatives as they contemplated even more decisive action during the August 1991 coup. And the many tens of thousands of defenders who surrounded the Russian White House in those critical days (whose actions are described more fully in the next chapter), left a decisive mark on the history of their country. Leaders and "great men" were not the sole actors on the Soviet historical stage.

But what kind of society did these broader elites, social changes, and mass movements produce? Clearly it was not a western-style civil society with effective parties, unions, business associations, church groups, and other organizations that could operate consistently and on a national basis to represent specific social interests. The Soviet system had destroyed and prohibited virtually all intermediate organizations that might function between individual families and the state, replacing them with a pervasive party-state apparatus. The sudden collapse of that system during the Gorbachev era left a social and institutional vacuum that was filled, at least for the moment, by short-lived "movements," local and regional elites relying on old connections, and rapidly expanding criminal organizations.[36] Whether that would be a temporary condition or a permanent state has been one of the key questions of the post-Soviet era.

Notes

1. For various Soviet understandings of this crisis, see Mary Buckley, *Redefining Russian Society and Polity* (Boulder: Westview Press, 1993), chap. 8.
2. The most accessible and thorough discussion of the economic crisis is William Moskoff, *Hard Times: Impoverishment and Protest in the Perestroika Years* (Armonk, N.Y.: M.E. Sharpe, 1993). This section draws heavily on that account.
3. Ibid., p. 60.
4. Anders Aslund, *How Russia Became a Market Economy* (Washington, D.C.: Brookings Institution, 1995), p. 52.
5. Moskoff, *Hard Times,* p. 89.
6. Aslund, *How Russia Became a Market Economy,* pp. 48–49.
7. Moskoff, *Hard Times,* p. 162.

8. See chart in the *New York Times,* March 6, 1994, p. 18.

9. Judith B. Sedaitis and Jim Butterfield, eds., *Perestroika from Below: Social Movements in the Soviet Union* (Boulder: Westview Press, 1991), p. 10.

10. Geoffrey A. Hosking, Jonathan Aves, and Peter J.S. Duncan, *The Road to Post-Communism: Independent Political Movements in the Soviet Union, 1985–1991* (London: Pinter Publishers,1992), pp. 16–22.

11. Kathleen E. Smith, *Remembering Stalin's Victims* (Ithaca: Cornell University Press, 1996).

12. M. Steven Fish, "The Emergence of Independent Associations and the Transformation of Russian Political Society," *Journal of Communist Studies* 7:2 (September 1991).

13. On the new parties, see John B. Dunlop, *The Rise of Russia and the Fall of the Soviet Empire* (Princeton: Princeton University Press, 1993), pp. 97–106.

14. A thoughtful assessment of these political movements is found in M. Steven Fish, *Democracy from Scratch: Opposition and Regime in the New Russian Revolution* (Princeton: Princeton University Press, 1995), on which this section draws heavily.

15. Cited in Moskoff, *Hard Times,* p. 190.

16. On the 1989 strikes, see Donald Filtzer, *Soviet Workers and the Collapse of Perestroika* (Cambridge: Cambridge University Press, 1994), pp. 94–100; and Simon Clarke et al., *What About the Workers? Workers and the Transition to Capitalism in Russia* (London: Verso, 1993), pp. 128–32.

17. Moskoff, *Hard Times,* p. 198.

18. Jonathan Aves, "The Russian Labour Movement, 1989–91: The Mirage of a Russian Solidarnosc," in *Road to Post-Communism,* eds. Hosking, Aves, and Duncan, pp. 138–39.

19. Gail Lapidus, "From Democratization to Disintegration: The Impact of Perestroika on the National Question," in *From Union to Commonwealth,* ed. Gail W. Lapidus et al. (Cambridge: Cambridge University Press, 1992), pp. 48–54.

20. N.R. Miuzneks, "The Daugavpils Hydro-Station and Glasnost in Latvia," *Journal of Baltic Studies,* 18:1 (spring 1987), pp. 63–70.

21. Taras Kuzio and Andrew Wilson, *Ukraine: Perestroika to Independence* (London: McMillan, 1994), p. 34.

22. David R. Marples, *Ukraine Under Perestroika: Ecology, Economics, and the Workers' Revolt* (New York: St. Martin's Press, 1991), pp. 212–13.

23. For this argument, see Kuzio and Wilson, *Ukraine,* chaps. 8, 9.

24. For a more detailed treatment, see Ronald G. Suny, *Looking toward Ararat: Armenia in Modern History* (Bloomington: Indiana University Press, 1993), especially chap. 12.

25. Hélène Carrère d'Encausse, *The End of the Soviet Empire* (New York: Basic Books, 1993), chap. 5.

26. Anatoly M. Khazanov, *After the USSR: Ethnicity, Nationalism, and Politics in the Commonwealth of Independent States* (Madison: University of Wisconsin Press, 1995), p. 120.

27. d'Encausse, *End of the Soviet Empire,* chap. 6.

28. Leokadia Drobizheva, "Perestroika and the Ethnic Consciousness of Russians," in *From Union to Commonwealth,* ed. Gail W. Lapidus et al., p. 101.

29. John B. Dunlop, "Russia: Confronting a Loss of Empire," in *Nation and*

Politics in the Soviet Successor States, eds. Ian Bremmer and Ray Taras (Cambridge: Cambridge University Press, 1993), p. 43.

30. Cited in Dunlop, *Rise of Russia,* pp. 16–17.

31. Aleksandr Solzhenitsyn, *Rebuilding Russia* (New York: Farrar, Straus and Giroux, 1991), p. 11.

32. Roman Szporluk, "Dilemmas of Russian Nationalism," *Problems of Communism* (July–August 1989), pp. 15–35.

33. For the extremist views, see Walter Laqueur, *Black Hundred: The Rise of the Extreme Right in Russia* (New York: HarperCollins, 1993).

34. Hillel H. Ticktin, "Review of *The Gorbachev Factor,*" *Europe-Asia Studies* 49:2 (1997), p. 319.

35. Thomas F. Remington, "Refom, Revolution, and Regime Transition," in *Dismantling Communism,* ed. Gilbert Rozman (Washington, D.C.: Woodrow Wilson Center Press, 1992), pp. 124, 126.

36. Alexander Dallin and Gail W. Lapidus, *The Soviet System: From Crisis to Collapse* (Boulder: Westview Press, 1995), p. 719.

Chapter 5

Passing into History: The Final Act of the Soviet Drama

For more than four years (1985–89), Mikhail Gorbachev had seized and largely held the initiative in the affairs of the Soviet Union. But in the final two years of the country's existence, he rapidly lost that ability to shape events as the democratic, labor, and national movements, together with a growing conservative backlash against them, took center stage in defining the country's agenda. For the first time since the revolution of 1917, society, rather than the state, was driving the process of change in Soviet life. But that society was increasingly fragmented, fractious, and polarized, pitting radical democrats against die-hard communists and nationalists of all kinds against Soviet "patriots." In this setting Gorbachev found himself reacting to multiple and conflicting pressures in an effort, growing ever more desperate, to hold the country together. The failure of that effort provides the "story line" of the Soviet Union's final and tumultuous two years. The political center, to which Gorbachev clung, contracted and then vanished amid the sharpening contradictions and conflicts of Soviet society. In the end, the ties that bound this sprawling country together no longer held.

Pressures from the Periphery: Responding to the Nationalist Challenge

Among the growing pressures Gorbachev confronted, none were more acute, or potentially threatening, than those from the Soviet Union's fifteen constituent republics, for those national awakenings (detailed in the previous chapter) called into question the very existence of Soviet statehood. The virtually universal judgment on Gorbachev's response to these movements has been: "Too little, too late." Gorbachev himself has admitted to seriously underestimating the strength of nationalist sentiment and moving too slowly to address it. Why should this have been the case?

One answer lies in how the Soviet leadership understood the Soviet state. Certainly, they did not view the USSR as an empire, the product of tsarist and Bolshevik conquests, in which Russians dominated other peoples. Rather, in their eyes, the Soviet Union was a multinational country, like many others in the world, bound together by ties of economic interdependence, intermarriage, a shared history, and a consciousness of "Soviet" identity. Nationalism, in this view, was primitive and backward looking, and the Soviet Union had largely transcended it. While Gorbachev's experience near the multiethnic Caucasus made him acutely aware of national differences and the need for great sensitivity in dealing with them, he came to power assuming that there were "no serious problems" on the national front. In 1986 the official CPSU program proclaimed that the national question had been "successfully resolved." And for decades little overt nationalist protest had surfaced to suggest otherwise.

Thus, Gorbachev initially saw no contradiction between his reform program and the continued unity of the country. Consequently, he largely ignored the nationalities question for the first several years while proceeding with glasnost and democratization. For this he has been much criticized, for as it turned out those reforms greatly stimulated national awakenings. Some have in fact argued that a "democratic Soviet Union" was a contradiction in terms, since the unity of the country relied so heavily on coercion. Even after 1988, when the nationalities question could no longer be ignored, Gorbachev continued to seek democratic reform while maintaining the country's unity in some form, with no sense that these were fundamentally incompatible goals. Nor was he alone in this belief, for as late as March of 1991, some 76 percent of the electorate responded "yes" to a referendum asking about "preserving the USSR as a renewed federation." If his policy of reform and unity failed, it was perhaps for reasons other than massive popular hostility.

By 1989–90, it was apparent to all that national issues were at least as urgent as economic and political reform. The "war of laws" and declarations of sovereignty raised in the most pointed fashion the relationship of the center to the republics and the balance of power between them. Widespread resistance to the draft and the unwillingness of some republics to contribute their prescribed share to the federal budget made the issue concrete. Yet until March of 1990 no republic had sought full independence. There was, apparently, room for negotiation.

By all accounts, Gorbachev's response to this deepening crisis was reluctant and hesitant. A meeting of the party's Central Committee to consider the nationalities question was repeatedly postponed and did not occur until September 1989. And even then its outcome was disappointing, particularly to the Baltic republics. While Gorbachev now acknowledged the need to create a "renewed federation," the party's program, although reasonably progressive, had been drawn up without consulting the republics. And that program rejected what was becoming their central demand: a new Union Treaty, negotiated directly with the republics, to replace the 1922 document on which the USSR was based. Furthermore, subsequent legislation to implement the theoretical possibility of secession created instead a series of almost insurmountable obstacles to it. Nor had economic reform granted the republics ownership or control of their resources and assets as they were demanding.

Two events in the first half of 1990 finally persuaded Gorbachev that writing a new Union Treaty was now the only way of saving the Soviet Union from complete disintegration. One was a series of republic and local elections that gave voice and electoral legitimacy to nationalists in many republics. The other was Russia's declaration of sovereignty in June of 1990, which put the Union's largest and most important republic on the side of autonomy. The negotiations that followed over the next year represented the first real effort in Soviet history to create a genuinely voluntary political association among the many peoples of the country and to move away from the highly centralized unitary state of Soviet practice. In these negotiations, Gorbachev's position was summed up in the slogan, "a strong center and strong republics," which in practice meant a renewed federation with substantial powers remaining to the central government while also granting real authority for the first time to the republics. The Central Asian republics, with a conservative leadership, generally supported Gorbachev's position. So too did many of the "autonomous republics" representing minority peoples within the republics, most of them in

Russia. They preferred the distant control of Moscow to the local imperialism of their republic's capital. Many Russians living outside the Russian Republic likewise favored a reasonably strong central government to counter what they saw as growing discrimination against them. And representatives of the major party-state bureaucracies pushed Gorbachev hard to hold out in these negotiations for the strongest possible central state. A diminished Union threatened their jobs and social positions.

Against this "unionist" coalition were ranged the growing forces of autonomy and even independence. The Baltic and Caucasian republics, as well as Ukraine and Moldavia, increasingly argued for a much weaker union or "confederation," in which the central government had only minimal functions granted to it by the member states. While they recognized the economic and military advantages of union, the rising tide of nationalist sentiment and fear of Moscow's retaliation pushed them to seek its weakest possible form. Lithuania, for example, had declared outright independence in March of 1990 but was forced to rescind it by a devastating economic blockade. A disintegrating economy and Moscow's failure to resolve interethnic disputes in the Caucasus further fueled bitterness against communism, against the center, and in some places against Russians.

But it was Russia's support for a weak Union that proved decisive in the negotiations. Under the leadership of Boris Yeltsin and reflecting a growing nationalist sentiment in the country's largest republic, Russia held out for a weak confederation, of which it would be the senior and most powerful member. Yeltsin supported the declarations of sovereignty by other republics and even encouraged autonomous republics and regions within Russia to take as much independence as they could handle. At a news conference in August 1990, Yeltsin stretched his arms wide apart and said, "This is the sort of center we have now." Then he narrowed his hands to within a few inches of each other and declared: "This is the sort of center we need."[1]

The shifting balance of power between the center and the republics found expression in four successive drafts of the Union Treaty, each of which featured a weaker center than the one before. The final version, scheduled to be signed on August 20, 1991, would have renamed the country the Union of Soviet Sovereign States. Thus sovereignty replaced socialism, and the defining element of the USSR for seven decades vanished from the country's name and was not mentioned in the Union Treaty. Furthermore, it would have been a smaller country, for the Baltic republics, Georgia, Armenia, and Moldavia had refused to take part in the negotiations. The central state envisaged by the treaty was but a shadow of the Soviet state it sought to replace. Even the tax rates to support the central government were to be "determined by agreement with the Republics." But it did preserve an international presence for a single successor state to the USSR and a measure of "common economic space" for its member republics. That treaty, of course, was never concluded, for its provisions so alarmed the country's conservative establishment that its leading members took forcible action to prevent its signing. Whether the Union Treaty could have long preserved a unified state remains an open question. It is clear, however, that the failed coup of August 19 virtually ensured the collapse of the country and thus produced the very outcome that it was intended to prevent.

Pressures from the Left: Responding to the Democratic Challenge

Both paralleling and overlapping the nationalist challenge to Gorbachev's program was the rise of a democratic movement (described in Chapter 4). Expressed in a multitude of informal organizations, in a series of competitive elections, and in a new and assertive parliament, that movement had been in many respects Gorbachev's own creation and represented his most obvious source of support for perestroika. By 1989, however, the democrats had become the opposition to Gorbachev's more measured reformist program, constantly urging him to move further and faster toward a western-style democratic politics and market economy. That movement articulated widespread disappointment with, and for many a burning hatred of, the entire communist system and its apparent reluctance to change. The May Day parade of 1990, voluntary and open to all comers for the first time, featured openly anticommunist placards, the red flag with the hammer and sickle ripped out, and chants of "down with the party" and "down with Gorbachev." Gorbachev later acknowledged that he had underestimated the speed with which this opposition took shape, the ferocity of its attack on the party, and the degree of support it attracted from both the intelligentsia and the working class.[2]

Furthermore, the democratic opposition had, by 1989, found in Boris

Yeltsin a leader and spokesperson, who rapidly became Gorbachev's chief political rival. A party boss in Sverdlovsk with a background in industry, Yeltsin had an earthy and populist style and an apparent disdain for the privileges of the Soviet elite that made him an early and enthusiastic supporter of Gorbachev's reform. On that basis he was brought to Moscow in 1985 as head of the city party organization, a candidate member of the Politburo, and a part of the Gorbachev team. There he rapidly became widely popular in the capital city as he took the bus to work, made tours of poor neighborhoods, and personally exposed the corruption of "the big shots." But his attacks on party privilege and his vigorous efforts to clean up Moscow's corrupt politics soon earned him the enmity of the local establishment. And, within the party leadership, he emerged as an impatient and impulsive liberal critic of Gorbachev's reform. At a stormy meeting of the Central Committee in October 1987, he lambasted the slow pace of reform, complained of the adulation accorded to Gorbachev, and directly criticized other members of the Politburo. That performance resulted in his humiliating dismissal from all of his leadership posts, which in turn created a lasting personal bitterness between the two men.

But Yeltsin found a way out of the political wilderness in the new democratic arena, in which being attacked by the party establishment proved a major asset. Campaigning on themes of social justice, opposition to the party elite, and a bit later, Russian nationalism, he was elected by huge majorities to both the Soviet and Russian parliaments, emerging narrowly as the chairman of the Russian body in 1990. In June 1991 he was elected president of the Russian Republic. Yeltsin thus achieved a kind of political legitimacy through popular election that Gorbachev never had.

The democratic movement, of which Yeltsin had become the de facto leader by 1990, involved prominent intellectuals and scholars, impatient urban activists, disenchanted communists, striking miners, and nationalists opposed to Soviet centralism. In 1989 and 1990, this coalition pushed Gorbachev hard on two major fronts. The first was a political issue of the highest importance: the repeal of Article Six of the constitution, which defined the Communist Party as the "leading and guiding force of Soviet society." With the moral authority of Sakharov behind them, democrats in the Soviet parliament argued strenuously in 1989 to end the party's legal monopoly and to move toward a multiparty system. While Gorbachev was not opposed in principle, he felt that it was premature: the new parliament was not prepared to assume full political responsibility, and the party elite was certainly opposed to such a drastic change. Circumstances, however, forced his hand. The growing strength of anticommunist democrats in Russia found expression not only in parliament but on the streets. A huge rally of some 250,000 people in Moscow in early February 1990 featured references to the "February Revolution," reminding everyone of an earlier upheaval that had toppled the tsar in the name of liberal goals. Furthermore, the collapse of communist parties all over Eastern Europe just a few months earlier provided a vivid illustration of what might happen if democrats' demands were rejected. In this context Gorbachev moved reluctantly to repeal Article Six; by March 1990, a party that had changed Soviet society but could not change itself had lost its political monopoly. The way was now open for the legal creation of alternative political parties.

The repeal of Article Six was a devastating and demoralizing blow to the party, marking a real watershed in Soviet history, and millions subsequently resigned their membership. But the party did not vanish overnight. Communist officeholders remained in their jobs; its property was not confiscated; no trials or reprisals befell its members; its network of communication and personal connections remained intact. And despite considerable pressure from democrats to resign as general secretary of the party, Gorbachev refused, fearing that conservatives intent on wrecking perestroika would take it over. "You mustn't let go of the reins of a mangy mad dog," he argued.[3]

A second issue on which democrats pressured Gorbachev, though less successfully, was economic reform. By late 1989, an enveloping economic crisis (described in the first section of Chapter 4) had persuaded Gorbachev and many others of the need to dismantle centralized state control and to introduce private property and the market as quickly as possible. But how, precisely, was this to be accomplished? In the flurry of commissions and recommendations that subsequently addressed this question, attention focused by the summer of 1990 on a set of radical proposals for a rapid transition to the market put forward by a young, maverick economist, Grigory Yavlinsky. Yeltsin eagerly embraced these ideas, thus buttressing his leadership of the democratic movement. Gorbachev, too, was impressed, particularly by Yavlinsky's desire to proceed on an all-Union basis. In a rare demonstration of their ability to cooperate, Gorbachev and Yeltsin temporarily put aside their rivalry and jointly established a working group to flesh out a concrete program based on Yavlinsky's ideas. A decisive moment, it seemed, had arrived for a bold experiment in economic transformation and a further step in the process of reform. And it had taken place with no involvement of the Communist Party!

By early September 1990, this group, headed by the free-market economist Stanislav Shatalin, produced a document known as the "500 Day Program." Containing not a word about socialism, the 500 Day Program unambiguously endorsed private property, called for a massive privatization of state enterprises, proposed ending state subsidies and price controls, recommended sharp budget cuts for the military and KGB, and would have devolved most economic power to the republics. It represented a decisive break with traditional Soviet economic thinking and drew heavily from the "shock therapy" program that Poland had recently undertaken. And, perhaps most important, it set a timetable for the program—500 days.

To those favoring radical change, a moment of truth had arrived for Gorbachev. Had he embraced the 500 Day Program with enthusiasm and continued to align himself with Yeltsin and the democrats, the process of Soviet renewal might have gained new energy and momentum. But he did not. Instead Gorbachev developed second thoughts: the timetable was unrealistically fast, and even worse, he believed the plan undermined the Union by giving so much economic power to the republics. The central government, under the Shatalin plan, had no independent taxing authority and derived all of its revenue from the republics. Endorsing such an economic plan, Gorbachev feared, would undermine the Union Treaty he was then trying to negotiate. But beyond his own reservations, Gorbachev found himself under enormous political pressure from an array of conservative groups representing the party apparatus, the industrial ministries, the military, and the KGB—all of whom stood to lose badly if the 500 Day Program were to be adopted. Under these circumstances, Gorbachev backed away from Shatalin's proposals and tried to blend them with less radical recommendations from a parallel government commission. The result was a compromise that did little to forward market reforms. As a consequence, Gorbachev's support from democrats and nationalists diminished even further, and Yeltsin emerged decisively as the spokesman for progressive forces.

In the struggle over Article Six in early 1990, Gorbachev had sided with the democrats and persuaded the party to accept disestablishment, thus transforming the Soviet political system in a fundamental way. But in the controversy over the 500 Day Program in late 1990, he opted for stability and order rather than gamble on a decisive transformation of the Soviet economic system. What had happened between March and October to account for this change in Gorbachev's posture? One factor surely was the growing nationalist crisis. Russia's declaration of sovereignty in June 1990, followed by that of other republics, made the threat to the Union immediate and stiffened Gorbachev's resolve to do nothing to weaken it further. The deepening economic crisis likewise put a premium on short-term stability rather than long-range reform. Furthermore, the democrats, despite Yeltsin's populist appeal, were organizationally weak and divided—"all chiefs and few Indians," according to one scholar[4]—and thus offered Gorbachev a limited and apparently diminishing base of support, especially within the now powerful Soviet parliament. But perhaps most important was the growing influence of Soviet conservatism—an increasingly powerful backlash to economic and national crisis and to a reform process that had clearly escaped state control.

Pressures from the Right: Responding to the Conservative Challenge

The deeper roots of this Soviet conservatism lay in the growth of a privileged but insecure bureaucracy of party and state officials during the Stalin years. Stalin had kept this communist elite off balance and subservient through terror and purges; Khrushchev attempted, less successfully, to do so through repeated reorganizations. Ultimately they deposed the capricious reformer and finally found the stability and security they yearned for in the conservatism of the Brezhnev era. Then Gorbachev's reforms, and all that followed from them, profoundly threatened this established system and, not surprisingly, prompted an increasingly politicized conservative awakening that bitterly contested many of those reforms as well as the democratic and nationalist movements that perestroika had spawned.

This conservative awakening initially took shape in the upper levels of the party apparatus and all-Union ministries, where virtually all of Gorbachev's early reforms were subject to great skepticism, outright opposition, and sabotage in the process of implementation. Reaching decisions on a reform program, Gorbachev remembered, was like "cutting one's way through jungle undergrowth," as both self-interest and "stereotyped thinking" required frequent delay and compromise.[5] Within the party leadership, the role of conservative spokesman came to focus on Yegor Ligachev, an upright party leader from Siberia who had been brought to Moscow by Andropov in 1983 and emerged as the second in command in Gorbachev's Politburo. No die-hard reactionary, Ligachev supported Gorbachev's early reforms but felt increasingly uneasy as glasnost, perestroika, and democratization began to transform, rather than simply improve, the existing system. Gorbachev, he felt, was being led astray by his radical advisers, and the reform process was moving toward dangerous extremes: anticommunism in political life, anti-Sovietism in the non-Russian republics, creeping capitalism in economic policy, and a radical press bent on slandering the Soviet legacy.[6] Both socialism and the Union were endangered.

Beyond the realm of party and bureaucratic politics, conservative sentiment found expression by 1987–88 in numerous "unofficial" organizations as well as in those newspapers and literary journals with sympathetic editors. In both the Soviet and Russian Writers Unions, conservative literary figures openly blasted the new policies, especially in the cultural arena, for permitting western mass culture to poison Soviet life with its commercialism, violence, pornography, and rock music. It was nothing less, wrote military novelist Alexander Prokhanov, than a "campaign of annihilation" against Soviet society and culture.

Soviet conservatism embraced a wide range of ideological positions. Some spoke from a Marxist-Leninist viewpoint and sought to uphold the traditions of the Bolshevik revolution. In a famous 1988 essay that became a conservative manifesto, Leningrad chemistry teacher Nina Andreyeva lamented the "ideological confusion" of many young people, deplored the "constant harping" on the negative aspects of Soviet life, defended a Stalinist era that "brought our country into the ranks of the great world powers," and broadly hinted that Jews, class enemies, and other "cosmopolitans" were responsible for the country's present distress. But also part of the conservative awakening were some who detested Marx, Lenin, and the revolution, finding in them the source of Russia's twentieth-century tragedies. But such conservative Russian nationalists shared with the "neo-Stalinists" a deep hostility toward the West, a commitment to the continued unity of the Soviet state, and a patriotism that saw a "separate path" for Russia as the core of a great empire. Given the threat posed by perestroika, it was enough to cement this strange conservative alliance of communists and nationalists.

In dealing with this emerging opposition, Gorbachev was haunted by the memory of Khrushchev, who had so offended his conservative elite that they unceremoniously ousted him from power. The lesson Gorbachev drew was that of centrism: stay in the middle of the political spectrum, balance the democrats and the conservatives, avoid a frontal challenge, and thus survive to move forward slowly. To his critics on the left, it was an unprincipled zigzag strategy of indecision and compromise. But Gorbachev, acutely aware of his own tentative position amid the entrenched power of an enormous party-state bureaucracy, saw it differently: "My caution stemmed from my desire to avoid open mutiny, which could have defeated political reform even before it got started."[7]

And for five years (1985–90), while perestroika bit ever more deeply into Soviet life, Gorbachev did prevent open rebellion and carried a largely conservative Communist Party with him, even as he was asking an entrenched elite to forgo its privileges and its power. It was a remarkable political feat. To achieve it, Gorbachev persuaded, charmed, and cajoled the conservatives, affirming his socialist commitment while stretching the meaning of socialism and invoking Lenin's support of NEP. He co-opted some of their issues, such as the anti-alcohol campaign and the restoration of the Orthodox Church, and appointed prominent nationalists and conservatives to prestigious positions. And he played on the deference traditionally granted to the general secretary of the party with threats to resign if his reforms were not supported. The most impressive evidence of Gorbachev's ability to deal with the conservatives lay in his persuading the party in early 1990 to accept the repeal of Article Six, thus ending seven decades of political monopoly and requiring it to function as an ordinary parliamentary party in a competitive environment.

But by the summer of 1990, with the economic crisis growing worse by the day, with a number of republics in virtual revolt against the center, and with Gorbachev apparently supporting a dramatic move toward a capitalist economy, conservatives mobilized for a major new offensive. Their most prominent spokesmen now were military politicians such as Colonel Viktor Alksnis, a brash deputy representing Soviet military forces in Latvia. Disgusted with Soviet weakness and overtly hostile to the West, Alksnis had helped to organize Soyuz (Unity), the assertive and conservative faction of deputies in the Soviet parliament, and he used that forum effectively to articulate his provocative and semifascist message. With an open disdain for democracy, conservatives of various stripes called for dictatorship, for presidential rule, for a state of emergency, for some decisive action to preserve the Union and resolve the country's crisis. Throughout the fall and winter of 1990–91, they hammered Gorbachev relentlessly in the Soviet parliament, in the newly formed and reactionary Russian Communist Party, and in a series of meetings with defense-industry managers and military officers. One such gathering in November found Gorbachev facing some eleven hundred officers who poured out a stream of bitterness and disappointment: they were humiliated by the Soviet withdrawal from Eastern Europe; they had been abused in many non-Russian republics; draft dodging and desertion were rampant; the honor of the military had been trampled. Within the Communist Party Politburo as well, hard-line conservatives demanded action: restore law and order; halt economic reform; curb nationalist movements; get control of a slanderous media; dismiss liberal advisers. Mysterious military maneuvers suggested preparation for a coup d'état, while the press speculated openly about that possibility. Whether stated or implied, an ultimatum had been thrown down before Gorbachev: Align with the conservatives, or suffer the fate of Khrushchev.

This was the context for Gorbachev's "turn to the Right" in the fall of 1990. The clearest expression of this new political posture lay in his backing away from the 500 Day Program. But there was more. Gorbachev got approval for increased executive powers, distanced himself from his more liberal advisers, and appointed or promoted to high positions a number of highly conservative figures, some of whom were later involved in the August 1991 coup. He cracked down on the independence of Soviet television, granted new powers to the KGB to combat economic sabotage, and authorized the army to take part in foot patrols in major cities. And he endorsed a draft of the Union Treaty that met few of the republics' demands and infuriated them in the process. "The most essential thing now," he declared, "is to restore order to the country."[8]

To democrats, the most ominous sign of this new political alignment came in January 1991, when Soviet security forces took violent and unprovoked action against separatists in both Lithuania and Latvia, killing nineteen people and wounding almost six hundred. It was a brazen attempt to remove elected, independence-minded Baltic governments and to begin a rolling crackdown on democratic and nationalist forces in the country at large. The extent of Gorbachev's prior knowledge and approval of these actions remains unclear, but the display of naked force reflected the new insistence on order that characterized his alignment with the conservatives. Sharp western criticism, large-scale protests by democrats, and his own aversion to bloodshed persuaded Gorbachev to halt military operations, but he did not condemn them publicly. He was still trying to hold the center and maintain the fragile balance of political power in the country.

But Gorbachev's turn to the Right, even if it was a temporary and tactical maneuver, polarized Soviet political life even further. It encouraged the hard-line conservatives to act more aggressively. And it prompted strong democratic protests. In the aftermath of the Lithuanian military action, Yeltsin came out firmly in favor of the Baltic states, even urging Russian troops there to refuse orders to fire on civilians and calling openly now for Gorbachev's resignation. The whole episode further eroded Gorbachev's political standing, for it earned him the profound distrust of democrats, while never really gaining the confidence of conservatives. Yet Gorbachev's actions may also have "tranquilized the hardliners" and delayed their attempt to seize power for almost a year. By the time they finally acted in August 1991, the democrats had strengthened their position and were able to face down the coup.[9] Had conservatives moved against Gorbachev and the democrats in the fall of 1990, the outcome might well have been quite different.

The spring and summer of 1991 witnessed new twists in the fluctuating and now white-hot political contest between the democrats and the conservatives. Mobilized by Gorbachev's apparent betrayal, democrats staged mass demonstrations in many cities and were joined in their anticommunist demands by a renewal of the coal miners' strike, which idled a third of the country's mines and threatened the country with economic ruin. A further indication of popular support for the democrats came in Boris Yeltsin's sweeping victory in the June 1991 Russian presidential election, in which he won 57 percent of the vote in a field of five candidates.

In this context, Gorbachev returned to his role as reformer and again lined up more closely with Yeltsin and the democrats. Most important, he finally agreed to a Union Treaty that decisively reduced the role of the center in favor of the republics and permitted six recalcitrant republics to opt out of the new arrangement altogether. He scheduled its signing for August 20. In addition, he signaled a renewed interest in serious economic reform, pushing the Communist Party to abandon Marxism and adopt a social democratic platform.

But if the democrats had a highly popular leader in Yeltsin, support from the West, and now a measure of agreement with Gorbachev, conservatives largely controlled the state apparatus, the military, and the KGB, and held a sizable presence in the Soviet parliament—all of which they used vigorously in the spring and summer of 1991. They continued to press Gorbachev to declare emergency rule and constantly fed him damning information about "radical democrats." The head of the KGB said publicly that perestroika was a blueprint for the country's destruction and opined that "we have had about as much democracy as we can stomach."[10] In June, Gorbachev's own quite conservative prime minister, Valentin Pavlov, sought parliamentary authorization to assume many of Gorbachev's powers, and without Gorbachev's knowledge. And military leaders deliberately undercut their president's efforts to achieve agreements with the West.

The tenor of conservative thinking in the summer of 1991 was reflected in "An Open Letter to the People," an impassioned, apocalyptic statement published on July 23 and signed by a dozen leading conservatives, including three who subsequently played active roles in the coup (see Voices, "Inviting a Coup"). Invoking the values of statehood and patriotism rather than Marxism-Leninism, it gave voice to a conservative awakening, long in the making, representing those whose principles, privileges, and power had been devastated by perestroika. It virtually invited the violent overthrow of the Gorbachev regime together with the suppression of the nationalist and democratic movements. Less than a month later, the conservatives struck.

Three Days in August

Gorbachev was winding up his summer vacation at the presidential retreat at Foros on the Crimean coast of the Black Sea. Late in the afternoon of August 18, he was confronted by an uninvited delegation of ranking party, military, and KGB officials representing the just-formed State Emergency Committee in Moscow. They demanded that

Voices

Inviting a Coup: "An Open Letter to the People"

Dear residents of the Russian Republic! Citizens of the USSR! Compatriots!

An enormous, unprecedented misfortune has befallen us. Our homeland and country, a great state that was given into our care by history, nature and our glorious ancestors is perishing, breaking up, and being plunged into darkness and nonexistence. . . .

What has happened to us, brothers? Why is it that sly and pompous rulers, intelligent and clever apostates, greedy and rich money-grubbers, mocking us, scoffing at our beliefs and taking advantage of our naivete, have seized power and are pilfering our wealth, taking homes, factories and land away from the people, carving up the country into separate parts . . . excommunicating us from the past and debarring us from the future—dooming us to pitiful vegetation in slavery and subordination to our all-powerful neighbors . . . ?

We turn our voice to the Army, which won mankind's respect for its selfless feat of saving Europe from the Hitlerite plague. . . . We are convinced that the fighting men of the Army and Navy . . . will act as a reliable guarantor of security and a mainstay of all the healthy forces of society. . . .

The Soviet Union is our home and our bulwark, built through the great efforts of all peoples and nations, which saved us from disgrace and from slavery in the times of black invasions. Russia—our only beloved—is calling for help.

From "An Open Letter to the People,"
Sovetskaya Rossia, July 23, 1991.
Published in English in the *Current Digest of the Soviet Press*
43:30 (1991), pp. 8–10.

Gorbachev sign documents legalizing a state of emergency and turn over his powers to Vice President Gennady Yanaev, a member of the Emergency Committee. He refused to do so, and for the next three days the Soviet president, together with his family and a few aides, was confined to Foros in complete isolation from the country he supposedly governed.

Here was the beginning of what democrats had long dreaded and conservatives had hoped for—a concerted effort to turn back the clock on radical reform, to return to the ordered society of the Brezhnev era or to the controlled and disciplined reform of Andropov. Under the leadership of KGB chairman Vladimir Kryuchkov, contingency planning for a coup had begun in November 1990, as the resurgence of conservative political influence took hold. Even then, however, leading conservatives had hoped to influence or intimidate Gorbachev into siding decisively with them and thus avoid an illegal seizure of power. But by midsummer that possibility was rapidly fading. Final agreement between Gorbachev and the major republics had produced a Union Treaty that conservatives saw as a catastrophe—nothing less than the end of the Soviet Union. Furthermore, taped conversations involving Gorbachev, Yeltsin, and Nursultan Nazarbaev of Kazakstan had alerted top-ranking government officials that they would be replaced soon after the Union Treaty was signed. The president's own discussions had been illicitly recorded. And Yeltsin had just banned Communist Party cells from workplaces on Russian territory, where they had long formed the basis of the entire party organization.

Thus, in early August operational planning for a coup began in earnest. The core conspirators, most of whom had been appointed to high office by Gorbachev personally, represented a cross section of the Soviet elite. In addition to Kryuchkov, they included the Soviet Union's vice president (Yanaev), prime minister (Pavlov), minister of defense (Dmitry Yazov), minister of interior (Pugo), Gorbachev's chief of staff (Boldin), and several top party officials. Representatives of the military-industrial complex, collective-farm administration, and armed forces, as well as the head of the USSR Supreme Soviet, also played important roles.

Despite much open speculation in the press and repeated warnings from many sources, the actual coup, announced in the early morning of August 19, came as a surprise. Timed to prevent the signing of the Union Treaty, the State Emergency Committee announced that Vice President Yanaev was assuming the powers of an ill Gorbachev, that a six-month state of emergency was in effect, that political parties, strikes, and demonstrations were banned, and that all governing bodies were subordinated to the committee. Astonished Muscovites awoke to find tanks and armored personnel carriers taking up positions throughout the central city. Liberal newspapers were shut down, and tight censorship was imposed on the Soviet press, radio, and TV. An arrest list of leading democratic political figures, former dissident intellectuals, private businessmen, and disaffected party and KGB officials indicated that a widespread crackdown was planned. So too did the preparation of several thousand arrest warrants and orders for 250,000 pairs of handcuffs.

With no mention of Lenin, Marx, or socialism, the committee justified its actions in terms of popular grievances: combating corruption and a sharp drop in living standards; fighting a rising tide of crime; restoring order; and preserving the Union. And they tried hard to present the new regime as operating within the framework of Soviet legality, apparently intending to gain approval from the Soviet parliament. Nonetheless, the coup was a serious effort to reimpose a highly authoritarian and repressive order on the Soviet Union.

Why then did it collapse within three days? In the first place, the conspirators, graying apparatchiks of the old order, were hardly an inspiring lot. Yanaev, the front man of the coup, was a known drunk and womanizer of limited capacity who had only reluctantly joined the conspiracy at the last minute. The image of his trembling hands at a televised press conference on the first day conveyed to many that these were not men to be feared. Nor was the planning for the coup very effective. Of those targeted for arrest—most notably Yeltsin—few were actually seized. Telephone links to his headquarters remained intact. Foreign journalists and TV services continued to report; their coverage of popular opposition to the coup was fed back into the country through BBC, Voice of America, and other western broadcasts, thus negating the Committee's censorship measures.

Furthermore, the legitimacy of the coup leaders was challenged at every point. Gorbachev's refusal to cooperate removed the cover of constitutional authority. Western governments soon condemned the coup as illegal, thus denying its perpetrators the international acceptance they sought. But of far greater importance was the emergence of Boris Yeltsin as a charismatic symbol of democratic resistance to the coup. Narrowly missing arrest, Yeltsin set up his headquarters in the White House, a building in central Moscow where the Russian parliament convened. There he unequivocally denounced the coup as reactionary and unconstitutional and posed his own authority, based on a democratic election, against that of men who sought to build a "throne from bayonets." Dramatically climbing on a tank outside the White

House, he proclaimed all decrees of the Emergency Committee illegal, demanded the return of the country's legal president, and asked for massive civil disobedience. His vice president, Alexander Rutskoi, a hero of the Afghanistan war, called on "my brother officers, soldiers, and sailors, not to act against your own people."

These appeals soon elicited a substantial and growing response. Well-known public figures flocked to the White House to lend their support: Eduard Shevardnadze, Gorbachev's foreign minister, who had resigned in December 1990 to protest a "coming dictatorship"; famed émigré cellist Mstislav Rostropovich; Sakharov's fiery widow, Elena Bonner; poet Yevgeny Yevtushenko. After some prodding, the patriarch of the Russian Orthodox Church issued a supporting statement. Even more impressive were the ordinary people, perhaps fifty thousand to seventy thousand at any one time, who came to defend the White House: students, a number of women, businessmen, priests, a small group of Afghan veterans, workers from offices and scientific or technical institutes, "detectives" from several private security firms. They built barricades, tracked the movement of troops, confronted soldiers and tanks, traded rumors, and waited for what they expected would be a deadly assault. Censored journalists published underground news sheets and posted them throughout the city, while courageous printers at *Izvestia* forced the publication of Yeltsin's decrees.

Among some seven million Muscovites, the number of democracy's active defenders was perhaps not overwhelming, but they showed that Soviet society had changed in ways that the coup leaders had not really understood. A segment of that society had acquired interests and values that persuaded them to stand firmly and with great courage against a return to the old order (see Voices, "On the Barricades"). To that extent, perestroika had succeeded.

Nor was resistance limited to the capital. In Leningrad—recently renamed St. Petersburg—well over a hundred thousand people gathered in the central city to show their defiance of the coup. While most local government and party authorities either supported the Emergency Committee or adopted a "wait and see" attitude, public demonstrations and workers' strikes took place in a number of cities, and some journalists found ways to print Yeltsin's declarations or broadcast news from Moscow. And, after some initial hesitation, the leaders of major republics such as Ukraine and Kazakstan came out against the coup. Polls subsequently showed that substantial numbers of people in fact

Voices

On the Barricades

What precisely motivated those who risked their careers and lives to defend the Russian White House? Here are statements from two participants, the first a fifty-five-year-old woman and the second a twenty-five-year-old man, reflecting different impulses and different generations.

I am ready to die, right on this spot. I will not move. I am 55 years old and for years nothing but obedience and inertia was pounded into my brain. The Young Pioneers, the Young Communist League, the unions, the Communist Party, all of them taught me not to answer back. To be a good Soviet, a bolt in the machine.

But Monday morning my friend called and said, "Turn on the radio." I didn't need to. I heard a rumbling and went out on my balcony and saw the tanks. . . . These monsters! They have always thought they could do anything to us! They have thrown out Gorbachev and now they are threatening a government I helped to elect. I will ignore the curfew. I'll let a tank roll over me if I have to. I'll die right here if I have to.

From the *Washington Post*, August 21, 1991, p. A1.

For us the putsch was not a matter of simple politics. Usually we hate politics, to tell you the truth. But this was the Pepsi generation under threat. Our very existence was in jeopardy. The bikers feared for their motorcycles. The young businessmen worried about their markets. The racketeers even thought about their bottom line and came to defend the White House. Prostitutes, students, scholars, everybody had an interest in this new life, and we were just not willing to give it all up to these old men. And also, it was like being in a great movie. Life and art were all mixed up together. My friends who were abroad were heartbroken . . . because they felt left out. They couldn't be in the movie.

From David Remnick, *Lenin's Tomb*
(New York: Random House, 1993), p. 479.

supported the committee, weary beyond measure of the upheavals and insecurity in their lives. But these people did not come out on the streets. Democrats did.

This spreading resistance raised dramatically the price in bloodshed the coup leaders would have had to pay to enforce their rule, and it bought time for that lesson to penetrate the various security forces who would be called upon to put down the resistance. Soon divisions and defections appeared within those forces. St. Petersburg's democratic mayor, Anatoly Sobchak, persuaded the local military commander to disobey orders from Moscow to move troops into his city. Small groups of tank teams and paratroopers in Moscow switched sides to support the White House. The commander of the Soviet air force threatened to shoot down helicopters assaulting the White House and even to launch air raids on the Kremlin. The uncertain loyalty of particular units caused hesitation, and officers found reasons to delay or even to refuse orders. The weather, too, seemed to favor the democrats, as a rainstorm in the early hours of August 21 prevented an airborne assault. The net result was that no sustained attack on the White House took place, and Yeltsin remained a figure of defiant opposition as the coup entered its third day.

By that point, the Emergency Committee was ready to retreat, its members divided and dispirited. Several were stone drunk and another had suffered a nervous collapse. Unlike the Chinese leadership during the Tiananmen Square protests in 1989, those centrally involved in the Soviet coup were either unable or unwilling to move beyond intimidation to violent repression and large-scale bloodshed. The horrible excesses of Stalinism, now fully exposed by glasnost, together with the affirmation of human rights, democracy, and "freedom to choose" during the Gorbachev era, had rendered violence and bloodshed so illegitimate that even the coup leaders shrank from using it. They too, it seems, had been influenced by perestroika.

With the end in sight, a small delegation of the plotters rushed to Foros to seek some accommodation with Gorbachev—who refused to see them. A team of Yeltsin's people likewise flew to Foros, and Gorbachev returned with them to Moscow and to what everyone recognized was a different country. The Emergency Committee, and others affiliated with it, were arrested, though several committed suicide. The coup was over.

Russian citizens erect a barricade near the White House in Moscow, August 1991. From Victoria E. Bonnell, Ann Cooper, and Gregory Freidin, eds., *Russia at the Barricades: Eyewitness Accounts of the August 1991 Coup* (Armonk, N.Y.: M.E. Sharpe, 1994), p. 73. Photograph by Gregory Freidin.

Coming Apart: The Final Days of the Soviet Union

Particular events sometimes markedly accelerate the pace of historical change. Such was the case with the August coup, which dramatically changed the balance of political forces in the Soviet Union and led, within four months, to the country's disintegration. Most obviously, the conservative awakening, resurgent since the fall of 1990, was now thoroughly discredited. Many of its leaders were in jail. Documents about Communist Party misuse of its funds came to light, suggesting to many that the party had long been a criminal rather than a political organization. Decrees from Yeltsin and Gorbachev legally banned the party, seized its property, and froze its assets. A committed reformer took over the KGB and substantially reorganized it; the military high command was purged. Triumphant democrats roamed Moscow toppling statues of Lenin, and the museum dedicated to the Soviet founder was closed, "pending reconstruction." At least temporarily, the political defeat of Soviet conservatism seemed complete and much of the Soviet legacy lay in shambles.

Gorbachev's political standing also suffered badly. He had, after all, appointed the "team of traitors" who led the coup. And upon his return to Moscow, he continued to talk, albeit briefly, about socialism and the renewal of the party, showing himself unaware of how sharply the political climate had changed. At a gathering of the Russian parliament, Yeltsin took his revenge on his longtime rival, forcing Gorbachev to read aloud the names of his own ministers who had betrayed him. It was a humiliating encounter. Gorbachev had been unable to change as rapidly as the country he led, and his strategy of balancing the democrats and conservatives, so effective at the beginning of his rule, had backfired at the end.

The chief beneficiaries of the coup, of course, were Boris Yeltsin and the democratic forces of the Russian Republic. Not only was Yeltsin the freely elected president of the huge republic, but now he was also the man who had bravely faced down the coup leaders, rallied the country, defended democracy and the gains of perestroika, and rescued Gorbachev in the process. With enormous personal popularity, he now proceeded to define the new Russia. At the broadest level, he declared that Russia "wants to proceed along a civilized path traversed by France, England, the United States, Japan, Germany, Spain and other countries."[11] Thus, Yeltsin aligned Russia with the West and explicitly disclaimed any unique and special role for the country. In doing so he broke with centuries of Russian and Soviet tradition. More concretely, and after some initial hesitation and infighting among his advisers, Yeltsin announced in October 1991 a program of radical economic reform aimed at creating a market economy, along the lines of the ill-fated 500 Day Program. And he appointed a young free-market economist, Yegor Gaidar, to implement it.

But the circle of Yeltsin advisers who drew up this program—his so-called Young Turks—also argued that Russia should proceed largely on its own. A "center" of almost any kind, they believed, would block or retard radical reform in Russia and would redistribute Russian resources to the poorer republics. Acting on this "Russia first" position, Yeltsin appropriated for Russia much of the economic base and many of the powers of the Soviet Union. He nationalized all energy resources—oil, gas, coal, hydroelectric, and nuclear power facilities—on Russian soil; he ceased all financial contributions to the center, except those Russia had explicitly agreed to; he took over the USSR Finance Ministry, the mint, major Soviet banks, and the prestigious Academy of Sciences, asserting Russia's right to control important Soviet cultural institutions. By November the USSR could not meet its payroll, and Russia took responsibility for that as well.

Finally, the August coup considerably heightened the nationalism of the non-Russian republics and made them even more skeptical about the value of any Union. After all, the Emergency Committee had attempted to reimpose strong control from Moscow and to revoke some of the new independence the republics had already gained. They wondered if it might happen again. More immediately, Yeltsin's insistent takeover of Soviet powers reinforced fears of Russian domination and stimulated a desire among many people for complete independence, despite obvious economic connections to their giant neighbor. Moreover, Russia's radical economic program threatened the more conservative leadership of the other republics. The Baltic republics, always a special case, received immediate recognition of their declarations of independence. Most of the other republics now upgraded their assertions of sovereignty to outright independence, though most remained willing to at least consider some form of loose association with one another and with Russia.

Discredited conservatives, a damaged Gorbachev, a triumphant Yeltsin, and invigorated nationalists—these were the immediate outcomes of the coup, and together they created a political environment clearly inhospitable to the survival of a unified Soviet state. Nonetheless, that is what Gorbachev attempted to retrieve from the fallout of the August coup. Invoking centuries of history, linked economies, and polls showing public support for union, Gorbachev relaunched the Union Treaty negotiations. Initially his efforts seemed to bear fruit. In October the leaders of ten republics signed a Treaty on an Economic Community of Sovereign States, intended to promote economic cooperation. It was vague and incomplete; still, they had agreed on something.

But parallel political discussions about a Union state were even more problematic. Everyone now agreed that any new Union would be a "confederation," in which the central state would be clearly subordinate to the collective will of its member republics. This obviously implied a dominant position for Russia, and Yeltsin was quick to demonstrate what that might mean. Russia wanted all nuclear weapons from the Soviet arsenal returned to Russian soil; republics not in the new Union would have to pay world market prices for the gas and oil they imported from Russia; Russia intended to defend the interests of Russians who lived as minorities in other republics; even borders between Russia and other republics might have to be reviewed. All of this antagonized the non-Russian republics and heightened their reluctance to take part in such a Union. Some even spoke of the possibility of war among the republics.

And then there was the old question about what kind of Union was possible. Would it be, as Gorbachev hoped, a "new state"—no matter how circumscribed in its powers—with its own president and legislature, sending and receiving ambassadors, and participating as a single unit in the international community? Or, as Yeltsin and some others seemed to desire, would it be a mere "association" of sovereign states, each of which acted independently in the international arena, with only the loosest of ties among them?

As late as mid-November, agreement on a much reduced "confederative state, " now named the Union of Sovereign States, seemed possible. But then all of the accumulated ambiguities, suspicions, and reservations surfaced and that agreement unraveled. On November 25, Yeltsin, supported by the presidents of several other republics, postponed initialing a Union Treaty, citing reservations in their parliaments. And then, in a December 1 referendum, in what was perhaps the final nail in the Union's coffin, Ukrainian voters opted massively for complete independence. Thereafter the Ukrainian leadership would endorse no Union whatever. It seemed clear that the Union Treaty negotiations had reached a dead end.

At that point, or perhaps even earlier, Yeltsin and the presidents of Ukraine and Belarus decided to act independently and without Gorbachev's involvement to resolve a tense and dangerous situation. Rumors of yet another coup, this time by Soviet military and police authorities, may have stimulated them to move quickly. Meeting in a hunting lodge in Belarus on December 7–8, the three presidents and their staffs cobbled together, virtually overnight, an agreement terminating the existence of the USSR and forming in its place a wholly voluntary Commonwealth of Independent States (CIS). With no executive authority, no legislature, no permanent coordinating bodies, no power to tax, and no mechanism to enforce agreements, the Commonwealth clearly was not a state in its own right. It did maintain temporarily a unified military command, commit its members to respect existing borders, and recognized international standards of human rights. For the rest, it was little more than a call for "cooperation," a framework for negotiation on a wide range of policy issues, and periodic meetings of top government leaders.

Gorbachev was furious, and he even made overtures to the military for support. Without a debate in the Soviet parliament or a countrywide referendum, it was in his view another illegal coup. How could three political leaders, acting on their own, in the space of a few days, and with no public discussion, dissolve a huge multinational state of centuries standing? On the contrary, the CIS founders replied, it was a considered act taken by constitutionally chosen presidents of the three states that had created the original Union in 1922. What those states had created, they could also dissolve. And the agreement creating the CIS was subsequently ratified by their parliaments. In short, it was both a legally sound and a politically necessary action undertaken to save what could be saved from the wreckage of the Soviet Union. Boiling nationalisms and competing interests compelled some resolution without further delay and would permit a no more elaborate Union.

Despite Gorbachev's dire warnings of ethnic conflict, economic chaos, and even civil war, by December 21 eleven republics—all except the Baltic states and Georgia—had signed on to the Commonwealth. Four days later, on December 25, 1991, Gorbachev formally resigned, transferring his control of Soviet military forces and the "nuclear briefcase" to Yeltsin. That evening, with both pride and sadness, Gorbachev addressed his now vanishing country for the final time, as the Russian tricolor replaced the hammer and sickle high above the Kremlin. The Soviet Union had passed into history.

Questions and Controversies: *Why a Peaceful Death?*

Among the most remarkable features of the Soviet collapse was the relative absence of bloodshed with which it occurred. There was, of course, widespread violence between Armenians and Azeris and sporadic interethnic clashes in Central Asia. And Soviet security forces saw action in several places, most notably Lithuania, Georgia, and Azerbaijan. Still, the disintegration of a huge multiethnic empire and the demise of an entrenched communist system occasioned far less violence and bloodshed than might have been expected: no bloody wars of liberation such as those in Algeria, Zimbabwe, Kenya, or Vietnam during their decolonization; no civil war of the kind that accompanied secessionist movements in the United States or more recently in Ethiopia, Nigeria, Sudan, or Sri Lanka; no revolutionary violence against the old order such as that which accompanied the fall of communism in Romania; and, except for the Armenian-Azeri conflict, no ethnic cleansing or massive, uncontrolled, and violent movement of population like that which occurred at the breakup of British India and at the disintegration of Yugoslavia. The August coup notwithstanding, the defenders of the established system, including an entrenched party elite, a fearsome KGB, and the military forces of a global superpower, put up an amazingly modest resistance against those who sought to end their power and their privileges.

A beginning point in explaining this peaceful death lies perhaps in the declining "self-legitimacy" of the Soviet elite. Over the several decades preceding Gorbachev's accession to power, a harsh Stalinist order had become a "corrupt and sloppy bureaucracy, full of cynicism and self-seeking," in which real commitment to Marxism-Leninism was increasingly rare.[12] Influenced by the relative security of their own positions, more communication with the West, the moderating of the Cold War, and the growing discrepancy between ideology and reality, many among the Soviet elite simply ceased to believe. The revelations of the Gorbachev era only diminished that belief further. Until virtually the end, defenders of the old order had the means to halt the reform process, for the structures of the party, the KGB, the internal security forces, and the military remained in place. What they lacked was the will to use them decisively.

Perhaps the need to use them was diminishing as well, for opportunities as well as threats beckoned in the new order. Not a few communist officials rapidly became nationalists and emerged as leaders of the new independent states. Those states needed skilled managers, and the party-state apparatus was virtually the only place to find them. Directors of state enterprises frequently became owners of those valuable assets as a largely uncontrolled and corrupt process of privatization began. For many in the Soviet elite, a change in the social system did not mean a loss of social position.

Gorbachev, too, deserves considerable credit for his country's peaceful demise. His unwillingness to countenance large-scale violence, his desire to humanize and democratize Soviet socialism and make it consonant with western values, his "freedom to choose" rhetoric, and the success of glasnost in discrediting the brutalities of Soviet history—all served to delegitimize the use of force as the basis for political order. It set a new standard for Soviet political behavior, which apparently affected even the leaders of the August coup, who ultimately chose not to resort to violence. Furthermore, the origin of the reform process at the very top of the political system, and with the immense authority of the general secretary himself, minimized opposition. So too did Gorbachev's much criticized zigzag strategy, which long kept conservatives off balance.

Finally, the surge of isolationist sentiment within Russia, particularly among the triumphant democrats, certainly eased the way to a peaceful divorce. By no means wholly altruistic, this anti-imperial viewpoint reflected the uniqueness of the Soviet empire, in which many of the dominant Russians had come to feel the empire was a burden and a drain that they sought to discard to their own advantage.[13] Furthermore, neither Russia nor any of the other new national states made any consistent effort to redraw boundaries or to gather all members of their nationality into a single state. Yeltsin's redefinition of Russia as a national state rather than the core of an imperial state helped the Soviet Union to avoid the fate of Yugoslavia, where Serbian irredentism triggered a downward spiral of bitter conflict.[14] In sharp contrast to its birth and to much of its life, the Soviet Union died a peaceful death.

Questions and Controversies: *Meaning and History*

How does the Soviet denouement of 1991 appear in the longer view of historical analysis? How can we assess the significance of those events in the context of Russian, Soviet, and even world history? Those who answer with appropriate modesty that "it is too soon to tell" do not merely mean that new archives must be explored, more memoirs written, and further interviews undertaken. They also mean that not enough has happened *since* the Soviet collapse to allow even the best-informed scholars to answer those questions with clarity or confidence. For it is a strange truth about historical reflection that our assessment of events is shaped as much by what occurs after them as by what happened before.

None of this, however, has stopped anyone, including serious scholars, from rendering their judgments. We are driven, it seems, to find meaning in contemporary affairs by placing them in historical perspective. By way of conclusion, then, here are four such perspectives on the demise of the USSR, all of which have implications for understanding the post-Soviet years.

The first views the Soviet collapse in a world context and finds its significance in the many global changes to which that event contributed. Most important perhaps has been the apparent end of the great global rift occasioned by the rise of communism that shaped so much of twentieth-century world history. In economic terms, it has meant the return to a single world economy in which Russia and China are now active participants. In political terms, it signaled the curtailment of Cold War hostilities and military encounters, the reunification of Germany and to some extent of Europe itself, a sharp reduction in the threat of a nuclear holocaust, and a reversal of the Soviet-American arms race, thus permitting, at least potentially, the diversion of resources to more humane and productive ends. In place of the bipolar structure of international relations, a more complicated world order of many competing centers seems to be emerging, in which economic strength counts for more than sheer military power. And in ideological terms, the Soviet collapse has brought to at least temporary closure the great debate about capitalism and socialism as distinct and rival systems. Controversy continues, of course, about the relative importance of state action in managing modern economies, but virtually all of the world's major nations now operate on the assumption of a prominent role for the free market.

At least from a western or American viewpoint, much of this has been overwhelmingly positive, giving rise on occasion to a triumphalism celebrating "victory" in the Cold War and the emergence of the United States as the sole global superpower. But not all of the global outcomes of the collapse of communism have been so beneficent. In both Eastern Europe and the former Soviet Union, ethnic tensions and hostilities, long held in check by repressive regimes, have exploded in violent clashes that threaten regional stability. The civil war in the former Yugoslavia is the most evident case, but violent conflict between Georgians and Abkhazians, Russians and Chechens, as well as the fear of Uzbek hegemony in Central Asia further illustrate the trend. The end of direct Russian control over Central Asia and the Caucasus has opened those regions to renewed international rivalry, with Russia, China, the United States, Turkey, and Iran as major players and with oil and religion among the issues at stake. The Soviet collapse has also raised deeply troubling questions about control over nuclear materials and the possibility of impoverished Russian nuclear scientists selling their services to the highest bidder. And widespread concerns about the stability of the former communist states derive from the enormous difficulties attending the unprecedented transition from state-controlled socialist economies to market-driven systems. Issues of social inequality, impoverishment, corruption, and criminality make that transition highly problematic and extraordinarily painful. These problems have left many in the international community almost nostalgic for the predictability and relative simplicity of the Cold War era.

Much of the debate about the significance of the Soviet collapse, however, focuses more narrowly on its importance within Soviet or Russian history. Thus, a second perspective sees the end of the USSR as nothing less than a revolution—a decisive break in the historical process and a sharp turning point for those peoples who had constituted the Soviet Union. Here is historian Martin Malia's argument:

> In 1991 the Communist Party was destroyed and a superpower was dismembered; "socialism" was renounced by the world's first socialist society in favor of the "restoration of capitalism"; and the most enduring fantasy of the twentieth century, the pseudoreligion-cum-pseudoscience of Marxism-Leninism, simply evaporated. . . . In normal parlance, all of this qualifies as "revolution." After all, the basic components of the Soviet system—the Party, the Plan, the political police, and the Union—were not transformed: they were abolished, and in the short span of three months after August [1991].[15]

Such a view sees the Gorbachev experiment as an abject and inevitable failure that served only to provoke revolution. But this upheaval, unlike its earlier counterparts in Russia, France, or England, disclosed no new classes or institutions that could credibly replace the old regime and the society it destroyed. Seven decades of Soviet rule had so pulverized civil society that after the "implosion" of 1991 only a "societal void" or "generalized institutional rubble" remained as its legacy.[16] In the view of Malia and others, this accounts for the enormous difficulties and disappointments that have beset post-Soviet Russia's efforts to construct a "normal society": fragmented and ineffective political parties, administrative anarchy, massive inflation, continued economic decline, ethnic conflict, an explosion of criminality, rising death rates. Nothing remained on which to build; Russians had to start from scratch and do everything at once. Russia's efforts to reconstruct itself as a market economy and a political democracy, Malia predicts, will take a generation or more and will occur under conditions far more difficult than those prevailing in 1914 before Russia's modernizing process was tragically interrupted by war and Bolshevik takeover.

A third perspective on the Soviet collapse, quite different in emphasis and tone, views it as part of a longer "transition," leading away from Stalinism toward more western forms of society, economy, and politics. That transition began with the social changes of a maturing industrial society in the post-Stalin era, but it was much accelerated during the Gorbachev years. Scholars such as Alexander Dallin, Gail Lapidus, and Archie Brown have argued that Gorbachev's reforms should be judged, not so much in terms of their own goals, but rather as "a vehicle for the transition" to a noncommunist regime. By that standard the Gorbachev record is far more positive. After all, he swept away the remaining Stalinist legacy, opened up a closed society, integrated an isolated nation into the world community, moved toward a mixed economy, and substantially democratized the political system—all with a minimum of bloodshed. The Soviet system did not "implode," as Malia would have it; nor was it "defeated," as American Cold War hawks proclaimed; rather, it was deliberately "dismantled." Even Gorbachev's greatest failure, the disintegration of a unified state, allowed the relatively peaceful emergence of fifteen new states. Obviously, in the brief period since the Soviet collapse, substantial reconstruction of a new society could hardly have been completed. But the skillful and largely peaceful dismantling of the old order was no small contribution to an extended and ongoing transition.

A "transition" perspective highlights the continuities between Gorbachev's reforms and the evolution of post-Soviet states, with an emphasis perhaps on the most positive outcomes. In Russia, for example, Yeltsin extended earlier economic reforms to include free prices and massive privatization of state enterprises in a process that left the new country with the elements of a market economy within five years. Optimists hoped that the endemic corruption and criminality of that economy, as well as its pattern of declining production and surging inflation, were the temporary growth pains of a more stable capitalism in the making. On the political front, four free and largely fair elections seemed to solidify at least this element of democratic practice begun in the Gorbachev years. In fits and starts, and with no small measure of human suffering, an extended transition continues.

A final perspective on the Soviet collapse might view that event as but an episode in much longer-lasting patterns of historical development. Such a view would caution us against seeing only a decisive break with an exhausted past and against an overly optimistic expectation of transition to a western-style society. Understanding the end of the Soviet Union as an episode reminds us that beneath the surface of dramatic change there often lie substantial continuities with the more distant past.

Elements of Soviet and Russian history, after all, seemed to survive in the new Russia. The Communist Party, banned in 1991, reemerged in subsequent years to win a substantial bloc of seats in the Russian parliament in December 1995 and to capture some 40 percent of the vote in the presidential election of July 1996. Furthermore, the primary beneficiaries of the privatization process that turned state-owned enterprises into private property were none other than the managers and directors of those very enterprises. And according Gavriil Popov, former mayor of Moscow, democratic activists did not control state power in Russia after the August coup and the Soviet collapse. Rather, elements of the old nomenklatura assumed power and rapidly learned to operate without the protective cover of the Communist Party.[17] In short, parts of the Soviet elite have survived, and often prospered, in the new Russia.

Nor were popular attitudes readily changed. Deeply rooted habits of dependence on the state, an aversion to the growing inequalities of Russian society, continuing ambiguity about western culture, and a distaste for political compromise remained entrenched in the minds of many. Considerable nostalgia for empire and stability found expression in the political rise of the semifascist Vladimir Zhirinovsky and in the revival of the Communist Party as the major opposition to the Yeltsin regime. So too did a widespread hankering for strong, even authoritarian, government in the midst of what often seemed like chaos. Democracy, in fact, became a pejorative term for many people, whose savings were wiped out, whose jobs were rendered obsolete, and whose standard of living dropped sharply. An experiment staged by a Russian newspaper in 1996 found "many more contributors" to a fund for a monument to Stalin than to one for his victims.[18] And, after a brief period of pro-western euphoria, Russian foreign policy adopted a more imperial posture: an assertive military and political presence in the "near abroad" of former Soviet republics, discussions about union with Belarus, and a challenge to the West on matters ranging from Serbia to NATO expansion. None of this suggests a revival of the Soviet Union, but it does remind us that centuries of Russian and Soviet imperial history will not be quickly swept away.

A witticism of the late Soviet period held that nothing was less predictable in the USSR than its past, referring of course to the many alterations in official history that accompanied changes in Soviet politics. Despite the transformations of recent years, that unpredictability of the Soviet past persists. In our continuing consideration of the Soviet Union's demise and all that led to it, we shall be guided not only by the evidence available to us but also by questions and perspectives deriving from our present circumstances. In short, the future will play a major role in shaping the various meanings ascribed to the Soviet experience and to its passage into history.

Notes

1. Rachel Walker, *Six Years That Shook the World* (Manchester: Manchester University Press, 1993), p. 180.

2. Mikhail Gorbachev, *Memoirs* (New York: Doubleday, 1995), p. 316.

3. Archie Brown, *The Gorbachev Factor* (New York: Oxford University Press, 1996), p. 196.

4. John Miller, *Mikhail Gorbachev and the End of Soviet Power* (New York: St. Martin's Press, 1993), p. 163.

5. Gorbachev, *Memoirs,* p. 230.

6. Yegor Ligachev, *Inside Gorbachev's Kremlin* (Boulder: Westview Press, 1996).

7. Gorbachev, *Memoirs,* p. 279.

8. Hedrick Smith, *The New Russians* (New York: Avon Books, 1991), p. 603.

9. Brown, *The Gorbachev Factor,* p. 271.

10. David Remnick, *Lenin's Tomb* (New York: Random House, 1993), p. 398.

11. *USSR Today,* September 8, 1991. Cited in John B. Dunlop, *The Rise of Russia and the Fall of the Soviet Empire* (Princeton: Princeton University Press, 1993), p. 282.

12. Vladislav Zubok, "The Collapse of the Soviet Union: Leadership, Elites, and Legitimacy," in *The Fall of Great Powers,* ed. Geir Lundestad (New York: Oxford University Press, 1994), pp. 157–74.

13. Victor Zaslavsky, "The Soviet Union," in *After Empire,* eds. Karen Barkey and Mark Von Hagen (Boulder: Westview Press, 1997), pp. 90–91.

14. Jack F. Matlock, Jr., *Autopsy on an Empire* (New York: Random House, 1995), p. 675.

15. Martin Malia, *The Soviet Tragedy* (New York: Free Press, 1994), p. 497. See pp. 496–513 for the argument summarized in the following paragraph.

16. James R. Millar and Sharon L. Wolchik, eds., *The Social Legacy of Communism* (Washington, D.C.: Woodrow Wilson Center Press, 1994), pp. 381–83.

17. Gavriil Popov, "August, 1991," *Izvestia,* August 21–26, 1992, in *Current Digest of the Soviet Press* 44:34 (1992), pp. 1–6.

18. *New York Times,* March 3, 1996, p. 10.

Suggestions for Further Study

The decline and demise of the Soviet Union have generated an enormous literature of analysis and commentary from participants, from journalists, and from scholars of all kinds. Here is but a tiny sample of that rich body of material.

Soviet history textbooks are a good place to find a broad context for the collapse of the USSR. Four of the best are Ronald G. Suny, *The Soviet Experiment* (Oxford University Press, 1998); John M. Thompson, *A Vision Unfulfilled* (Heath, 1996); Geoffrey Hosking, *The First Socialist Society* (Harvard University Press, 1993); and Michael Kort, *The Soviet Colossus* (M.E. Sharpe, 1996). Martin Malia's *The Soviet Tragedy* (Free Press, 1994) is also a full treatment of Soviet history, arguing that the Soviet collapse was "only a question of time," given its utopian socialist ideology. And Robert V. Daniels, *The End of the Communist Revolution* (Routledge, 1993), begins with the collapse and tells the story backward.

Journalists' accounts by western reporters stationed in Moscow are usually well written, engaging, rich in stories and telling detail, though short on analysis. Hedrick Smith's *The Russians* (Quadrangle/The New York Times Book Co.,1976) is a classic description of Soviet society in the Brezhnev era; Smith's *The New Russians* (Avon Books, 1991) recounts the Gorbachev era with vivid illustrations. So, too, does David Remnick in *Lenin's Tomb* (Random House, 1993), which focuses on the last two years of the Soviet Union and includes a fine description of the August coup. His *Resurrection* (Random House, 1997) depicts the effort to construct a "new Russia" on the ruins of the Soviet Union. Donald Murray has portrayed the development of embryonic parliamentary institutions in *A Democracy of Despots* (Westview Press, 1996), while Scott Shane, *Dismantling Utopia* (Ivan R. Dee, 1994), focuses on the role of information in the Soviet collapse.

First-person accounts by participants offer an insider's view of events, though told in an often self-serving fashion. Mikhail Gorbachev's *Memoirs* (Doubleday, 1995) offers an account of his rise to power and an extended defense of his record in office. Boris Yeltsin's *Against the Grain* (Summit Books, 1990) and *The Struggle for Russia* (Times Books, 1995) tell his side of the rivalry with Gorbachev and show the evolution of a party official into the leader of the democratic movement. Yegor Ligachev, *Inside Gorbachev's Kremlin* (Westview Press, 1996), provides insight into the thinking of the conservative opposition to Gorbachev's reforms. Georgi Arbatov, *The System: An Insider's Life in Soviet Politics* (Times Books, 1992), presents the views of the USSR's leading American expert. Stephen F. Cohen and Katrina vanden Heuvel, *Voices of Glasnost* (W.W. Norton, 1989), offer a series of interviews with major reformers of the early Gorbachev era.

Translations of articles from Soviet newspapers are available in the weekly publication *The Current Digest of the Soviet Press,* while the Foreign Broadcast Information Service provides translations of selected radio and television broadcasts. Excerpts from the Soviet press of the Gorbachev era have been collected in book form in Isaac J. Tarasulo, ed., *Gorbachev and Glasnost* (SR Books, 1989) and *Perils of Perestroika* (SR Books, 1992). Christopher Cerf and Marina Albee have collected a number of provocative letters to the editor of *Ogonyok* magazine in *Small Fires* (Summit Books, 1990).

Biographies of leading participants represent yet another source, though so far these are limited largely to Gorbachev and Yeltsin. Dusko Doder and Louise Hanson's *Gorbachev: Heretic in the Kremlin* (Viking, 1990) offers a readable account by two journalists, while Archie Brown's *The Gorbachev Factor* (Oxford University Press, 1996) is a thorough and appreciative study by a leading political scientist. John Morrison has chronicled Yeltsin's evolution in *Boris Yeltsin: From Bolshevik to Democrat* (Dutton, 1991), as has Vladimir Solosev in *Boris Yeltsin: A Political Biography* (Putnam, 1992).

The collapse of the Soviet Union has obviously attracted enormous attention from historians, political scientists, economists, sociologists, and others who have found in the USSR's final decades a laboratory for testing their own theories and approaches and for carrying on long-standing academic debates. Several collections of essays, articles, and excerpts from larger works provide a means to sample those materials. They include Alexander Dallin and Gail W. Lapidus, *The Soviet System: From Crisis to Collapse* (Westview Press, 1995); Robert V. Daniels, *Soviet Communism from Reform to Collapse* (Heath, 1995); and *The Breakup of the Soviet Union: Opposing Viewpoints* (Greenhaven Press, 1994). Also useful is the Spring 1993 issue of *The National Interest,* which presents, generally from a conservative point of view, a series of short essays under the rubric, "The Strange Death of Soviet Communism."

Political scientists have produced several comprehensive accounts of the Gorbachev years. These include Philip G. Roeder, *Red Sunset: The Failure of Soviet Politics* (Princeton University Press, 1993), and Carol Barner-Barry and Cynthia Hody, *The Politics of Change: The Transformation of the Former Soviet Union* (St. Martin's Press, 1995). Both of these attempt to illuminate late Soviet history through the lens of social science theory. More straightforward in their approach are Rachel Walker, *Six Years That Shook the World* (Manchester University Press, 1993), and Stephen White, *After Gorbachev* (Cambridge University Press, 1993). Walter Laqueur, *The Dream That Failed* (Oxford University Press, 1994), presents the reflections of a distinguished scholar on the collapse of the Soviet Union and on the various approaches to the history of the USSR that have competed for attention in the West.

Any number of more specialized treatments of particular aspects of late Soviet history are now available. On the Brezhnev-era background to perestroika, there is Robert F. Byrnes, ed., *After Brezhnev* (Indiana University Press, 1983), and Seweryn Bialer, *The Soviet Paradox* (Knopf, 1986). Early Gorbachev reforms are treated in Stephen White, *Russia Goes Dry* (Cambridge University Press, 1996); Alec Nove, *Glasnost in Action* (Unwin Hyman, 1989); Moshe Lewin, *The Gorbachev Phenomenon* (University of California Press, 1988); and Mary Buckley, *Redefining Russian Society and Polity* (Westview Press, 1993). For the economics of perestroika, see Marshall Goldman, *What Went Wrong with Perestroika?* (W.W. Norton, 1992); William

Moskoff, *Hard Times: Impoverishment and Protest in the Perestroika Years* (M.E. Sharpe, 1993); and Anders Aslund, *Gorbachev's Struggle for Economic Reform* (Cornell University Press, 1991).

The social awakenings of the Gorbachev era have been the focus of much academic work. The rise of "unofficial" organizations and the democratic movement are detailed in Michael Urban, *The Rebirth of Politics in Russia* (Cambridge University Press, 1997); M. Steven Fish, *Democracy from Scratch* (Princeton University Press, 1995); Geoffrey Hoskings, *The Awakening of the Soviet Union* (Harvard University Press, 1990); and Judith B. Sedaitis and Jim Butterfield, *Perestroika from Below* (Westview Press, 1991). Donald Filtzer's *Soviet Workers and the Collapse of Perestroika* (Cambridge University Press, 1994) treats the labor movement, while Lewis Siegelbaum and Daniel J. Walkowitz, *Workers of the Donbass Speak* (SUNY Press, 1995), presents workers' points of view in their own words.

On the nationalities question, there are general treatments such as Ronald G. Suny, *The Revenge of the Past* (Stanford University Press, 1993); Hélène Carrère d'Encausse, *The End of the Soviet Empire* (Basic Books, 1993); and Anatoly M. Khazanov, *After the USSR* (University of Wisconsin Press, 1995). More specific studies include Taras Kuzio and Andrew Wilson, *Ukraine: Perestroika to Independence* (McMillan, 1994); Anatol Lieven, *The Baltic Revolution* (Yale University Press, 1993); and Gregory Gleason, *The Central Asian States: Discovering Independence* (Westview Press, 1997). John B. Dunlop addresses the growth of Russian nationalism in *The Rise of Russia and the Fall of the Soviet Empire* (Princeton University Press, 1993), which also contains a detailed account of the August coup.

The relationship of the late Soviet Union to the wider world has been the subject of much study and commentary. Raymond Garthoff has examined the end of the Cold War in detail in *The Great Transition* (Brookings Institution, 1994), while relations with the Third World are explored in W. Raymond Duncan and Carolyn Ekedahl, *Moscow and the Third World Under Gorbachev* (Westview Press, 1990). Anthony Arnold's *The Fateful Pebble* (Presidio Press, 1993) argues that the Soviet invasion of Afghanistan contributed much to the country's collapse. Gorbachev's *Perestroika: New Thinking for Our Country and the World* (Harper and Row, 1987) outlines his early ideas about needed changes in Soviet foreign policy. And Jack F. Matlock, the American ambassador to the USSR during its final years, has provided an insightful account of those years and the American role in them in his *Autopsy on an Empire* (Random House, 1995).

Finally, a number of works have sought to place the final years of Soviet history in a larger historical or comparative context. Nicolai N. Petro, in *The Rebirth of Russian Democracy* (Harvard University Press, 1995), argues that Russian and even Soviet history provide some foundation for democratic practice in the post-Soviet era. More pessimistically, Tim McDaniel, in *The Agony of the Russian Idea* (Princeton University Press, 1996), suggests that a two-hundred-year history of abortive reforms helps to explain Gorbachev's failure and offers little hope that Yeltsin's Russia will do any better. Comparative approaches to the Soviet collapse can be found in Geir Lundestad, *The Fall of Great Powers* (Oxford University Press, 1994); Richard L. Rudolph and David F. Good, *Nationalism and Empire* (St. Martin's Press, 1992); Gilbert Rozman, ed., *Dismantling Communism* (Woodrow Wilson Center Press, 1992); Karen Dawisha and Bruce Parrott, eds., *The End of Empire* (M.E. Sharpe, 1997); and Karen Barkey and Mark Von Hagen, eds., *After Empire* (Westview Press, 1997).

Index

S

T

U

V

W

Y

Z

Robert Strayer was educated at Wheaton College and the University of Wisconsin. He has been teaching history at the State University of New York College at Brockport since 1970 and is a 1997 recipient of the SUNY Chancellor's Award for Excellence in Teaching. Professor Strayer has also written *The Making of the Modern World* (2nd ed., 1995) as well as two books on African history. He has been a frequent visitor to Russia since the 1980s.